Liberation and Orthodoxy

Liberation and Orthodoxy

The Promise and Failures
of Interconfessional Dialogue

Yacob Tesfai

ORBIS BOOKS

Maryknoll, New York 10545

Manufactured in the United States of America.

Library of Congress Cataloging in Publication Data

Tesfai, Yacob.
    Liberation and orthodoxy : the promise and failures of interconfessional dialogue / Yacob Tesfai.
        p.   cm.
    Includes bibliographical references and index.
    ISBN 1-57075-088-2 (alk. paper)
    1. Theology—Methodology.   2. Dialogue—Religious aspects—
Christianity.   3. Ecumenical movement.   4. Christianity—Developing
countries.   I. Title.
BR118.T45   1996
280'.042—dc20   96-24932
                                                                CIP

To
Miriam Mehzun,
partner of more than a quarter century
in times of pain and joy,

and to our children,
Selam
Abel
Bekit
Sewit
Lwam

Contents

Preface

This book is a result of a personal study project that I conducted at the Institute for Ecumenical Research in Strasbourg during the years 1989-1993. As its title shows, it attempts to deal with the question of the relationship between the interconfessional dialogues and the Third World theologies and churches.

For a number of years now, the rate of participation of Third World members in multilateral and bilateral doctrinal (interconfessional) dialogues has been gradually increasing. Theologians and church leaders from the Third World have become members of these groups formerly composed of mainly Western theologians. Their involvement has been increasing at a steady rate even though it cannot yet be said to be decisive. As their numbers increased, they also became vocal and began to ask questions as well as to make proposals regarding the contents, goals, and methods of the dialogues. Gradually, the specific emphases they advocated began to take shape. These emphases often revealed the differences that obtained between their aims and those of the dialogues. They thus contributed to the tensions that arose within the forums of the interconfessional dialogues. I therefore saw the need to assess this new development in view of what it may mean not only to the Third World churches but to the ecumenical movement as a whole.

The initial interest of the study centered on a limited problem, namely, to find out how or to what extent the results of international interconfessional dialogues were "received" or not by the churches of the Third World. At the start of the study, "the process of reception" was coming into vogue in view of the results—especially of the bilateral dialogues—that were accumulating. Gradually, however, I recognized that the study must go further than the issue of "reception" if it is to deal with the dialogues and the questions posed by Third World churches and theologians.

As the study progressed, therefore, the need to widen it was becoming increasingly necessary. In the course of time, two concerns called for attention: first, the desirability and helpfulness of a critical assessment of the whole enterprise of interconfessional dialogues. This would certainly need to be preceded by a presentation of the dialogues, their aims, achievements, and failures. In passing, such a presentation of the dialogues would contribute to the introduction of the initiate to this theological exercise, which is often done in the company of experts. Second, it became important to collate and present the reactions of Third World theologians and churches to these dialogues and their opinions on doctrines, confessions, and ecumenism. This would aim at bringing into the discussion the views of Third World theologians, views which are not heard very often in relation to the dialogues.

At the end, I try to present in summary form the main points that I saw increasingly drawing the attention of all concerned in the ecumenical discussion. To my surprise, I found the emergence of a number of themes that were attracting a commonality of interest in the otherwise different camps. Needless to say, that was the main pleasure of the study: to find out and show that, in spite of many differences, which are real, there are also points of convergence which are crucial in the understanding of the Christian faith and in the future prospects of the ecumenical movement. I bring the study to a close with some observations regarding what I see as the changing presuppositions and context of the ecumenical debate.

For some readers, the notes may prove cumbersome and intimidating. There are two reasons behind the ample notes that I have provided. First, I wanted to give inquisitive readers as many resources as possible to enable them to pursue their inquiries further. Second, I wanted to engage as many people and views as possible in the discussion.

Abbreviations

AFER	*African Ecclesial Review*
ARCIC	Anglican Roman Catholic International Commission
ATJ	*Africa Theological Journal*
ARCIC	Anglican-Roman Catholic International Commission
BEM	Baptism, Eucharist, and Ministry, Lima Document
CCPD	Commission of the Churches' Participation in Development
CWCs	Christian World Communions, World Confessional Families
DC	*Documentation Catholique*
EATWOT	Ecumenical Association of Third World Theologians
ER	*The Ecumenical Review*
ET	*Ecumenical Trends*
EvKomm	*Evangelische Kommentare*
EvTh	*Evangelische Theologie*
F&O	Faith and Order
F&V	Foi et Vie
HK	*Herder Korrespondenz*
IKZ	*Internationale Katholische Zeitschrift*
IRM	*International Review of Mission*
JES	*Journal of Ecumenical Studies*
JPIC	Justice, Peace, and the Integrity of Creation
K&D	Kerygma und Dogma
KNA	Katholische Nachrichten-Agentur
L&V	Lumiere et Vie
LM	*Lutherische Monatshefte*
LQ	*Lutheran Quarterly*
LWF	Lutheran World Federation
MSt	*Mid-Stream*
NRT	Nouvelle Revue Theologique
OR	*Oekumenische Rundschau*
OIC	One In Christ
PCR	Program to Combat Racism of the WCC
RCC	Roman Catholic Church
SdZ	*Stimmen der Zeit*
ST	*Studia Theologica*
US	Una Sancta
VOTW	*Voices of the Third World*
WARC	World Alliance of Reformed Churches
WCC	World Council of Churches
ZfM	*Zeitschrift für Mission*

Introduction

There were two speeches that were delivered at the Seventh Assembly of the World Council of Churches (WCC) in Canberra, Australia, in February 1991 which drew unusual attention from the participants and a wider public. The two presentations were viewed as being sharply opposed to one another. They came one after the other and dealt with the same topic: "Come Holy Spirit: Renew the Whole Creation." The speeches were received in different ways by the audience and they gave rise to a variety of reactions. What one can observe is that these two speeches are very important because they are the very examples which illustrate an important aspect of the antagonism and controversy that is increasingly characterizing the ecumenical movement. No two items of the same agenda could more aptly epitomize the tension to which the movement is being subjected. This antagonism and tension concerns what I will call *Liberation* and *Doctrinal Orthodoxy*.

The second speech, which happened to become one of the most dramatic and controversial events during the Canberra assembly, was the one delivered by the South Korean female theologian Chung Hyun Kyung.[1] The presentation of the speech was accompanied by both Australian aboriginal and Korean dancers. After the presentation, Chung was accorded a standing ovation by the audience. While there seemed to be approbation by the majority in the plenary hall, the speech was immediately followed by some sharp criticisms. There were a number of critical voices which evoked the same word: "syncretism." The critics were alleging that some assertions of Chung deviated from the correct teaching of the Christian faith.[2]

It is interesting to note that many of the criticisms that evoked the term "syncretism" were expressing the apprehension that the theology of the Christian churches who were members of the WCC (as well as those outside) was in danger of being diluted as a result of a theology propounded by theologians such as Chung. They were expressing the fear that the "true and pure faith" was in danger of being mixed up with "pagan" thoughts. In the view of such people, "the ghost of syncretism"—as one commentator called it—that reared its ugly head in Canberra was to become an ecumenical problem within the WCC.[3] Some were further scandalized by the fact that the spirits of those who had passed away were called upon and that the East Asian goddess of compassion and wisdom was related by Chung to the Holy Spirit.[4] What is at stake for such people is to what extent Christianity can borrow concepts from other religions "without itself risking falling back into heathenism." Right after the speech, the Orthodox delegates especially raised their critical voices and they were later followed in the assembly by others.[5] Subsequent references to the speech show also that it is not only the Orthodox that were affected but other churches and theologians as well, especially in the West.

Even a cursory reading of the speech of Prof. Chung shows that her main thrust was liberation.[6] The kernel of her presentation was the participation in and the overcoming of suffering that is caused by poverty and all kinds of oppression. All the people who struggled to gain freedom and justice throughout history were invoked and made present. Contemporaries were called to be part of this movement in search of justice and liberation. But when she brought in the question of the nature of the Spirit, there were cries of deviation from the right Christian doctrine, "syncretism." As one writer put it, "From this perspective, the very integrity of our biblical faith is at stake."[7]

The presentation by Chung was preceded by another speech. The latter was the epitome of "orthodox" faith presented by an Orthodox himself. It was written by none other than Patriarch Parthenios of Alexandria.[8] By the proponents of doctrinal orthodoxy—and these are by no means confined to the Orthodox Church or theologians—his speech seems to have been taken as a pure doctrinal exposition of the Holy Spirit based on the tradition of the Church. Even though he presented his thoughts on the Holy Spirit in the garb of a human language that was based on a particular philosophical tradition and thought forms, it did not raise any objections from the quarters that accused Chung of "syncretism."[9] It never dawned upon such people, and neither did they find it appropriate, to pose the question of whether the Western Christian tradition, which was presented in Hellenistic philosophical garb, could itself also be "syncretistic," as the Evangelicals in Canberra also admitted. In any case, both presentations became representative positions of a confrontation in ecumenism that has been brewing and had to come into the open at some time or another.

It must be recalled that the incident at Canberra did not simply come out of the blue. It could be said that it has been in the making for a number of years.[10] The fifth WCC Assembly at Nairobi (1975) had already recognized the presence within the ecumenical movement of what it called "diverse activities" which "do not always assist and enrich one another, and sometimes they are in tension with one another." The report goes on to identify two tendencies within the ecumenical movement which are at odds with one another. There are, on the one side, those who are committed to the "faithfulness to the truth" of confessional traditions and, on the other side, the tendency which primarily comes from the Third World.[11] Ever since the late sixties, the ecumenical movement has been affected by such tensions. In the light of such a situation, what happened at Canberra was only a symptom of that which has been haunting the ecumenical movement for some time and came out into the broad daylight here.[12] In other words, the thrusts for liberation and doctrinal orthodoxy, which at times pull in different directions within the ecumenical movement, have already been manifest with greater visibility especially in the last three decades.

But it is well to expect that these two tendencies will generate more tensions in the context of the ecumenical movement in the coming years. Not only will they cause tensions, according to some views, they will even become the occasion for a new Church division much greater than the one that divided the other Christian churches in the West. The prospect that this would happen was clearly enunciated at the Assembly itself. "Perhaps the most dramatic intervention came from Archbishop Kirill of Smolensk (Eastern Orthodox, Russia). It is quite clear, he contended, that liberal, radical, and contextual theologies have a dominant place" in the WCC. As a result of such developments as the ordination of women and a "tendency to syncretism," we are witnessing new divisions in the church. The WCC is acquiescing to majorities instead of "holding to the apostolic faith."[13] This conviction is corroborated by one reviewer of the WCC Assembly at Canberra, J. M. R. Tillard, who said: "It even occurred to us to be afraid that we may be moving—for lack of lucidity and depth—towards a new rupture, perhaps much more impossible to mend than the one which at present divides the East and the West, the Catholic East and the reformed Catholic: this time round, a rupture between the churches of ancient Christianity and the churches of the countries evangelized by them."[14] Tillard continues to reiterate this view elsewhere: "This is the real problem after Canberra. During the Assembly, it was evident that there is a danger of a new division. . . . It will be the division between the Churches which brought the Gospel to the African, Asian and Polynesian continents and the Churches which were born as a result of this evangelisation."[15] During the assembly, a similar warning was also echoed from the opposite side by Chung in uncompromising terms: "Beneath all the talk of syncretism," she said, "is the question of power. Western, male theologians have set the limits of the Spirit's work. We have been listening to your intellectualism for 2,000 years. . . . Please listen to us . . . Third-world theologies are," she maintained, "the new paradigm, the new wine that can't be put in your wineskins . . . yes, we are dangerous, but it is through such danger that the Holy Spirit can renew the church."[16] The confrontation between liberation and doctrinal orthodoxy and the challenges they pose to each other within the ecumenical movement cannot, it seems to me, be put in sharper terms.

If present trends continue—and there are no signs that they will diminish in the foreseeable future—the tensions between the tendencies for liberation and doctrinal orthodoxy will increase. These are assured by the fact that there are developments within the worldwide Christian Church itself which will contribute to them. On the one hand, there are the given conditions of Christians and Christianity in the Third World which gradually push the emphasis on liberation and justice. We shall look at the numerical increase of Christians in the Third World and its implications for ecumenism. Tied intimately to this is the growing theological dynamism being manifested there.

On the other hand, there is the traditional wing of the ecumenical movement which understands the aim of the movement as overcoming the divisions of the churches by reaching consensus in doctrine and agreement in the one unadulterated and true faith. In this camp are to be included the WCC's Faith and Order Commission (F&O) and its multilateral dialogues, as well as the bilateral dialogues and the Christian World Communions (CWCs) that sponsor the bilaterals. With these two realities in view—Third World churches and the Faith and Order wing in the ecumenical movement—the tensions between the concern for the Gospel as a force for liberation and the Gospel as expressed in the preservation of right and true doctrine will increasingly clash the one against the other.

It may be helpful to mention here that there are some voices which look at these differences in approaches as continuations of differences that characterized the previous history of the ecumenical movement.[17] In this line of argumentation, even though the special contributions of the Third World are recognized, the continuity of their concerns with the current of Life and Work seems to be emphasized. It is my contention, however, that there is something new which was introduced into the ecumenical movement with the entry of the Third World in the sixties.

It is to be recalled that the ecumenical movement is the result of three main currents which originally existed separately. The first was the Life and Work movement, which had its first conference in Stockholm in 1925. In the light of the wars fought between "Christian nations" in Europe, the movement aimed at organizing the churches together to work on social issues which would contribute to peace. The second was the Faith and Order movement, which had its first meeting in 1927 in Lausanne. The aim was to bring the churches together to study the doctrinal issues that both unite and separate them and in this way to proceed towards visible church unity. (The third current, the International Missionary Council, which became part of the WCC in 1961, will not concern us here.) The two movements merged in 1948 to form the WCC. Even so, the different emphases of the movements have been visible even within the WCC up to the present, sometimes as competitors. But it must be said that just as the two movements were firmly rooted in the Western Christian tradition, they also had many things in common in spite of their slightly different emphases.[18] They were both anchored in the Western context, in which theological traditions of the Western Church played an important role. One can even see that there was a significant rapprochement between them in the course of their history. That is to say that, as time went by, their presuppositions, concerns, and methods were becoming confluent. As Nils Ehrenstroem put it: "Life and Work increasingly recognized the importance of theological factors, and thus steered a course which gradually brought it into convergence with Faith and Order."[19]

But the emphasis on liberation which is rooted in the experience of the Third World provides one with an altogether different thrust and brings a new pressure on the ecumenical movement. Let us then look a bit more closely at the factors that will contribute to the antagonism and confrontation between the tendencies of liberation and doctrinal orthodoxy.

Changing Texture of the Christian Church

Significant and far-reaching changes are taking place in the texture of the Christian Church in the contemporary world. Ever since the beginning of the 1980s (some even say in the middle of the twentieth century), the balance of Christianity has switched in favor of the Third World. The statistics show that the number of Christians in the Third World is increasing—in some places by leaps and bounds—and that the greater number of Christians now live in the Third World. "We are in the middle of a process of change as a result of which the Church, at home in the Western world for almost 2000 years will, in a short time, have shifted its centre of gravity into the Third World, where its adherents will be much numerous."[20] Some statistics have it—to take just one example—that as much as more than half of the worldwide membership of the Roman Catholic Church is now found in Latin America.[21] This led Leonardo Boff to assert that "the future of the Catholic church, given the diminution of the European population, is undeniably in Latin America."[22] For the first time in the greater part of the history of the church, the Christian faith is becoming "a non-western religion."[23]

One uniting factor in this new majority of the worldwide Christian Church is that it is becoming literally "the church of the poor."[24] It has been recognized for some years now that three-quarters of the world's population counts itself among the poor while less than a quarter of its inhabitants are rich and enjoy more than three-quarters of the riches of the planet. In a world that is increasingly divided between the rich and the poor, the majority of the Christians of the Third World are finding themselves within the ranks of the poor. This has far-reaching consequences in the relationship of the rich and poor Christians on the one hand and the theological implications of the issue of poverty on the other.

Theological and Christian Dynamism

There is another equally important factor that one must take into consideration when one deals with the confrontation between liberation and doctrinal orthodoxy. This is the fact that a great deal of theological and Christian dynamism is manifesting itself in the churches of these parts of the world.[25] In the first place, in the course of the past few years, we have seen a surge of liberation theologies that come out of Africa, Asia and Latin America.[26] Even though there is still some resistance in some Western circles to accept these theologies as "scientific" or as theologies in their own right,[27] there is no question that they have already made their impact felt. For generations (or so it seemed) new theological insights were born in Germany, gradually made their way to Britain and hence to the United States, perhaps or perhaps not to gain a foothold in what was later called the "Third World" beyond the shores of Europe and North America. But today, if one asks, "Where are the new theological currents originating?" the answer comes readily: "In the Third World, in Latin America, Asia and Africa, usually in a variant of liberation theology."[28] As a result, some of the best minds in modern theology are rightly acknowledging that there has been an important "paradigm shift" in theology in favor of the theologies of the Third World.[29] The center of theological activity is no longer Europe, but there are now many other centers that vie with it. It is no longer Europe that calls the shots in theology. "Its [i.e., liberation theology's] endurance is shown by the fact that its message has grown brighter in clarity and in depth as it has spread throughout the world, while some of the many new theologies of the First World have flickered and grown dimmer as the years have passed."[30] The legitimacy of other theologies arising outside the Western world is no longer to be questioned. In fact, it seems that the case is the other way round. It is in this spirit that C. S. Song makes bold in affirming: "Christian theology has become decentralized. This is another paradigm-shift of tremendous magnitude. Tubingen is no longer the centre of the theological world. North American theologians may still catch a cold when German theologians sneeze, not third-world theologians."[31] This trend is summarized aptly in the opinion expressed by Ernst Kaesemann, who is quoted as saying: "I am convinced that the great time of Western theology has come to an end, that it is near its ultimate border. Like Moses, it can see the promised land but will not enter it. The Holy Spirit has left work to be done by the theologians from the Third World."[32]

A phenomenon of great significance has been the mushrooming of the ecclesial base communities in the Third World. While they have strong bases in the Latin American context, they also manifest their activities in other Third World areas as well. These communities are mostly composed of the poor and marginalized of their societies. They belong to the lower classes. Their spiritual life is centered around the reading of the Bible through their eyes and its interpretation in the light of their situation. A very strong characteristic of these communities is the application of their biblical insights to the particular life situation in which they live. Questions that have to do with the social and economic condition of these poor are thus viewed and interpreted in the light of their reading of the Bible. These usually lead to concerted action in the direction of a radical change of their situation of oppression. Even though they function within the institutional church, they also serve as renewal movements and sometimes as competitors.[33]

The question, of course, arises regarding the extent of the independence and authenticity of the Third World churches and theological centers, especially in the light of their deep financial, theological, and institutional dependence on foreign (mainly Western) churches. It is not only the question of financial dependence which affects their capacity to determine their own priorities that is the crucial issue here. It is also the question of the freedom and responsibility, nay duty, to develop and to disseminate their own theology in the centers of theological education of the Third World churches. In the light of the continuing dependence of a great number of these churches both on foreign financial resources and personnel and, consequently, on Western theology, the seemingly provocative question "Do we really have Third World Churches in the full theological sense of the term 'church'?"[34] is not totally inappropriate. It rightly raises the question as to what extent these churches can be called full-fledged churches inasmuch as many of them cannot even entertain the idea of organizing their life in a self-reliant and independent manner—in the Pauline tradition—let alone think in terms of developing their own theological perspectives different from those of their "mother churches" in a way that reflects their particular situation.

Even without losing sight of such valid questions, however, one cannot deny what the growth of these churches in numbers and the overwhelming impact of the dynamism of their form of Christianity and the growing influence of their theologies will imply. The growing confidence of these churches is partly illustrated in the boldness of a Third World theologian arguing the need for holding another council of the Roman Catholic Church (RCC). His main reasoning is that the transformation of Christianity due to the radical changes that are taking place in the Third World churches is such that the situation calls for another Vatican council to respond to the needs and visions of the new majority. Such a council would lead to the recognition of a new self-understanding of the RCC and to reach decisions based on it. In the light of the actual situation, he is of the opinion that a Western leadership of the church is an anomaly. A change, therefore, is imperative. "A smooth transition to a Church of the Third World must be carried out with clear foresight and spiritual insight."[35]

The Concern for Liberation

This numerical strength, coupled with the intense activity on the level of Christian life and theology, has not been without its effect on the ecumenical movement. This contribution, part of which will concern us here, is also not negligible. To appreciate the change, it is necessary to recall that the Third World churches as principal actors were practically absent in the earlier history of the ecumenical movement.[36] They did exert their influence on it in one way or another but it was not through the conspicuous presence of their constituencies, especially in the formation of the ecumenical organizations.[37] One of the first strong manifestations of their presence in an international ecumenical forum was the Geneva Conference on Church and Society held in 1966. Here, the new voices of the churches of the Third World were heard loud and clear. While their representation was significant in that they formed half of the participants, their concerns and their priorities were also dominant.[38] The fourth WCC Assembly in Uppsala in 1968 went further in recognizing this influence of the upcoming Third World. From this time on, the impact of the Third World churches began to increase in the WCC. Henceforth, their presence has been increasingly visible. It was in recognition of this fact that the Assembly structure committee advised the WCC to note the new balance of membership. It was explicitly stated here that the future of the ecumenical movement has to acknowledge the shift that has taken place with regard to the membership of the WCC. In its own words, the WCC was to keep in mind in the future "the effect of the Council's growth away from the North Atlantic region which gave it birth towards the Third World."[39]

This trend has some connection with both the beginnings of the ecumenical movement and its present history. "It was out of the pressures of the churches in missions and mission that the ecumenical movement received its initial impetus." This indirect Third World contribution of the past is being augmented at present by the direct participation of the leaders of these churches. "Today it is often through Third World Christians that new visions of the Church and missions are emerging. . . . It would be difficult to exaggerate the importance of Third World persons for generating fresh and compelling theological, ethical, ecclesiological and liturgical insights for the life of the whole Church."[40] With the election of Philip Potter as the general secretary of the world body, the Third World came into the center of the movement in full force. Further, through the WCC's programs, especially the Program to Combat Racism, the Third World began to have a strong impact on the movement. Through such a program, the concept of church unity that defined the vision of the ecumenical movement was seriously challenged. In the light of such developments, some have even gone so far as to accuse the WCC and the ecumenical movement of being dominated solely by the Third World and its concerns. In so doing, they argue, the WCC has forfeited its churchly character and betrayed the original goals that started it in the first place.

With the increase in the number of Third World Christians and the dynamism of their Christian life and theology, the question of liberation has thus come into the center of the ecumenical agenda. This particular emphasis brings them in line with the many concerns which have been in the forefront of a number of WCC programs as well as Third World theologies. In the words of the former general secretary of the WCC, Philip Potter, the intention of the WCC programs has been in line with that of Third World theologians: "All that the Third World theologians have been saying and writing has been the substance of the statements, programmes and activities of the World Council and have been its task and calling since its inception."[41] Concurring with this viewpoint, there are those who are of the opinion that the work of the WCC is influenced by the theology of liberation and that this theology has consequently become "an ecumenical challenge."[42]

The Concern for Doctrinal Orthodoxy

But it is also a fact that the search for doctrinal orthodoxy has been a continuous concern of a part of the ecumenical movement and the WCC. This contributes to the controversial encounter between the two factors. It must be reckoned that, besides the strength of the "coming Third Church"— to use Buehlmann's pregnant phrase—there is this other factor that concerns us here: it is the Faith and Order wing of the ecumenical movement. This movement has been one of the oldest and most important arms of the ecumenical movement. In accordance with the terms of its constitution, adopted at Amsterdam at the time of the founding of the WCC, the F&O Commission has among its aims "the study of questions of faith, order and worship . . . in their bearing on the unity of the Church." The function of the Commission consists in "drawing churches into conference . . . to explain their convictions to others." Through such activities, it hopes to "act as the handmaid of the Churches in the preparatory work of clearing away misunderstandings, discussing obstacles to re-union."[43] The commission has concentrated on engaging the various Christian churches in doctrinal dialogues which hopefully will lead to better understanding among themselves and the resolution of the doctrinal differences that separated them from one another in the first place and will prepare the way for their possible unity.

True to its mandate and goal, the Commission has used most of its energy in promoting doctrinal dialogues among representatives of divided Christian churches. These so-called multilateral dialogues (which involve many representatives from a variety of Christian confessions, both members and nonmembers of the WCC) have been the main emphasis and task of the Commission. The work of many years resulted in the now famous Baptism, Eucharist, and Ministry (BEM) document which was released by the Commission at its meeting in Lima, Peru, in 1982.

Within the WCC, which has often been referred to as "the privileged instrument of the ecumenical movement," the F&O line has a distinct "personality," so to speak, because of the fact that it always maintained its specific nature within the Council through its own Commission. Therefore, it has been able to pursue its main concern even after the merger within the WCC structure. Through its special Commission and meetings, it has been applying itself to its original mandate. Its continuity shows that it is one of the strongest and most enduring currents of the ecumenical movement.[44]

The same cannot be said of the "Life and Work" stream, which is not graced with the benefit of having its own continuous organizational structure. Its concerns have rather been picked up here and there by certain program units of the WCC. Sometimes, such concerns have been developed and dropped abruptly without having engendered any continuity. This had led the longtime head of the WCC Commission on the Churches' Participation in Development (CCPD), C. I. Itty, to observe that "of the movements which preceded the formation of the WCC, the Faith and Order and the Missionary movements still have considerable visibility, while the Life and Work movement is almost forgotten."[45]

There is an additional element that should be noted here. This is the fact that the various proponents of F&O even argue that it is the stream of the ecumenical movement which properly defines and truly deserves the term "ecumenical." There are many activities within the WCC which vie for the appropriation of the term. But it must be reminded, these proponents argue, that the original intention of the ecumenical movement, as inscribed in the constitution of the WCC, was the search for the visible unity of the Church. And this goal can be achieved mainly through the resolution of the doctrinal differences that have led to the separation of the churches.[46]

To this ideal, F&O has remained faithful through the years. In outlining the future role of the Commission within the ecumenical movement, for example, its director has stated as follows: "In this situation, the central role of the theological work of Faith and Order consists above all in being a constant reminder of the mission and goal of the most important fact of the history of the church in the twentieth century that we call the ecumenical movement."[47] It is argued that F&O has the duty to give focus to the scattered activities of the WCC. It is the arm which helps to maintain the churchly character of the activities of the Council.[48]

A clear presupposition lay behind the endeavors of the F&O line of the ecumenical movement as they are reflected in the pursuits of multilateral and bilateral dialogues. This is the conviction that the apostolic faith is an objective whole which has been delivered to the Church in the course of its history. This tradition has been formulated at certain points in the history of its development. There are, of course, differences in value among the various points in this historical process. For instance, the period of the early church and the conciliar documents as they were fixed in the fourth century as well as the Reformation era have special significance. It is also the case that each Christian church would add or subtract other doctrinal formulations to these documents which become binding. It follows that each Christian church living in any given epoch can remain faithful to its identity only insofar as it conforms to the givens of this formulation.

The dialogues are therefore aiming at seizing through the doctrinal discussions the objective truth as formulated in the doctrines. Here they are led by a specific assumption: "The dialogues assume that there is a possibility of deepening and widening the expression of the objective, established truths of the apostolic faith, and seek new forms of expression. . . . They assume that there is an apostolic faith handed down to us which can be known in our day. . . . They envision . . . a common expression of the full apostolic faith—and this is the consensus both presumed and sought."[49] In the definition of Dunn, orthodoxy amounts to the following: "Orthodoxy has traditionally been thought of as in conformity to the apostolic faith. It . . . implies that a clear distinction can be drawn between truth and error.

Orthodoxy implies that there is a pure, uncontaminated faith, a correct teaching."[50]

There are, of course, those who argue that such a search for clarity in doctrine does not in any way reflect the situation that prevailed in the early church. "The early Christian communities do not appear to have regarded precise and elaborate doctrinal formulations as essential to their self-definition."[51] Even an Orthodox writer admits that this was indeed the case, that is to say, that the church did not lend itself to the preoccupation with dogmatic elaborations of its faith: "The ancient church had not troubled itself so much with exact formulations [of dogmatic definitions] because its existence as a living organism was convincingly obvious."[52]

Even so, the search for doctrinal agreement has as its main basis the understanding that the Church throughout the centuries has been characterized by the need to formulate its creeds and faith in a verbal form. The church has done so and succeeded in this task. This formulation has its own canon or measuring stick. It has a standard to which generations of Christians and churches have to submit. This presupposes that they must seize it anew in every generation and articulate it in conformity with the ancient norm. The task of the doctrinal dialogues finds its very place in such a search for doctrinal purity and normativity. This is what we have called doctrinal orthodoxy.

Third World and Faith and Order

As in other areas of the ecumenical movement, the F&O Commission has also opened itself up to the participation of theologians from the Third World. As their numbers and the level of their participation have increased, they have begun to express their dissatisfaction with the overall emphasis on only doctrinal discussions. They have gradually brought the concerns of the theologies of the Third World into an otherwise hitherto limited circle. As a result, there are signs of growing tension even within the F&O itself. Third World voices want to register their own priorities in the agenda of the movement. They harbor impatience in the face of concentration on "that endless process of speculative re-interpretation which is the main stock-in-trade of much contemporary theology, both Protestant and Catholic."[53]

F&O on its part naturally wants to continue to define the goals of the movement in terms of its own priorities. It interprets faithfulness to the original intentions of the founders of the ecumenical movement in terms of finding unity in the confession of the one faith. As has already been stated, these two opposing perspectives lead to increasing tensions, and even clashes, in the ecumenical movement. As was the case in the Commission meeting at Budapest in 1989, the raising of this new criticism in a Commission which otherwise represented a homogeneous search for doctrinal agreement has become a source of "open conflict" and "tension" within the F&O Commission itself.[54]

The presence and impact of the Third World churches and their theologies has thus been growing in the ecumenical movement in general as well as within the F&O. In light of these developments, it is true to say that what happens there, and their opinion on all aspects of the ecumenical movement, becomes significant, important, and even decisive.[55] As the WCC Assembly in Canberra has amply shown, if current trends continue, what happens in the Third World churches and what they say may radically affect the shape of the ecumenical movement, or lead it to unbearable tensions.

Another Arm of Faith and Order

But there is another equally important element that should be added to this list, and that widens the battleground and contributes to the intensity of the tension. The multilateral interconfessional dialogues, which were originally confined to the F&O Commission, were augmented at a later date by the bilateral dialogues. These are the doctrinal discussions which are conducted between two Christian bodies with the view of reaching agreement on doctrinal issues that separate them. These dialogues were picked up intensively by the Christian World Communions and national churches (mainly in the West) in the late sixties as a means of reaching agreements on the doctrinal issues that separate them from one another.[56]

As we shall see in more detail later, there was initially the fear that the multilaterals and the bilaterals may compete one against the other. As time went on, however, they began to see each other as complementary. Henceforth, the coming of the bilaterals gave the F&O wing of the ecumenical movement increased force and momentum in the movement. In the course of time, the doctrinal conversations in the form of bilateral dialogues have been extremely influential among numerous CWCs and widely used by them and have become one of the strong expressions of the ecumenical movement. In the view of George H. Tavard: "The major characteristic of the ecumenical movement in the 1970's has been the work of the bi-lateral dialogues."[57]

The choice of opting for the bilaterals by the CWCs is of a far-reaching consequence. By choosing this form of ecumenism as their priority, the CWCs affirm the importance of the confessional factor in their existence.[58] They thus commit themselves to resolving the differences that arose during the course of the history of some of their member churches. It is a deliberate choice that shows clearly where their ecumenical priorities lie. In the words of one of its strongest proponents, Tillard, the aim of bilaterals is expressed in the sharpest possible way:

Questions immediately at stake are not, ordinarily, the sometimes burning problems of relations between North and South, the common commitment of all Christians in the difficult search for justice and peace, or common defense of human rights. Rather, they are questions about the true faith in Jesus Christ, the meaning and role of sacraments, the right understanding of the nature and function of the church. This means that bilateral dialogues are mainly concerned with dogmatic issues.[59]

In these words, we find summarized in a clear way the contradictions in the definition of the goal of the ecumenical movement.

The sharp contrast which Tillard draws between the emphasis on the bilaterals and what may be called Third World concerns are illustrative of the kind of ecumenical battle that is announcing itself. Tillard further argues that the bilaterals are concerned with "the true faith in Christ Jesus." From what he says, it is clear that the issues of peace and justice, defense of human rights, difficulties between North and South, whatever they may be, do not have much to do within the context of the bilaterals, which are concerned with the true faith. Following this line of thinking, the bilaterals rightly keep them out of their sphere. Their aim is not to deal with the questions that have to do with the works of charity or love. They have, in their opinion, a far greater and more serious problem to deal with, namely, attacking the issue of the separation of the Christian churches.

For Tillard, the churches should have one overriding goal: to repair their division. "Given the present division among Christians . . . the most significant task of the churches . . . is to become what Christians are supposed to be: a true 'communion' grounded in the common confession of the one same faith, sealed by the one Spirit of God, and bound by the common partaking of the one eucharist of Christ." It is true that the churches should speak to the world on the dramatic events that take place in the world. Tillard does not deny that the church should have a word for the world and should take part in the efforts to ameliorate human life. But this is secondary to the main goal, namely, "the realization of the Gospel and its koinonia within the church itself."[60]

For Tillard, the weakness of Christians is not their absence in the world. They can be as active as possible in their efforts to save human beings; they may join together in caritative work. But that is a secondary matter. To agree to do something on the basis of praxis is easy enough. But the search for agreement in the finding of the true faith is a taxing endeavor. This is the merit of the bilaterals.

To deal with problems as justification, baptism, eucharist, ministry, and authority amounts to a recognition of the essential importance of the inner being of the church of God, among the realities with which Christians have to be concerned here and now. It reveals the necessity to repair the greatest scandal, which is not the lack of generosity of the people of God in its service of humanity. Even before the tragic situation of our world, the most difficult and urgent issue among the ecclesial dossiers is not an issue of charity or love. It is, rather, as it was at the beginning of the church, the question of faith.

Tillard then drives home the importance of the bilaterals when he writes: "This insistence of the bilateral dialogues on dealing with the divisive doctrinal issues is, then, very important for the future of the ecumenical movement, which more and more is forced, or at least tempted, in the midst of the tragedies of our times to concentrate almost exclusively on evangelical praxis."[61]

Tillard draws a sharp wedge between an ecumenism that seeks to serve humanity and one that concentrates on the healing of the division of the churches on doctrinal lines. He is in no doubt that there is the temptation for the ecumenical movement to weigh its choice in favor of the first option. Tillard disagrees with this choice on ecclesiological grounds. This would deny the original calling of the Church. The bilaterals are a welcome instrument in the fight to preserve the integrity of this unique mission of the church. They send us back to dealing with the real ecclesiological issues that have to do with the essence and calling of the church. The bilaterals are the most important instruments at hand to deal with the burning issue facing the church: the overcoming of its division through agreement on doctrines.

Wolfhart Pannenberg also carries forward this line of reasoning. For him, the doctrinal dialogues which will lead to the unity of the churches are absolutely necessary in the light of the secular culture of the Western hemisphere. In his opinion, it is the division of the churches that became the source of this secular culture in Europe and America in the first place. The churches have damaged their common witness and in this way contributed to the strength of secularization and to their weakness. As a result, the secular culture has become independent of the churches; it has evolved into a culture over against the churches and gradually posed itself as a threat to "the religious question of being human." Only a united witness of the churches can forestall the danger of this secular culture. The doctrinal dialogues, especially in their bilateral form, are therefore important in this respect not only because they will lead to the unity of the churches but because they will also contribute to the renewal of Christianity and "our civilization." In his own words: "Therefore, a renewal of Christianity in our culture and a renewal of our civilization itself can only take place in the context of its religious roots when the churches overcome their divisions."[62]

For Pannenberg, the task of the churches in the modern world does not "in the first place have to do with the problems of the world." On the contrary, it has to do with that which the world does not talk about. This is "the most important and specific theme of the churches and the Christian faith."[63] In the face of the secularized world which threatens the basic question of the religious meaning of life, the churches have to rally together to address it. That is why Pannenberg is opposed to what he sees as a "politicization" of the ecumenical agenda by the influences of liberation theology from the Third World. According to him, the ecumenical agenda has to do strictly with the unity of the churches. And it is the overcoming of the divisions through doctrinal dialogues that is the appropriate means to reach the ecumenical goal of church unity. Any deviation from this specific line is a betrayal of the ecumenical cause.[64]

In this connection, the ecumenical "muscle" that the bilateral dialogues wield should be given the utmost consideration. First of all, they are the preferred channels of church communication and ecumenical relationships of the biggest Christian church, the Roman Catholic Church. Ever since the end of the Second Vatican Council (1962-1965), the RCC has used these dialogues as the preferred method of its ecumenical relations with and rapprochement to other Christian churches. At one time, it was involved in no less than fourteen conversations with various groups. As a result, it has given an unexpected boost to the confessional dialogues. "The entry of the Roman Catholic Church into the general ecumenical movement did not only contribute to the stimulation of the Faith and Order Commission. But it had far-reaching consequences especially for the second type of interchurch conversations, namely, the bilateral dialogues."[65] Second, the bilaterals are also sponsored by the CWCs, which embrace a great number of Christian churches, both members and nonmembers of the WCC.[66] The steps taken by the RCC have in turn strengthened the position of the confessional families (CWCs). They were encouraged to enter into theological "conversations" which "constitute a new element in the ecumenical movement."[67] As a result of this new development of the bilateral dialogues, the CWCs' relationship to the WCC in particular and the ecumenical movement in general has been viewed as ambiguous at times. They were suspected of serving as "bastions of confessionalism" and were even viewed as potential rivals of the WCC. In the course of time, however, a modus vivendi has evolved, even though some questions remain, as we shall see in more detail below.[68]

Faith and Order and Bilateral Dialogues

It is the F&O Commission which has succeeded not only in increasingly establishing a good working relationship with the CWCs but in coordinating what gradually came to be seen as their common ecumenical task. In coordinating their efforts, they have mutually reinforced their task and one another. The Commission has been closely related to the CWCs and has been responsible, among others, for the organization of the Forum on Bilateral Dialogues, of which more will be said later.

In the post-Vancouver period (1983 onwards), one of the roles of F&O was envisaged as consisting in "holding in close relationship to one another the ecumenical strivings of the World Christian Communions (confessional families) and the WCC."[69] F&O should see to it that there is "complementarity" between the bilaterals, which express the "new significance of the World Christian Communions" in the ecumenical endeavor and the multilaterals. It is noted that it is only in the F&O work of the WCC that one of the biggest "Communions," the RCC, participates as a full member. The RCC, as we have already seen, is also heavily involved in the bilaterals. "A weakening of the cooperation of the churches in the WCC as well as the theological concentration on the question of the unity of the churches would unquestionably have as a consequence an increasing transfer of the theological struggle for the unity of the Church from the WCC on the CWCs. Such a development would not be in the interest of the WCC in the long run and would go against the ecumenical intention of these families."[70]

Liberation versus Doctrinal Orthodoxy

The growing tension between liberation and doctrinal orthodoxy once more emerged in sharp focus after the Canberra Assembly of the WCC, as already mentioned at the beginning of this chapter. As a result, there were some voices which expressed openly the conviction that the WCC may no longer be the instrument to bring the churches together in the search for unity. These voices were distressed by the lack of "doctrinal orthodoxy" and consequent fall into "syncretism" which the Canberra assembly manifested. As a result, there is expressed a visible disappointment with the WCC. In order to remedy the situation and to salvage the ecumenical movement, one of the proposals that has been suggested is to strengthen further the proponents of F&O, whether they be the multilaterals or the bilaterals. In the words of Tillard once again: "After the 7th Assembly of the World Council of Churches at Canberra, this (i.e., 'to rediscover the authentic Christian truth') is sometimes crucial for the future of ecumenism." But, in his opinion, this is no longer guaranteed in view of the ecumenical developments within the WCC. He goes on to emphasize the crucial importance of the doctrinal dialogues in the face of the growing threat coming from the "syncretistic" tendencies of Third World Christianity as manifested, in his view, at Canberra. The F&O arm of doctrinal dialogues has therefore to be strengthened by forming a new united front to counteract the danger. In his own words again:

To conclude, I only want to launch an idea to be discussed at different levels: after Canberra it is, for me, evident that the future of ecumenism will depend on the way the results of the bilateral dialogues will be "received" by the World Council of Churches. At the 7th Assembly, the manner some very crucial problems—such as contextualization, mission, inculturation—have been dealt with shows that the World Council can no longer be considered as having the capacity to lead the churches towards visible unity if it is not connected with other ecumenical institutions devoted to study deeply and peacefully the ecclesiological issues. Faith and Order itself has to rediscover its vocation as movement . . . and to act as a servant of the ecumenical movement *as such.* But bilateral dialogues, in strong connection with Faith and Order, are probably the group where the researches of this Commission and the studies undertaken in the diverse traditions may bear fruits.[71]

It is too early to say how fast this idea will be picked up and what long-term effects it will have on the ecumenical movement at large if it is implemented. The point that needs to be made in the present circumstances is that the CWCs exercise a great deal of influence and pressure on the ecumenical movement through both their structures and their member churches.[72] And, just like the RCC, the CWCs have proven their commitment to the bilateral dialogues by placing in them a considerable amount of financial resources and energy. This factor makes them a formidable force in the ecumenical movement. By remaining outside the WCC and supporting fully the bilateral dialogues, they have given a tremendous boost to the concerns of F&O. This gives a special character to the nature of the endeavor to which Tillard is calling forth and the further polarization that we have highlighted between the concerns for liberation and doctrinal orthodoxy in the ecumenical movement.

The CWCs and the Third World

The importance of the CWCs in the encounter with the Third World is another element that contributes to the confrontation between liberation and doctrinal orthodoxy. This concerns the uneasiness that obtained earlier between them and Third World churches. At a number of points and in different forums, some Third World churches had raised important questions regarding the CWCs. As Kinnamon noted, "They (especially those from Asia, Africa and the Pacific) fear that CWCs export theological motifs (and quarrels) inherited from Western culture that hinder truly united churches from taking authentic root in their settings. The divisions of sixteenth-century Europe, they argue, need not be normative for the worldwide church in this era."[73]

Beginning at the New Delhi Assembly of the WCC, the CWCs had been suspected by Third World churches of hardening the confessional borders and strengthening the confessional consciousness by various means. During the years following the Assembly, there was special criticism from Asia which also posed some questions regarding the CWCs' relationship to and influence on Third World churches related to them.[74] The fear had existed that the CWCs may exert undue pressure and stifle these churches in one way or another. Some had even expressed harsh judgements. "The real growing points of ecumenicity today are in the life of the younger churches. The real driving force in this organized confessionalism which is in danger of hardening into ecumenical sectarianism lies in the older christendom."[75] The Nairobi WCC Assembly (1975), for its part, had also noted that, with regard to the CWCs, "the critical questions raised by the churches engaged in the ecumenical movement, especially the churches of the Third World, have not lost their validity."[76] These questions were further pursued in the framework of the uniting churches. The latter were often of the opinion that the confessional families hampered some of their member churches—particularly those which depended financially on them—in their moves towards organic union with other confessions in their respective regions. We shall see later that the controversy on these and related issues did continue in a variety of ways.

By way of summary of what we have been driving at so far, we observe that, on the one hand, the concerns of the Third World churches are being increasingly vocalized both inside and outside the F&O and in the larger ecumenical movement. These concerns do not often mesh with the aims of the interconfessional doctrinal dialogues and consequently pose serious questions. On the other hand, we also observe that the multilateral dialogues conducted by F&O and the bilateral dialogues of the CWCs go together and strengthen one another. Both agree in the overall goal of searching for the unity of the Church through the achievement of doctrinal agreements. As the concerns polarize, they affect deeply the ecumenical movement and contribute first to its crisis, and then to fears of its possible rupture.

In the light of the above, one of the questions that arises is how these doctrinal dialogues have been viewed by the Third World churches and theologians, a Third World which, over a number of decades now, has been increasingly claiming to exert its own impact on the ecumenical movement. The question therefore becomes acute as to how such an exercise of ecumenism meshes or clashes with the one advocated by the interconfessional dialogues. I am convinced that the best way of contributing to the ecumenical movement is to bring closer these two currents, which often seem to be worlds apart, and to subject them to closer scrutiny. What do interconfessional dialogues have to do with the dominant concerns of the Third World?

As we have been able to see above, sometimes one would not be far from the truth if one were to describe the ecumenical scene as a divided camp where each part seems to hold dearly to its area of interest and is ready to defend it at all costs. In view of the subject at hand, the two ecumenical concerns seem to be moving parallel with one another without daring to encounter one another. But a critical confrontation is a must if the ecumenical movement is to be served.

Due to an awareness of and concern with this state of affairs, there have been growing calls for the need to engage in dialogue. On the one hand, there have been complaints that not enough has been done to generate the much-needed dialogue.[77] But there have also been attempts here and there to respond to the challenge. To this attempt belong the meetings of First

World and Third World theologians.[78] There are also specific calls to this effect within the ecumenical movement. "The truth can only be genuine when it is sought together. In this search, the critical and conflictive dialogue with the ecumenical theology of the Third World is considered indispensable if one is to arrive at the truth."[79] It is admitted by the advocates of such a rapprochement that Third World theologians have to be intentionally admitted into this process of discussion. A "hermeneutic of coherence," argues Houtepen, can only be possible "above all through the participation of the younger churches of Asia, Africa and Latin America. They have to become participants with equal rights within the Christian hermeneutical fellowship. . . . The Ecumenical Association of Third World Theologians (EATWOT) should be brought in in the capacity of an expert group in this cooperative work."[80]

My aim in this book is hopefully to contribute to the clarification of the nature of the confrontation, to delineate as much as possible the issues that are at stake, and, in this way, to further the dialogue. I propose to do this in three parts: first, I shall have a close look at the interconfessional doctrinal dialogues held on the international level that have characterized one important section of the ecumenical movement. In order to do so, I shall first try to introduce (mainly the bilateral) dialogues to the reader. What are they? How do they operate? Who sponsors them? What have they accomplished? What are their problems and prospects? What stage have they reached at present? Where are we now with such dialogues? These chapters will serve as an introduction to those who are not well acquainted with this aspect of ecumenism. They will also hopefully sharpen the reader's awareness of the issues involved. I shall, of course, include many of the criticisms that have been made of the doctrinal dialogues. Let me also add that the multilaterals will not be neglected.

Second, I shall present some of the voices of the Third World regarding the numerous aspects that touch on the important issues that the dialogues deal with as well as their overall concerns and priorities. How do Third World theologians assess them? What do they say about them? In what way do they agree or oppose them? What arguments do they use for or against them? What are the leading ideas and concepts which they put forward in relation to doctrinal dialogues? The chapter will try to gather the opinions expressed mainly by Third World theologians on this subject.

Third, in the next-to-final section, I shall present some of the meeting points, some elements of the argument where the two protagonists of liberation and doctrinal orthodoxy seem to be treading what may be called the same ground. An attempt will be made here to give a sort of synthesis by focusing on some particular issues which have drawn the attention of both parties and have emerged as predominant ones in the course of ecumenical discussions. A number of issues will be highlighted which have, in varying degrees, been treated by both. The aim is to show that, even in the face of the divergences in starting points and goal, there are a number of agreements on particular faith issues that draw the separate groups together. I shall bring the work to an end by offering some concluding remarks which will build on and draw from what had been said earlier.

In any Christian theological undertaking, it is the interpretation of the Christian faith that is at stake. Whether one leans heavily towards liberation or doctrinal orthodoxy as the main exigence of the Gospel, one is intimately engaged in the definition of the faith that stands on the person and message of Jesus Christ. It is thus an attempt to interpret the Gospel. There is no question about the fact that different interpretations of this Gospel are at play in all these theological enterprises. Therefore, a critical encounter of such theological trends is a useful exercise in the continuing effort to respond authentically to the engagement with the Gospel.

In concluding this introduction, it is perhaps in order to say that the following thoughts neither claim nor purport to provide a definitive answer to the vexing question regarding the right way of exercising ecumenism and the definition of its goals. The aim is rather modest. It consists in an attempt to summarize the opinions in this regard from the perspective of the author and to facilitate some dialogue by giving some resources. If it succeeds in doing so, then the wishes of the author will have been more than fulfilled.

— 1 —

The Interconfessional Dialogues: What Are They?

Writing in 1977, Harding Meyer, who has personally accompanied the bilateral dialogues and has contributed a great deal towards their success through his voluminous writings and personal engagement,[1] made the following observation: "One of the most significant developments within the ecumenical movement over the past fifteen years has been the evolution of a far-flung network of bilateral interconfessional dialogues. Of course, bilateral conversations between confessional churches have existed before as well. But it is only in recent times that they have become so concentrated and extensive that they can indeed be seen as a new kind of ecumenical encounter."[2] In what follows, I shall try to present this new element in the ecumenical movement.

The Bilaterals and the CWCs

A significant aspect of the international bilateral dialogues is that they are sponsored by the so-called World Confessional Families or Christian World Communions. These organizations embrace member churches throughout the world, which, generally speaking, adhere to a common confession of faith and share similar traditions, ways of worship, or, sometimes, church polity. These international organizations regroup under their umbrella the Anglicans (Anglican Communion), Lutherans (Lutheran World Federation), the Reformed (World Alliance of Reformed Churches), the Baptists (World Baptist Fellowship), etc. The communions sponsor these dialogues as representatives of their church constituencies. While the majority of these communions take part in the dialogues, there are some who have not yet done so.

Another aspect is that these dialogues are conducted independently of the WCC. The various CWCs use their own infrastructures and people in conducting the dialogues. These do not form part of the multilateral dialogues which are sponsored by the F&O Commission of the WCC, which have a longer history and in which many experts from various confessional backgrounds (Catholics, Protestants, Anglicans, Orthodox, etc.) are involved at one and the same time. In contrast to the WCC-sponsored multilateral dialogues, the bilaterals have one main practical reason: two confessional bodies—say, Catholics and Lutherans—are enabled to focus on dealing with specific doctrinal issues that divide them.[3] As a result of such double sponsorship, the bilaterals have sometimes been looked at askance by some proponents of the ecumenical movement. In the first place, there are those who question their efficacity. They are of the opinion that they may not be as fruitful as the multilaterals.[4] In addition, at one time, the bilaterals were viewed as running parallel to and even rivaling the multilateral dialogues on the one hand and threatening church union negotiations on the other (we shall say more about the latter later). There has thus been a lot of discussion on the relationship of the two forms of dialogue and their contribution to the ecumenical movement.[5] In the course of time, as regards content, both the bilaterals and the multilaterals have been seen as strengthening each other. It was recognized that the issues studied by one or the other dialogue and the results reached served as valuable resources to the other. They have thus been viewed as contributing to the success of both. This is also the case with regard to their structure. A close cooperation has developed between the (WCC) F&O Secretariat and the CWCs. This is evident in that the Commission is sometimes invited to send observers to some bilateral dialogues. At the same time, the F&O Secretariat has been instrumental in organizing the Forums on Bilateral Conversations, where the CWCs meet regularly (almost annually), among other things, "to promote the interaction between the bilateral and multilateral dialogues and to study the implications of bilateral findings for the ecumenical movement as a whole."[6] In their meetings, the secretaries of the CWCs summarize the achievements of the dialogues, assess their progress, pinpoint difficulties that may be encountered, and offer better organizational facilities to enhance their smooth running.[7] This Forum is a unique meeting place of the secretaries of the CWCs. It has been going on for more than two decades and shows the importance the CWCs attach to the doctrinal dialogues. The fact that the secretaries of the CWCs have never organized a regular meeting on such a high level on any other ecumenical issue says how central a role the doctrinal dialogues play in their vision of the ecumenical movement and their task.[8]

The Rise of the Bilaterals

There are a number of reasons that contributed to the rise of the bilateral dialogues. Some of these were general and others specific. On the whole, these factors pressed on the CWCs the need to engage in bilateral conversations. Among these reasons may be mentioned the following three:

First, in spite of the uneasy relationship that initially characterized the bilateral and multilateral dialogues, the former did profit significantly from the ecumenical atmosphere which had been created thanks to the latter. Having a longer history behind them, the multilateral dialogues had helped greatly in clearing the air of a great deal of misunderstanding that existed among the churches of different confessions. They had also contributed to strengthening and increasing the interaction among members of various churches who met through the forums of the F&O movement. By discussing many of the topics that would later be rediscussed in the bilateral dialogues, they have also contributed a great deal of material to build upon. "In this way, they [the multilateral dialogues] have prepared the ground for an encounter in the form of the bilateral dialogues of the individual churches, an encounter which is more direct and having specific goals."[9] Partly through the discussions and interactions that were made possible by the multilateral dialogues, the eyes of many church members were opened to the contributions of the doctrinal discussions in the search for the unity of the Church. Part of "the Affirmation which was adopted by a standing vote at the Edinburgh Faith and Order conference of 1937" states: "We are thankful that during recent years we have been drawn together: prejudices have been overcome, misunderstandings removed, and real, if limited progress has been made towards our goal of a common mind."[10] In their turn, the bilaterals also influenced and contributed to the multilaterals. On the one hand, they dealt with fresh issues and came to conclusions which could serve the multilaterals. On the other hand, they picked up the same topics and studied them in a much deeper and singular manner.[11]

Second, some of the CWCs were prodded by events taking place in some of their member churches. The role played by Third World churches in this regard is significant. Some of the latter were involved in union negotiations with member churches of a different communion.[12] In this case, the church union conversations which had started in India and East Africa were particularly significant.

There were practical reasons for setting up the various dialogues with the . . . confessions and churches: union negotiations between Lutheran churches and those churches in Southern India and Tanzania which have been strongly marked by the Anglican tradition provided the impulse for *dialogues with the Anglican Communion*. The problems which emerged in these union negotiations seemed to have immediate implications for the relationship of the negotiating churches to their confessional families. In the interests of a proper clarification of these problems, the Lutheran World Federation (LWF) decided to engage in dialogue with the Anglican community.[13]

For one reason or another, these local churches engaged in union negotiations gave the communions the necessary push to approach their counterparts on the international level. The Pullach Report of the Anglican/Lutheran conversations confirms this fact when it states that "in particular the involvement of Anglican and Lutheran churches in union negotiations led to the proposal of official conversations between the Lutheran World Federation (LWF) and the Anglican Communion."[14]

The conversations between the Baptists and the Reformed also take note that church union negotiations taking place among Third World member churches of their respective confessional families did influence their desire to talk officially to one another in the form of a bilateral dialogue. Among these developments, they list "the emergence of church union consultations and indeed one union now consummated in North India in which Baptist churches are fully involved"[15] as one of the reasons behind the beginning of their bilateral discussions. It is noteworthy that impulses from the Third World churches played an important role in these cases.

Third, the Second Vatican Council of the Roman Catholic Church (1962-1965) became a very important source for the flowering of bilateral conversations.[16] First, many non-Catholic observers had the "remarkable" possibility of being invited to be present during the deliberations of the Council.[17] The friendships that were made possible through the meetings in the Council proved invaluable in the establishment of the bilaterals. This was an unprecedented occasion. It gave many of the observers the unique opportunity to establish valuable contacts with the leaders of the Roman Catholic Church who were members of the Council. As was the case with the Lutherans, "binding terms were thought and defined for systematic dialogue as the direct result of the intensive contacts and increased mutual trust between the Lutheran delegates/observers at the Second Vatican Council and a number of leading representatives of the Catholic Church."[18] Second, the invited guests gained a rare inside view of the RCC. A channel of communication was opened through which they brought valuable information about the RCC to their churches. To take just one example, "The presence of Orthodox Church observers [at the Council] played a very important role both for the reflection which took place within the Catholic Church, and for the direct information they brought back to their own Churches about the Catholic Church's new attitude."[19] Third, according to the reading of many, a fundamental shift in the RCC's understanding of other Christian churches found expression in the Council. With the promulgation of the Decree on Ecumenism, the RCC referred to Protestants as "separated brethren" and encouraged Catholic theologians to engage in research work and dialogue with them.[20] The decree opened up the RCC for participation in the ecumenical movement, which, up to that time, was a predominantly Protestant movement. As Harding Meyer has written in evaluating the significance of the Council's decision and the decree: "What the promulgation of the Decree on Ecumenism achieved for Roman Catholic/Protestant relationships was the momentous conversion of a history of deepening division and estrangement lasting for four centuries into a history of growing contact and mutual understanding."[21] On the whole, the Decree on Ecumenism which paved the way for the official entry of the RCC into the ecumenical movement (not membership in the WCC) also had a decisive effect on the bilaterals.[22] As the Lutherans have admitted: "The official entry of the Roman Catholic Church into the ecumenical movement has had a powerful influence on the World Confessional Families including the Lutheran World Federation. Since Vatican II many bilateral contacts and conversations have resulted at world, national and regional levels. Stimulated in part by these Roman Catholic relationships a number of dialogues have also been initiated with other churches and world confessional bodies."[23]

It must be mentioned in passing that such a positive interpretation of the impact of the Decree on Ecumenism is also contested by some. While it is here argued that through the decree, the RCC opened up a new era of ecumenism, there are those who see that it was also an ambiguous if mixed blessing; it is a double-edged sword. It is argued in this perspective that "the conciliar decree on ecumenism will be a source of hope and a stone of stumbling to the ecumenical movement."[24] This is to say that its message was not as clear and as forthright as one would wish with regard to the RCC's ecumenical opening to the other confessions. This is seen in the sometimes opposite or contradictory interpretations to which the famous phrase "subsists in" is given even by highly placed Roman Catholics themselves. This has also given rise to conflicting signals coming out of Rome itself with regard to its ecumenical direction, depending upon who is interpreting the decree at one given time.

The Aims of the Dialogues

What are the aims behind the bilaterals? What do the CWCs and the churches involved in the process expect from them? There is indeed a variety of aims and expectations. It is true that sometimes the bilaterals have been accused of not having a clear goal and of being "initiated in a relatively arbitrary and haphazard way."[25] Nils Ehrenstroem lists an amalgam of reasons, some of which are not always accompanied by the best of intentions. "The deeper aspirations are often obscure and diffuse: an instinctive desire to join the bandwagon, a feeling of excited curiosity . . . in the face of the unheard-of opportunity to 'dialogue' for the first time with the Roman archantagonists, a convenient alibi for denominational self-promotion, and, at a more serious level, the sense of a kairos, a historical moment of divine presence and promise, which one dare not neglect."[26] The reasons stated clearly by the parties in the dialogues follow.

The first aim that one observes is the acquisition of a better understanding of one another's beliefs and practices, the removal of prejudices, and the opening of channels of communication. Conversations with such an aim focus on particular issues that have proven to be causes for misunderstanding between two communions. For example, the main aim behind the Baptist/Reformed dialogue is to gather up-to-date information on developments within the two communions, to discuss some divisive issues such as baptism, and "to explore together the nature of our disagreements and how best we may overcome our differences."[27] This is also the case with the aims of the RCC/Baptist conversations. It is "the purpose of these conversations to come to a better understanding of similarities and differences in Baptist and Roman Catholic doctrinal, ecclesial, pastoral and mission concerns. They also aim at identifying existing prejudices and improving relations between their communities."[28] Such cases can be multiplied.

Closely related to the above but of a still different category is the second form of bilateral dialogue, which does not aim at addressing any structural questions. It is more or less interested in using the forum of the dialogues to foster cordial relations between churches and interconfessional movements. A typical example is the RCC/Pentecostal dialogue. There is no intention here to move beyond the maintenance of useful and constructive contacts. This is accomplished by discussions on broad issues of common concern, such as the Holy Spirit, baptism, or Scripture and tradition. In this case, the dialogues do not possess any "authority" because the Pentecostals are not delegated officially by a body which is representative of their movement. The Pentecostal members engage in the dialogue only in their capacity as respected members of the movement. They are appointed by individual congregations. Therefore, the aims of the conversations involving them are stated in general terms, that is, "that prayer, spirituality and theological reflection be a shared concern at the international level in the form of dialogue."[29]

Third, there are communions that set a higher goal for the discussions by aiming at "a mutual recognition and fellowship." Some of the best examples are perhaps the Lutheran/RCC dialogues. Their goal was earlier defined as restoring "communion."[30] Even though this was not defined clearly at that stage, it was agreed that it is a goal which would be reached gradually by taking one step at a time. It is admitted that this is an open process in which "the Holy Spirit will show us the steps and lead us in paths which for the most part we cannot at present envisage."[31] As the latest product of the dialogue puts it, the goals of the conversations consist in achieving "unity in the truth, the elimination of divisive differences, and thus the achievement of church fellowship—these have been and are the main concerns in the dialogue initiated in 1967 between the Lutheran World Federation and the Roman Catholic Church." Subsequent meetings have taken the opportunity to spell out as clearly as possible the models of unity that are available for Roman Catholics and Lutherans and the steps that lead to unity. The results of this attempt are perhaps the most ambitious and at the same time the most concrete delineations of the steps to unity that have ever been made by two communions. In their joint report FAC-ING UNITY, Lutherans and Roman Catholics went very far in defining the various "concepts of unity and models of union." Furthermore, they sought "to outline step by step how such church fellowship could become a reality."[32]

A more concrete even though verbally ambiguous goal is also set by the Anglicans and Roman Catholics. At several points, they state their goal as the achievement of "organic union." Before the start of the dialogues, the leaders of the two churches, namely, the Pope and the Archbishop of Canterbury, agreed that they would aim at restoring unity between the two churches. They declared, in their own words, that "they resolve for a future in which our common aim would be the restoration of full organic union . . . of our two communions." At a later date, another related concept comes up—"corporate union." Even though this concept was interchangeable with that of "organic union," it is now made to carry a slightly different meaning. This is seen when a clarification is offered in which it is stated that the term "corporate" is not used in its classical sense, meaning "organic." It has been rephrased to mean "union in diversity" or, as is said, a unity of churches "which remain churches and nevertheless become one church."[33]

The Catholics and the Orthodox have also stated their goal in a clear manner. They put it as follows: "The purpose of the dialogue between the Roman Catholic Church and the Orthodox Church is the re-establishment of full communion between these two churches. This communion founded on the unity of faith according to the common experience and tradition of the ancient Church, will find its expression in the common celebration of the Holy Eucharist."[34] It may be added here that the RCC gives a high priority to its dialogue with the Orthodox[35] even though the dialogue "has never been an easy one."[36] Compared to the churches of the Reformation, the Orthodox have been accorded a special place since Vatican Council II. They are also viewed as being closer to the teachings and traditions of the RCC even though they have a defect because they do not recognize the primacy of the Pope. Even so, the going of the dialogues has been rough.

The Topics of the Dialogues

There has been an extremely wide range of topics that have been discussed in the bilateral dialogues. Ecclesiological, christological, and other doctrinal issues have, at one time or another and in varying degrees, found their way into the conversations. On the whole, however, there are a number of particular issues that have caught, so to speak, the minds of the bilaterals. These appear in the agendas of a number of conversations. In many cases, they are topics which were causes of division of the churches in the past. We mention below three of the important topics which formed the subject matter of many dialogues and some of the agreements reached on them. These are the issues of authority, the Eucharist, and ministry.

The Issue of Authority

One of the most difficult topics in the bilateral dialogues is the question of authority. In the words of Harding Meyer: "This problem [authority in the Church] is even now one of the biggest problems and themes of the dialogues! . . . There are very clearly three themes in the dialogues which stand in the center and which one meets time and again. To these belongs besides the Eucharist and church ministry the question of authority in the church."[37] Under this general rubric come the many questions that have to do with the sources and extent of authority of the church within as well as outside itself. Under this topic are also encompassed a vast array of subjects such as the authority of the Gospel, the Scriptures, and tradition. The question of how all these are related to one another, their levels of authority, the interpretative principle(s), if any, which guide one through the diversity of Scripture, and how the various traditions of the church are related to Scripture are subsumed under this heading. The reformation principles of "Scripture alone" and "faith alone" as well as the authority of the confessional writings of the churches, the creeds, and councils come up for discussion under this topic. The controversial issues of the papacy and the nature of its authority also belong to it.[38]

In some aspects of this topic, it has been claimed that some far-reaching agreements have been reached. On the one hand, the normative character of the Scriptures is affirmed. The Bible—the Old and New Testaments—is acknowledged as the only norm of faith and life. It has thus a primary authority over and above any other text(s). On the other hand, it is affirmed that the sharp distinction that often obtained between Scripture and tradition is now practically superseded. There is general recognition that both belong together even though it is acknowledged that tradition should be viewed in the light of Scripture and be subject to it. As the Malta Report of the Lutheran/RCC dialogue puts it: "The Scripture can no longer be exclusively contrasted with tradition, because the New Testament itself is the product of primitive tradition. Yet as the witness to the fundamental tradition, Scripture has a normative role for the entire later tradition of the church."[39] Furthermore, the Apostles' and Nicean-Constantinopolitan Creeds are seen as faithful expressions of the apostolic faith handed down to the Church.[40] They are seen as faithful summaries of the Christian faith as it has been handed down through the ages. It is even asserted that the Reformation principle of "justification by faith" is no longer posed as a divisive issue between Protestants and Catholics even though the claim that it is the sole key to the Scriptures is still contested. But we shall say more about the nature and significance of the agreements on this particular issue later.

The Issue of the Eucharist

A second topic that has extensively engaged the bilateral discussions is the Eucharist. It is necessary to point out here that the separation of Christians at the table of the Lord has weighed heavily on many churches. Many have been asking why Christians who confess their faith in one Lord have been content with continuing to shut out their fellow Christians from the Lord's Supper administered in their respective churches. Serious efforts were thus expended to reach agreements on this point. But the issue of the Eucharist is further complicated because it is tied to that of ministry. That is to say, it is bound up with the question of who is authorized to administer the sacraments in a valid way? Can a pastor/priest who is not ordained "properly" administer the sacraments? Can one who does not belong in the "apostolic succession" by not being ordained by a duly ordained bishop do so? If so, are the sacraments so administered valid for salvation? As the RCC/Lutheran conversations conveniently put it: "Greater agreement on the Eucharist requires the overcoming of the hitherto existing differences concerning the ordained ministry."[41] It is often stated that substantial agreements reached on the issue of the Eucharist could not lead to further steps to unity mainly because of remaining differences on the nature of the ministry.

It is significant to note that important convergences have been attained with regard to the understanding of the Eucharist, especially between Catholics and the churches of the Reformation tradition.[42] It is also worth noting that most of the parties to the conversations agree on the terminology to use. The Eucharist was often referred to by different names: Mass, Lord's Supper, holy communion, holy mysteries, etc. It seems now that the term "Eucharist" has the upper hand.[43] Agreements have been recorded concerning the real presence of Christ in the Eucharist and the once-for-all nature of the sacrifice of Christ. There have been controversies going back to the Reformation on the manner of the presence of Christ in the Eucharist. Do the bread and wine change (transubstantiation) or do they remain what they are while they convey Christ's presence all the same (consubstantiation)? What is the role of the word of the presiding priest in the celebration? Are the elements symbols of the presence of the ascended Christ or are they his true body and blood? Some of the agreements on these and related issues have been viewed as being so solid that some dialogue groups have come to the bold conclusion that interim eucharistic hospitality (sharing the Eucharist sometimes) under special circumstances can and should be allowed. That is to say that members of different churches should be allowed to take part in the Eucharist administered in churches other than their own.[44]

There are other convergences in terms of the frequency of celebrating the Eucharist. There is general agreement, in line with the recommendation of the Lima Baptism, Eucharist, and Ministry document, that celebration take place at least once a week.[45] There is also general understanding on the contents of the liturgy in which the Eucharist is celebrated. Here are included the invocation of the Holy Spirit, the sermon, the confession of faith and sins, etc., as important elements. There are of course some points that still remain unresolved. These have to do with the sacrificial nature of the RCC Mass. This is meant to address the question of whether the Eucharist is a repetition of the sacrifice once accomplished by Christ on the cross or not. And as mentioned above, the relationships of the Eucharist and the ministry are also outstanding problems which have not been resolved to the satisfaction of all.[46]

The Issue of Ministry

The third issue is that of ministry. The issues of the nature of the ministry of Christ and that of the church as a serving community fall under this rubric. In addition, the priesthood of all believers and its relationship to the ordained ministry and the question of whether the latter belongs to a different category from the former, and in what way, are debated. Is the ordained priest or pastor different from the laymen, does one have a higher relationship to God and thus authority by virtue of one's ordination? Or is the special status of the pastor/priest due to the congregation or church which confers on him/her a special responsibility which is, in the final analysis, accountable to it?

This issue of ministry becomes a particularly difficult point in some dialogues. This is precisely the case because it is tied to the question of the recognition by the RCC of the validity of the ministry exercised by the Anglicans and the Reformation churches. That is, the RCC contests on the basis of its doctrinal positions the correctness of the ministry exercised by these churches. This means that the ministers ordained in these churches are not recognized as true ministers who have the capacity, among other things, to administer the sacraments. The RCC line of argument is based on the judgement of the situation that arose due to the Reformation. It is illuminating to hear in this connection the opinion of a Roman Catholic on the change that came about regarding the understanding of the ministry after the Reformation:

> Was there a new doctrine on the sacraments and a new conception of the Church, which would have deprived the Lutheran and Reformed Churches, and, starting with Edward VI and Elizabeth, the Church of England, of sharing the true being of the Church? Catholics generally answered in the affirmative, and so found themselves unable to recognize the ministry of Lutheran and Calvinist pastors as the ministers of the Church, and their ordination as ordination to the Christian priesthood. The Reformer's theology and the breaking of communion combined to make the Protestant ministry unrecognizable to Catholics.

. . . Catholics rejected the ordination and the ministry of Lutheran and Calvinist pastors, and eventually (but not so clearly at first) those of Anglican bishops and priests.[47]

Even so, there are agreements on some other touchy aspects of the issue. With regard to the concept of apostolic succession, for example, the understanding, in some dialogues, of the succession in terms of an uninterrupted apostolic teaching and faithful preaching of the Gospel by the church through the ages has opened up new possibilities.[48] It is also generally agreed that the threefold pattern of ministry—episcopal, presbyterial, and diaconal—is largely believed to have been developed after the close of the New Testament era.[49] Still, its usefulness for present church order is acknowledged and recommended.[50] The sharp differences that obtained earlier between the mainly functional understanding of the ordained ministry in the churches of the Reformation tradition and the "sacramental" understanding in the RCC have largely attained a measure of understanding. In plain terms, some Reformation traditions insisted that the minister is one among equals. S/he is chosen by the congregation to be responsible for a special task assigned to her/him by the congregation. In the Orthodox and Roman Catholic churches, however, the priest is divinely appointed. Due to his part in the apostolic succession, made possible through the ordination by a bishop who himself belongs in that succession which goes back to Jesus, the priest belongs to a special category. As a result, there are religious tasks which only a priest can perform, especially the administration of the sacraments.

The question of the papacy still remains a point of contention, for example, with the Methodists.[51] There have been no dialogues on the international level which have specifically broached the subject other than in the context of other issues. It must, however, be mentioned that Lutherans and Anglicans have generally consented that a reformed papacy would serve the unity of the church: "But in various dialogues, the possibility begins to emerge that the Petrine office of the Bishop of Rome also need not be excluded by Lutherans as a visible sign of the unity of the church as a whole, 'insofar as [this office] is subordinated to the primacy of the gospel by theological reinterpretation and practical restructuring.' "[52] This does not mean that such a would-be understanding has received the blessing of all Lutherans. There are those who are vehemently opposed to undertaking such steps.[53] With regard to the Anglicans, following the lead given by the Archbishop of Canterbury—the primate of the Anglican Communion—the Anglican partners and their Catholic counterparts have stated together: "We believe that the primacy of the bishop of Rome can be affirmed as part of God's design for the universal Koinonia in terms which are compatible with both our traditions."[54] The serious problem for the Orthodox lies in the papacy and Mariology. Their understanding of the church is opposed to having one head over all the churches.[55] Such an opposition from the Orthodox side led one writer to raise the following difficult question, revealing the intricacies of the dialogue: "Most important of all, can a stage be envisaged of mutual recognition and full communion without Orthodox acceptance of Roman Catholic retraction of (for example) Marian dogmas and Papal infallibility, and without Papal jurisdiction over Orthodox local churches?"[56]

On the question of episcopacy, there has been a good deal of agreement. The result is that a number of communions which do not practice the "historic episcopate" are willing to introduce it. This is the case with the Lutherans who do not practice it yet, for example.[57] It is argued that such a succession can be "a sign of the unity and continuity of the church."[58] A number of practical steps are proposed for the process of introducing the episcopal ministry, e.g., the participation of episcopal bishops in the ordination of nonepiscopal ones, the practice of the laying on of hands, etc.

There remain a number of other issues which have not been discussed yet. The issue of Mary is highly contested by Protestants. In most cases, they have even resisted Catholic attempts to bring it up as an issue in the dialogues. On the whole, the RCC emphasis on Mary is taken as a hindrance to agreements with other Protestant confessions. There seems to be an apparent unity among non-Catholic confessional groups in resisting the RCC position on this issue.[59] There are, however, some attempts to open some doors for understanding from the Protestant side.[60] In contrast, the question of the infallibility of the Pope is a highly contested issue from the Protestant side.[61] In some instances, the papacy is claimed as being one of the most intractable issues standing in the way of church unity.

Overall, it is argued that amazing convergences and agreements have been reached on a number of doctrinal issues. Many elements that divided the churches have been discussed and "substantial agreements" obtained. To take one case as an example, the Lutheran/RCC dialogues have tabled a number of doctrinal issues and claimed to have reached understanding on them. The issues of the Eucharist, ministry, the church, aspects of the teaching on the papacy, and others have been dealt with. As already mentioned above, some have even dared to outline the steps to be taken to achieve the unity of Lutherans and Roman Catholics. The agreements are such that some are convinced that a concrete step must be taken by the hierarchies of the churches. That is to say, since the theological commissions have done their job, it is now up to the church authorities to take concrete steps that shape the lives of the two bodies.[62]

Such a conviction is present on the Catholic side as well. But the dilemma is clear, as one observes in one dialogue: "On the one hand, an amazingly high degree of mutual understanding has been reached in Lutheran-Catholic dialog. . . .; on the other hand, the documents handed over to the churches fail to provide the basis on which the struggle to attain the visible unity of the Church in the sense of 'sister churches' can make headway."[63]

At the center of this ambivalence or the reservations visible in the responses of the churches to the results of the dialogues stand the concepts of unity held by one or the other church. These have therefore constituted one of the main discussion points in the whole range of the bilateral dialogues. We shall therefore now turn to them.

Concepts of Unity

Over and above the many issues that have engaged the bilaterals, there is one overriding issue that has gradually come to be recognized as central. This is the definition of the vision of the unity of the church. We have seen above how quite a few of the bilaterals have agreed that their work was aimed at restoring the unity of the one Church (Anglicans/RCC), the realization of visible unity in Christ (Disciples of Christ/RCC), and the pursuit of the "hope of the reunion of separated Christians." But what kind of unity are all the partners in dialogue talking about? Do they have the same concept of unity? If not, what are their specific understandings of this concept? It has been acknowledged that in order to work towards achieving unity, it is imperative that a common vision of this unity be developed first. As Bangalore stated it: "On the basis of their understanding of the nature of the Church, the various traditions hold and promote different concepts of the unity of the Church. If the churches are to advance towards unity, they need to develop a common vision of their goal."[64]

It was in recognition of this fact that the Forum on Bilateral Conversations at its first meeting dealt with this issue. It defined its task as follows: "The churches have to engage in a serious effort in order to agree on the nature of the unity we seek. Yet such agreement is required in order to advance together: hence comes the need for those engaged in bilateral conversations to participate in the constant effort to clarify their concepts of unity and to reach agreement on a fundamental concept of unity which may afford criteria for evaluating models of union."[65] One must admit, however, that, even though much work has been done for so many years in this regard, there is still "a great deal of confusion on the shape of the visible unity we seek."[66] The RCC/Lutheran dialogue, which has consistently tackled the task of defining the concepts of unity more than any other group, has also admitted that here the danger of terminological confusion and misunderstanding is great.[67] Nevertheless, intrepid minds have not been deterred by such difficulties from attempting to present, if not a definition, at least an outline of the concepts of unity sought after. Among the many models that have been developed, one notes the following examples.[68]

Organic Union

The concept of "organic union" is one of the original concepts which marked the goal of the ecumenical movement from its early days.[69] It lies behind some of the church unions that took place in some parts of the world.

This concept envisages the union of once separated churches into one body. The confessional distinctions and organizational differences are transcended and merger takes place. The new union consists in a common confession of faith, a common ministry and sacraments, and a new organizational structure that replaces the old. The resources of the merging churches are brought together and become common property, and the new church henceforth forges one identity under one name.[70] The merging churches thus give up their specific denominational characteristics and identities and opt for a new church life together in union.

Unity as Conciliar Fellowship

The concept of the church as a "conciliar fellowship" is closely related to that of organic union.[71] It is sometimes viewed as a further elaboration of the concept of organic union. Having said this, one notices that there are some slight but significant nuances that may be said to separate the two concepts. The basic idea underlying the concept of conciliar fellowship is that a number of churches that are found within a particular region or country recognize one another as churches. There are four basic requirements for the constitution of this fellowship: 1) the sharing of one faith, 2) mutual recognition of one another's baptism, Eucharist, and ministry, 3) the ending of mutual prejudices, hostilities and condemnations, and 4) the establishment of ways and means of deciding together. The special characteristic of this concept is that the churches agree to conduct their affairs in common under one council. "Conciliarity expresses the interim union of the churches separated by space, culture or time, by living intensely the unity in Christ and seeking from time to time, by councils of representatives of all the local churches at various geographical levels, to express their unity visibly in a common meeting."[72] Such a meeting is expected to take place whenever the need arises in the churches to deliberate on and to arrive at decisions on issues that affect their lives as churches.[73] There is some unclarity here, but it seems that, in this model, each church retains its own particular individuality. There is room for diversity and "even conflict."[74] "To accept conciliarity as the direction in which we must move means deepening our mutual commitment at all levels. This does not mean moving in the direction of uniformity. . . . On the contrary . . . , if the unity of the Church is to serve the unity of mankind, it must provide room both for wide variety of forms, and for differences and even conflict."[75] The churches which participate in this conciliarity are "sister churches" and maintain "sustained and sustaining relationships with one another."[76] "Different members in each local community, and different local communities, do and should manifest a rich diversity, and develop their own proper personality."[77] In an attempt to differentiate between the concepts of organic union and conciliar fellowship, it is said that "in relation to the present debate, it has shown itself in a fear that 'organic union' could mean the development of oppressive structures hindering the freedom and spontaneity proper to the Christian life. By contrast, the 'conciliar' model emphasizes the elements of variety and individuality. Councils are gatherings of churches which are different from one another and respect their differences."

Unity in Reconciled Diversity

The third model that has emerged is that of "unity in reconciled diversity." This concept is closely related to the CWCs because it was developed in the context of their Forum held in 1974.[78] Initially, it seemed that it was mainly developed in reaction to the concepts of organic union and conciliar fellowship. The CWCs were of the conviction that the range of these two concepts was too narrow. These concepts presupposed the death of confessional identities as we know them, with their particular pieties, specific traditions, ways of worship, and doctrinal convictions. The communions argued that there are indeed healthy and positive confessional nuances and emphases which need to be retained even within a united church. The concepts of organic union and conciliar fellowship, in their opinion, do not take these concerns into consideration. The aim was thus to find a model of unity which accommodated legitimate and edifying confessional diversities.[79]

In subsequent discussions, the communions have argued that this concept was not specifically developed to counter or pose as a rival to that of conciliar fellowship.[80] They argue instead that the concept of reconciled diversity was immediately related to that of conciliar fellowship and regarded from the beginning as a complementary and corrective concept and in no sense a "rival" one. It simply tries to enlarge the vision. The four requirements for conciliar fellowship are recognized as necessary and valid. Even so, the concern is that the confessional expressions should not simply die out in favor of uniformity, a line of thought which is affirmed in the Lutheran/RCC 1980 document, WAYS TO COMMUNITY: "It is against the nature of the search for Christian unity to level down all differences in the realm of church life. . . . The operative principle must here be that the changes reciprocally risked by increased cooperation must be balanced by a legitimate concern to preserve the identities and special characteristics which each side derives from its tradition."[81] But in being retained even in a united church, the hope is that the doctrinal and other differences will lose their divisive character; it is expected that they change and be transformed to reflect the reconciliation that is at the heart of the unity of the churches in the first place.[82]

At one time, this concept generated a heated debate. It was accused of aiming at preserving the confessional differences under the guise of unity. It was attacked as a dangerous concept which tried to evade the responsibilities and demands of unity by sanctioning and perpetuating the divisions that characterize the various confessions. Its opposition to the concept of conciliar fellowship was highlighted, and its emphasis on the legitimacy and the need to continue the existence of the confessional specificities even after the realization of unity was severely criticized.[83]

In light of the criticism, it has been argued that the concept was presented as a corrective to concepts of unity which tended to emphasize uniformity which may preclude meaningful diversity. This explanation was offered in the first Forum on Bilateral Conversations of the CWCs in 1978. Their Report states: "It has now been made very clear that unity in reconciled diversity is to be an expression of the organic unity of the church as the body of Christ—that the reconciliation of diversities and the overcoming of their separation is the basic aim."[84]

It is interesting to note subsequently that the very people who advocated the concept of unity in reconciled diversity in the first place are recognizing that a serious question mark is being put beside this concept. Harding Meyer states: "It is no exaggeration, I fear, to speak of an emerging crisis over the concept of 'unity in diversity.' "[85] The problem consists in stretching too far the words "unity" and "diversity." The danger was, according to Meyer, that the diversity recommended may be so wide that the limits are never clear. In the process, the idea of unity is somewhat left behind or drastically attenuated. "It is hardly possible to reconcile this view of the unity we seek with the understanding of unity held within the ecumenical movement with great unanimity in spite of certain differences of emphasis."[86] Echoing the criticism hurled earlier at the concept by Duchrow, Meyer sees that the insistence on the aspect of diversity might be seen as endorsing the status quo. The conclusion may be wrongly drawn that the concept supports the continuation of the confessional differences and divisions without any change. Such an interpretation of the concept is, its proponents argue, contrary to its intention.

It was finally agreed by the WCC and the CWCs that the concepts of conciliar fellowship and unity in reconciled diversity are interdependent and that they do not necessarily exclude each other.[87] It was claimed that they do not provide conflicting models of unity but complement and correct each other by providing sharpness and emphasis on particular points. They are viewed as re-enforcing one another and creating a healthy synthesis.[88]

Church Fellowship in Concord

The fourth model of unity is that of "church fellowship in concord." This is the model that has been developed and taken up by some eighty churches coming out of the Reformation tradition in Europe and elsewhere who took steps to realize church fellowship among themselves. This has involved mainly Lutheran, Reformed, and United churches as well as the Waldensians in Italy and a Lutheran church from as far away as Argentina. The basic document of this fellowship in concord was completed and sent to the participating churches in 1973 for confirmation.[89] The participating churches acknowledge that they benefited from their historical distance from the Reformation period. This distance has had a beneficial effect on their present relationships. For it had led them to declare that the mutual condemnations of the Reformation period are no longer valid in that they do not pose themselves as obstacles to church fellowship. On the doctrinal level, they agree that the message of "justification by faith" is the measuring stick of the church's preaching and is "the heart of Scripture." They also agree on the basic essentials of the faith, such as the recognition of the validity of one another's baptism and Eucharist. Having reached broad agreements on other doctrinal issues that were bases of contention in the Reformation period, they acknowledge that differences in styles of worship, traditions of spirituality, and church order remain. But such differences no longer constitute church-dividing issues. On the basis of such consensus, they agree to establish church fellowship, which means that "churches with different confessional positions accord each other fellowship in word and sacrament, and strive for the fullest possible cooperation in witness and service in the world." Here, individual churches are left with the freedom to continue to adhere to their confessional traditions. This does not entail organizational changes, for these remain intact. All the same, the churches commit themselves to common witness, service, study of theological problems, and the promotion "of the ecumenical fellowship of all Christian Churches."[90]

In the course of time, the strengths and deficiencies of the Leuenberg agreement have been visible. While there have been positive developments on the basis of the agreements in some areas, there has also been no significant movement in some. As Andre Birmele observed:

> The search for a common commitment in the face of ethical, social, and political changes (Witness and Service, LA 36) and the possible establishment of common structures at the level of the national or regional church have hardly given rise to noteworthy developments. On the other hand, the other two elements, namely the continuation of theological dialogue and the attempt to understand Leuenberg in a more general ecumenical context, have been at the center of research over the years.[91]

As the discussions continue, one also sees different interpretations of the agreement and its implications for the wider ecumenical movement, which surface among the adhering churches. Another persistent criticism "states that the Agreement has not brought any change in church life. The great challenges of society are not taken up; interest seems to center on certain non-urgent theological questions." A far more severe criticism is heard when it is said that "the realization of church fellowship is not satisfactory. In too many instances, the Agreement serves as a pretext for cementing the status quo." Even in view of its negative aspects, however, it is claimed that it is "one of the only models of church fellowship that has reached the stage of any concrete implementation."[92]

In rounding up the discussion on the models and concepts of unity, one has to admit that only a sketchy picture can be given here. As was stated in the beginning of the section, the discussion on these particular issues is not very clear. First, the list of the various models which claim to be such is not clear-cut. The lines of demarcation are not as clear as one would expect. Sometimes the concepts are so related to one another that a different count would either shorten or lengthen the list. Second, for a would-be impartial observer, there are many points of contact among the various concepts. That is, there are points that are found in one which can be included in the other. The differences seem to lie in their particular emphases. Third, one also observes that there is a great deal of verbiage, which sometimes seems to contribute more to the clouding of the issues at stake. This defect cannot of course be entirely avoided, especially when dealing with an elusive topic such as the unity of the church in view of the long history of divisions of the Christian churches. The unclarity that accompanies them does not in any way lessen their positive contribution in the overall discussion concerning the goal the churches are aiming at.

Questioning the Concept of Unity

It is worthwhile at this juncture to point out some of the arguments that shake these descriptions of unity. A common presupposition that underlies them all and the whole search for the unity of the church is that there is something which the church has lost and which needs to be restored. At a certain point in her history, the Christian Church was united or manifested a certain shape of unity. In the course of time, this unity had been lost for various reasons. The uppermost reason for the division is the confessional, or doctrinal, differences. It follows from this that, in order to attain unity, one has to focus mainly on doctrinal discussions to remove the confessional disagreements. There is the explicit presupposition that church divisions were caused by differences in doctrines. The unity that we seek will thus entail attacking these dividing issues. The removal of the doctrinal differences through the conversations thus stands at the center of the search for, and the recovery of, the lost unity. But there are also questions which are being raised with regard to the presuppositions that underlie such a quest for unity. These come from different quarters. It is worth our while to cast a brief glance at some of the prominent ones.

Questioning from Faith and Order

The first questioning comes from within the Commission of F&O itself. In the "Unity and Renewal" study of the Commission, there have arisen proposals which argue that there needs to be a revision of the concepts of unity which have been closely identified with the movement. It is interesting to note that the elements that are listed in forming the model of unity do not even include some of the elements which require doctrinal agreements. As a report of the Singapore consultation organized by the Commission puts it:

It now seems clear that any model of unity which hopes to be taken seriously, or which is offered as a basis for ecumenical work, must include or enable the following elements:
* the common confession of Jesus as Lord
* the welcoming of diversity
* a common witness which articulates and strengthens justice
* eucharistic sharing, understood as spiritual empowering to serve those suffering injustice
* common action for justice
* mutual correction, leading to common repentance and renewal.[93]

This line of thought is corroborated and reenforced by another consultation that was held in Porto Alegre, Brazil, and which followed the same study theme. This consultation also gave proof of the fact that the nature of the unity that is being thought by the churches has to change. There are new developments which pressure the old concepts to reevaluate themselves. "Lastly, there was a recognition that the terms of the unity debate have changed: the traditional divisions of the various confessions . . . which have been transplanted to Latin America in different historical periods, have been dramatically altered by the political commitment which is searching for justice for the poor. This is the new matrix in which the common task for church unity, and the common search for justice, is now located."[94]

It is clear from the above that the issue of justice increasingly becomes indispensable in the envisioning of unity. The community which finds itself searching unity must see to it that justice becomes an integral aspect of its constitution. Justice becomes an indispensable criterion for legitimizing any form of unity. In the absence of this factor, the unity towards which the churches strive becomes truncated, incomplete.

Closely related to this need to include justice in the definition of the concepts of unity is the need to expand them in the light of church situations in the nonwestern world. There are other experiences of unity which should be added to the ones already listed and which rest mainly on the experience of the church in the West. The United and Uniting churches, for example, while agreeing that the factor of justice be included in the definition of unity, also make reference to other experiences of church unity. The new ones would include "a) the experience of the church in the People's Republic of China, b) the life of the base communities in Latin America, c) the various forms of local and national covenanting . . . as well as the concept of 'unity as solidarity.' "[95]

Questionings from the New Testament

The second challenge comes from the study of the New Testament. There are quite a few voices which are arguing that the multiplicity of the New Testament understanding regarding faith and church organization be taken into consideration. The conviction has been growing that the early church was not as homogenous doctrinally and organizationally as has often been understood. In fact, the opposite is now believed to have been the case. "In the light of the basis of proclamation and faith of the [early] church, unity in diversity was from the beginning an essential and, ecumenically, an exceedingly significant theme."[96] But there are three contributions especially to the concepts of unity which should be mentioned at this juncture. This comes especially from the study of the New Testament and the early church. These ideas, presented by prominent New Testament scholars, have argued consistently that the church in the New Testament era did not envisage a unity in doctrine and institutional organization.

The first challenge to the vision of unity had already been represented strongly by the German theologian Ernst Kaesemann as far back as 1951. He asked the question point-blank: "Does the unity of the Church find its basis in the canon of the New Testament?" After a cursory examination of a number of factors that characterize the New Testament, he noted especially three elements. First, there are diversities in the kerygmata in the New Testament; second, there a variety of theological positions; and third, they are not all prone to unification. He then stated his major conclusion as follows:

> The New Testament canon as such does not establish the unity of the Church. On the contrary, as it is, i.e., as it is accessible to the historian, it establishes the multiplicity of confessions. The variability of the Kerygma in the New Testament is an expression of the fact that already in earliest Christianity an abundance of different confessions existed side by side, following upon one another, merging with each and making distinctions between themselves.[97]

The negative effect of this assertion was very strong at the time of its enunciation. It is said to have shocked the first general secretary of the WCC, who is reported to have said: "H. Berkhof said with reference to this remark in his Berkelbach lectures of 1975: 'A little while later I met a death-stricken

Visser't Hooft, who said to me: "It is terrible how such a person like Kaesemann truly deals a death blow to my lifelong work.' "[98] The thesis of Kaesemann was hard to take in view of the presuppositions on the unity of the early church which were often taken for granted. The point is that, as far as the New Testament is concerned, there is no unity of the church in terms of uniform doctrine and organization.

Second, the noted New Testament scholar Oscar Cullmann has also proposed what he calls "this fundamental conception . . . that every Christian confession has a permanent spiritual gift, a charisma, which it should preserve, nurture, purify and deepen, and which should not be given up for the sake of homogenization." He reaches this conclusion after a study of the New Testament. He contends that "the one church of Christ is present in a special form as the body of Christ in every Christian confession."[99] He views all the ecumenical endeavors from the perspective of whether they preserve this reality or not.

Cullmann accepts the fact that "the challenge of ecumenism can be expressed in one word: unity" (p. 13). But the unity which is meant is not uniformity but diversity. The unity that is meant is a "unity in plurality." In this light, Cullmann says that "what I advocate, not as a preliminary state, but as an ultimate goal of all our strivings toward unity, is a union of all Christian churches within which each preserves its valuable elements, including its structure" (p. 15). For lack of a better term, he earlier advanced the word "federation" to define this goal but later dropped it in favor of the term "a community of (harmoniously separated) churches." (p. 35) This implies that the unity sought should be "unity in diversity, or even better, unity *through* diversity." (p. 16) In other words, the enriching aspect of the diversity must be retained and fusion and anarchy avoided. "There was no uniformity even in earliest Christianity" (p. 29). The sin of the divided churches is not the fact that they are separated but that they separated from one another with hatred. "From the beginning, human sinfulness has transformed the richness of church's diversity into hostile, fighting church groups and has even generated terrible persecutions and wars. This is the great historical sin of Christians." But the diversity that we need "has its own theological significance from the point of view of the history of salvation," and ecumenism need not mean the removal of such diversity (p. 31).

To support his argument, Cullmann refers to the work of the Holy Spirit, who engenders unity through diversity. He refers to 1 Cor. 12:4-31. The riches of the church and its members consist in their having a multiplicity of gifts (charismata) and not in their uniformity. The Holy Spirit creates and sustains this diversity for the sake of the unity that ties all the members together. Each church, wherever it finds itself with is own problems and possibilities in view of its particular situation, has a mission of its own within the overall working of the Holy Spirit. Cullmann argues that Protestant, Catholic, and Orthodox churches have their own "charisms," specific to their traditions, which they should preserve as well as share with other churches.

While Protestant churches have what he calls the "concentration on the Bible" and "freedom" and the Catholic Church "Universalism and Institution," the charisms of the Orthodox churches are said to be "the theological deepening of the concept of the Spirit . . . and the conservation of traditional liturgical forms" (p. 20).

When it comes to the doctrinal aspects and their relation to unity, Cullmann picks up the concept of the "hierarchy of truths," made famous through Vatican Council II of the RCC. He says that in all confessions, there is the tacit or openly acknowledged position that all doctrinal affirmations cannot be treated as equal but their importance is placed on varying levels. It is good that all the confessions agree on the rank of the importance of faith affirmations to which they hold. There are of course ambiguities here and there. If they can agree, well and good. But if there are points on which they cannot agree, the churches belong together in spite of their differences. This is argued by Paul himself, for whom "this requirement of tolerance is truly a very important concern . . . even when differences cannot be overcome" (p. 27).

In summing up his argument, Cullmann makes it crystal clear that he is for the continuation of the confessional separations as they exist at present. "What I propose is a real community of completely independent churches, that remain Catholic, Protestant, and Orthodox, that preserve their spiritual gifts, not for the purpose of excluding each other, but for the purpose of forming a community of all those churches that call on the name of our Lord Jesus Christ" (p. 33).

Third, James Dunn on his part has been consistently applying himself to answering the question of what the foundations of the unity of the church are in the New Testament. One of his basic conclusions is that, as far as the New Testament is concerned, it is characterized by diversities. These are such that they allow the existence, one beside the other, of various expressions of the faith. There was of course "the centre which determined the circumference."[100] But the circle was wide enough to accommodate a great number of differences and conflicting ideas. There were even tensions among the various currents of the understanding of Christianity which were possible. "To recognize the canon of the NT is to affirm the diversity of Christianity. We cannot claim the authority of the NT unless we are willing to accept as valid whatever form of Christianity can justifiably claim to be rooted in one of the strands that make the NT" (p. 376).

Dunn argues that differences in the expression of the one faith were commonplace in the New Testament. In fact, there was a place for highly controversial tensions within the body of the early church. "The point is that diversity is not some secondary feature of Christianity, not just a sequence of temporal husks which can be peeled away to leave a virgin, pure, unchanging core. Diversity is fundamental to Christianity. As fundamental as the unity and tension. Christianity can only exist in concrete expressions and these concrete expressions are inescapably different from each other. In order to be Christianity it has to be diverse."[101] Confirming the argument of Cullmann, Dunn contends: "But what perhaps needs to be given more attention is the fact that NT contains the archetypal model of 'unity in diversity'—viz. the body of Christ."[102]

The conclusion that one draws with regard to the unity of the church is the following: A greater part of the ecumenical movement has been inspired by the vision of the rediscovery of the unity of the one church of Christ. In the background of this search for unity was the understanding that the unity was lost. It was lost through the divisions that wrack Christianity. There was also the presupposition that the division was caused primarily by the disagreement on doctrinal matters. In order to go back to the original unity that characterized the Christian church, the path to be followed by the various confessions was viewed in terms of arriving at doctrinal agreements. The endeavor of the ecumenical movement—especially the multilateral and the bilateral dialogues—thus focused on the achievement of consensus in doctrine. Unity was to be re-constructed on the basis of a common expression of the faith.

The merit of the contributions from New Testament scholars is that they demonstrate that there was no such as a thing as a united church to begin with. On the contrary, the entire history of Christianity, including its beginnings, is full of differences and tensions. The distinguishing mark of Christian faith was diversity both in its formulations of the faith and in its structures. This does not deny that there was a core which stood in the center and which served as a unifying point of reference. But this was a person and not a particular formulation or proposition.

It is, in part, in the light of these significant developments that there are increasing calls that the vision of unity of the ecumenical movement be redefined. On the one hand, this has been recognized even within the Central Committee of the WCC. This is evident in the fact that it requested the F&O Commission in 1987 to "undertake a new clarification of the question of unity."[103] The result was presented at Canberra and adopted by the Assembly. On the other hand, other calls persist that the ecumenical movement's traditional presuppositions and conceptions of division and unity, defined in terms of doctrines, have been too limited and restrictive. They need to be widened in the light of new developments and understandings. More will be said later about this need for redefining the goal of the movement in the context of our discussion of the Third World. But now, let us look at some of the problems and the promises of the dialogues.

— 2 —

Problems and Promises of the Dialogues

Interconfessional doctrinal dialogues, and especially the bilaterals, have by no means been conducted without problems. In the course of their history, they have faced numerous difficulties and challenges. Quite a few critical questions have been raised.[1] It is not possible here to go into all of them and discuss them in detail. But it is necessary and will be illuminating to mention some of the criticisms that have been raised with regard to their methods and goals and some of the difficulties they have encountered. We shall also highlight some of their prominent achievements, the promises they raise, and the problems consequent on the promises.

In this chapter, we shall deal with the difficulties the interconfessional dialogues encounter and the solutions they propose. We shall begin with an analysis of some aspects of the relationship between the multilateral and bilateral dialogues and that of the CWCs and the United and Uniting churches. This will be followed by a discussion of other critical questions which some concepts and events pose to the dialogues. We shall conclude the chapter by reviewing some of the achievements of the dialogues, concentrating mainly on the BEM document and the results of discussions on justification by faith and the further problems raised by these same achievements.

Bilaterals and Multilaterals

We have mentioned earlier that while the bilaterals conducted on the international level are sponsored by the CWCs, there are also interconfessional dialogues which take place under the auspices of the WCC. These multilateral dialogues are the responsibility of the F&O Commission of the WCC. Many theological issues have been discussed in these international fora. The main aim is to facilitate direct discussions among confessions and lead them to a better understanding of one another's faith and tradition. The intention is that, in this manner, the churches will be able to get to know each other better and come closer to one another and be enabled to move towards unity. The members originate from different confessional backgrounds, so that several confessional strands are engaged in discussion at one given time. The members of the F&O Commission are not necessarily official representatives of their churches. Even so, they involve a greater number of confessions in one dialogue. Even the RCC, which is not a member of the WCC, has about 12 members in the 120-member F&O Commission.

When the bilateral dialogues were started, fears were expressed that they might rival the multilaterals.[2] It was even asked whether the bilaterals do not contribute to a "crisis of ecumenism." There was, however, a sustained attempt to bring the two closer to each other. This is evidenced by the resolution passed by the WCC Nairobi Assembly, which envisaged a close cooperation between, and coordination of, the two forms of dialogue: "16. The Assembly *welcomes* the proposal that World Confessional Families, in close collaboration with the Faith and Order Commission of the WCC, should establish a Forum for the regular evaluation of bilateral conversations."[3] It is further recognized here that the bilateral dialogues have come to "significant conclusions" but that their relations to the work of the WCC is not clear. After a great deal of subsequent debate, however, the general agreement was reached that the multilateral and bilateral forms of dialogue were not exclusive of one another. They, rather, benefited from each other's researches and findings and thus contributed to the advancement of the one ecumenical movement.[4]

The Fourth Forum on Bilateral Conversations emphasized this aspect when it stated as follows: "In the period since 1980 we note that critical questions concerning the bilaterals becoming an independent ecumenical method in competition with multilateral dialogue (within the framework of the WCC) have receded into the background. There is a growing appreciation that both bilaterals and multilaterals are serving the one ecumenical movement."[5]

This rather optimistic assessment by the secretaries of the CWCs is tempered by the opinion expressed in the Report of the Central Committee to the Sixth Assembly of the WCC in Vancouver. Written in 1983, the Report makes it clear that the fear of the rivalry between the bilaterals and the multilaterals had not subsided as fast as one would have wished. The Committee Report refers to the danger still posed by the bilaterals, especially in the light of some confessional currents which might encourage anti-ecumenical tendencies. In the words of the Report:

> The future style of relationship between the WCC and all Christian World Communions will demand special attention in the post-Vancouver period, in view of the increasing tendency towards confessionalism and bilateral relationships between denominations within the WCC fellowship. Understood in the context of the current search for identity and

sense of belonging together, this tendency poses a challenge to the ecumenical movement and the adequacy of already existing ecumenical structures.[6]

But the Vancouver Assembly sensed a marked improvement of the situation. Going beyond the apprehension of the Central Committee Report, it acknowledged that there was now "a deeper partnership" between the WCC and the CWCs.[7] It is acknowledged here that the partnership takes place in the different activities of both. What is referred to as "this period of growing partnership and mutual trust" is said to be characterized by a variety of formal discussions on various topics. But the discussions on the place of bilateral dialogues in the ecumenical movement here become important. It is in this light that it was recommended and adopted that "the Assembly recognize the ecumenical importance of the CWCs and the Conference of Secretaries of CWCs as partners in the quest for the full visible unity of the Church."[8] The F&O line is strengthened when it is agreed that the definition of the goal of unity and the promotion of the reception of the BEM document can be furthered by the cooperation of both the WCC and the CWCs. It is interesting to note here that the CWCs' contribution is closely tied to the concerns of the F&O, i.e., the interconfessional dialogues.

This growing and positive relationship is acknowledged once again for the period between the assemblies in Vancouver (1983) and Canberra (1990). Again, the report presented by the Central Committee to the Assembly notes that there were serious questions that had been raised earlier about the CWCs. By the time of the assembly, however, it was recognized that the cooperation between the WCC and the CWCs had reached such a level that there was expression of satisfaction on the part of the Committee. There was no longer any mistrust on either side. While it is noted that there was a great deal of cooperation on a variety of levels, it must be noted here also that the work done with F&O is highlighted and its importance underlined. The important place of the bilaterals is noted clearly: "The number of bilateral dialogues has increased since Vancouver. They represent on the international, regional and national levels a major expression of present ecumenical endeavor." The close cooperation with and involvement of the F&O in this endeavor is highlighted. The Forums on Bilateral Conversations that it organizes "dealt with the coherence between the different dialogues and with their complementary relationship with the multilateral dialogues of the WCC."[9]

Canberra takes this good relationship further. It acknowledges that "the relationship with the CWCs has been marked by growing participation, mutual trust, and closer cooperation." The increase of the bilateral dialogues is noted, and the fact that "they are now regarded as normal events in ecumenical relationships" and that the bilateral and multilateral dialogues are "complementary" is welcomed.[10]

We note, then, that the work of the WCC and the CWCs is increasingly moving closer. It is also to be noted further that the relationship is closer when it comes to the doctrinal dialogues which are the mandate of F&O of the WCC. As this relationship is strengthened, the common interests of both F&O and CWCs on the doctrinal dialogues become important and strong. The multilaterals and the bilaterals strengthen each other, and this further contributes to the strengthening of the F&O current of the ecumenical movement.

United and Uniting Churches, CWCs, and Dialogues

In the modern history of the ecumenical movement, there have been numerous churches which have resolved to bury their denominational differences and to opt for church unity. As a consequence, at one time or another, these churches have had problematic relationships with the CWCs. This was due to the fact that the two entertained different perspectives about the goal of the ecumenical movement and, more specifically, about church unity. The importance of this issue is stated by Michael Kinnamon: "It is not an exaggeration to say that dialogue between united churches and the Christian World Communions (CWCs), formerly called the World Confessional Families, is at the heart of the ecumenical movement; it deals with nothing less than the final shape of the unity we seek."[11]

The issue is rendered sharper when one notes that the two followed different models of unity. While the United and Uniting churches opted for the model of organic union, meaning that they left denominationalism behind, the CWCs seemed to persist in emphasizing continuity in one or several confessional traditions. Furthermore, with regard to the bilateral dialogues, it is stated by the United and Uniting churches that they had a negative effect on union negotiations. "Bilateral theological conversations between Rome and various CWCs (or between two non-Roman Catholic CWCs) began to take the spotlight away from local church union negotiations."[12]

Disagreements along this line were noted as far back as the WCC Assembly in New Delhi by some Third World churches. It was argued here that there are "those who see the world confessional bodies as a threat to wider unity in particular areas, a view which some Asian and African Christians have often expressed with vigour."[13] Even after the WCC Assembly in Nairobi (1975), it is observed that this tension had increased, especially with regard to the CWCs' program of bilateral dialogues. For example, the WCC Nairobi Assembly had noted that "the critical questions raised by the churches engaged in the ecumenical movement, especially the churches of the Third World, have not lost their validity." This statement was made in a direct reference to the questions raised at the Salamanca Consultation of F&O in 1973 by the United and Uniting churches, especially those of the Third World. The consultation had addressed pertinent questions to the CWCs, among others, "whether their structures, policies, and activities in fact encourage and support their member churches as they move towards union, and do not prevent local ecumenical commitment."[14] Taking note of these and other such concerns, Kinnamon writes: "The danger remained that local union negotiations and international bilateral conversations would be seen as competitive, and not as complementary parts of one movement. When one adds the multilateral efforts of Faith and Order to this picture, it becomes complex indeed."[15]

Over and above these apprehensions, strong fears were also expressed on the part of United and Uniting churches, particularly from the churches in the Third World. Reflecting this apprehension in their report from Toronto (1975), these churches had harsh words concerning the CWCs. "We have also experienced the way in which the strong tradition of the WCFs (CWCs), coupled with the strength and financial power of their older member churches, have been an unintended threat or even sometimes directly exercised hindrance to the achievement of union."[16] These fears are expressed in the light of real experiences where the intrusion of CWCs or confessional bodies had a negative effect on efforts towards unity. These were accused of using their power and influence on local churches, to the end that the union efforts of these churches were brought to nought.[17]

In order to address such issues, the United and Uniting churches called, at several occasions, for conversations with the CWCs. Their Colombo, Sri Lanka, meeting especially noted the positive result that could come out of such an encounter. It raises especially the problems related to the funding by CWCs of churches in the Third World which were believed to hamper moves toward unity by dependent churches. It was alleged that, "in some places, large amounts of funds are given by independent mission boards to dissident groups in order to strengthen opposition to church union." This is referred to as "a tragedy."[18]

But—and this is a new development—the Toronto meeting had a favorable attitude towards the bilateral dialogues, which, in its own words, "have become an important part of the ecumenical movement." It affirms the need for the United and Uniting churches to share their experiences with those of the bilaterals, especially as the latter face the problem of reception. The hope is expressed that they can both strengthen each other. To this end, they specifically request the CWCs to let them participate in the bilateral dialogues.[19]

The concern with the pressure exerted by the CWCs was expressed to the latter openly. As a result, some of the CWCs took the concerns seriously, to the extent that they discussed them. Some of them even came up with assurances that they have no intention of standing in the way of church union negotiations but that they both encouraged and supported them.[20] But there were also some others which were not at ease in their relationship with United and Uniting churches. One of the glaring examples was the rejection of the entry of the United churches of South India, North India, Pakistan, and Bangladesh into the Anglican Communion. Some of these churches had been united as far back as 1948, as was the case of the Church of South India (CSI). This church had requested membership in the Anglican Communion as a united church, since local Anglican churches formed part of it. But its requests were consistently rejected.[21]

Such an exclusion of a United church prompted the Potsdam, Germany, meeting of the United and Uniting churches to address the Anglican Communion with the request to reconsider its decision.[22] Some of these united churches were finally received into the Anglican Communion in 1988, after almost forty-five years of waiting.[23] This goes to show that there were a number of issues that became contentious between the CWCs and the United churches. The following may be noted.

First, the United and Uniting churches understand that denominationalism has to give way to unity. The separate identities of the confessional bodies must die and give birth to a new, united Church. The one, new identity must replace the older and many identities. The communions are intensely opposed to such a trend. They continue their activities on the basis of the conviction that confessional traditions should not die to give way to something new. They argue that there are many positive elements in these confessions that need to be preserved. There is the need for their transformation but not for their disappearance.[24]

Second, a direct consequence of this point was that the United and Uniting churches saw both the CWCs and the bilateral dialogues they espoused as helping in fostering and strengthening the separate confessional positions. They were of the opinion that this did not augur well for the eventual unity of the churches. In the light of such disagreements between them, there was once again a proposal that a discussion take place. Among the items proposed for discussion between United and Uniting churches and the CWCs (WCFs) was "d) a fresh analysis and assessment of bilateral conversations to clarify how they contribute to and also distract from the quest for organic union." These churches even go so far as to propose the following item for the agenda of the discussions between the two groups: "g) The consideration of the criteria and timetable for altering and terminating the functions and eventually the existence of the WCFs."[25] Such proposals go to show how far the United and Uniting churches were convinced of the provisional character of the CWCs while the latter thought the contrary. It also goes to show the problems which the United and Uniting churches attached to the exercise of the bilateral dialogues.[26]

Dialogues and Institutional Identities

Taking such factors into consideration, the late former general secretary of the WCC, Dr. W. Visser' t Hooft, on his part raised some questions. He asked first whether the international bodies that sponsor the bilateral dialogues can really be taken as representing the doctrinal positions of their member churches. This problem applies to almost all the churches except the RCC. In this regard, he writes: "In this connection the question arises whether a complete consensus is necessary (a) for going on with the task of dialogue, (b) for any form of communion or unity." He also raises the problem of reception, that is, whether the churches are ready to accept the results of the dialogues as their own. He expresses his doubts and concludes by saying that "the whole future of bilateral conversations is at this moment still uncertain."[27]

Closely related to this point is whether the members of the dialogue teams can accomplish much—that is, whether they are in a position to change the confessional landscape. This includes the question of whether such confessional discussions do not, in the last analysis, contribute to reenforcing the confessional identities of the participating churches rather than contributing towards the unity that is sought. Looking at it from a sociologist's perspective, Roger Mehl argues this point. He says that, in such ecumenical dialogues, the quest for unity is almost always accompanied by an opposite desire to defend one's own confessional identity and thus contribute to the continuity of the confessional institution. He observes a paradox in that "even as a direct result of institutionalized ecumenism, there has been a very clear confessional hardening."[28] Mehl poses the question of why the confessional bodies have preferred the bilateral dialogues instead of the multilaterals. While he acknowledges that the bilaterals enable the partners to deal with issues that concern them directly, which cannot be done in the multilaterals, he nevertheless asks: "Without questioning these reasons, the sociologist must however ask: do not these methodological and theological considerations also hide considerations of a strategic nature?" (p. 195).

A further problem in these dialogues, which involve many churches at the same time, is that the churches are often confronted with the choice of approaching one church at the expense of the other. Hard choices need to be made in terms of getting close to one church by sacrificing the other. (This is the problem of what has been referred to as "the compatibility of the dialogues.") Therefore, there are strong questions of strategy that are raised. Mehl even goes so far as to consider the formulation of the following hypothesis: does a church—and in this case the RCC, which favors the rapprochement with the Lutherans to that with the Reformed—"sometimes play off the Lutherans against the Reformed thanks to the bilateral dialogues in spite of the existence of the Leuenberg Concord (which is the basis of the Communion between them in Europe)—or does not at least such a temptation exist?" (p. 197). Furthermore, in the view of Mehl, "there is a linguistic ambiguity" which accompanies the dialogues. This is characterized by a strategy of the leaders which sees to it that no significant agreement which changes the institutional relationships takes place (p. 193). The confessions have come to the point where they have developed ground rules where diplomacy leading to peaceful coexistence is the order of the day. In this case, the hierarchies are not officially opposed to the continuation of the dialogues. They even manifest dramatic public gestures to witness their support of the ecumenical process. But they do everything to frustrate the achievement of the results of the dialogues by using a variety of tactics.

One can say that the composition of the members who are charged with conducting the dialogues is not innocent: even though they are nominated by church authorities on the highest level, these teams do not really commit their respective churches; they can be repudiated, their reports rejected or, as is most often the case—in view of the fact that open disavowals are not well received by public opinion—buried in the archives of the chancelleries of the churches. Everything takes place therefore as if the hierarchies, always disposed to dialogues, fear at the same time that the dialogues are not pushed to the extent that a premature blurring of the identity of the partner churches occurs. (p. 194)

Limitations on Representation and Subject Matter

The questions of how far the dialogues reflect the concerns and the priorities of the worldwide churches also come to the fore. These are accompanied by the concern whether representatives of various churches are allowed to express their views. In other words, the fear is often expressed that the conversations are limited in terms of their subject matter and representation. In terms of the former, they deal with historical doctrinal questions which have to do mainly with Western church history.[29] They focus on the doctrinal issues that separated the historic Western churches in the course of their life. Therefore, they seldom discuss the burning issues that may be questions of life and death to the churches in the nonwestern world.

In line with the choice of the subject matter, it follows logically that the majority of the members of these bilateral groups are Western theologians. The dialogue teams are composed of experts on various theological disciplines of the Western theological tradition. In the process, a great chunk of the theological endeavor of the Third World is practically judged out of limit. At the same time, the few scattered "spices" from the Third World easily get lost in the labyrinthian discussions about a specific theological, philosophical, and historical tradition. This fact had been noted by Philip Potter as far back as 1961. He stated then that "the Churches of Asia and Africa would have more interest in Faith and Order if its discussions were not so involved in the 'presuppositions of Western Schoolmen.' "[30] In the light of such apprehensions, even the call of the Second Forum on Bilateral Conversations which felt urged to "strongly suggest that attention be given to adequate representation from all parts of the world,"[31] will hardly contribute to the redressing of the imbalance. Such criticisms of the limits in the representation of traditions in the dialogues is also reflected in some dialogues. It is made, for example, with regard to the RCC/WARC (Reformed) dialogues. In the evaluation, it is stated: "Among the questions and criticisms of a more general nature, the following were noted: the representative nature of the commission, and therefore of its work (lack of representatives of the so-called Third World; lack of women members)."[32]

Doctrinal Dialogues and Secularization

One of the most difficult issues with regard to the interconfessional dialogues is the possibility of their being out of touch with the social reality in which they operate. This is to say that, especially in the Western context (and it is precisely here that the interconfessional dialogues are supported), the church in general and its doctrines in particular have lost ground ever since the Enlightenment. The churches have since been subjected to increasing marginalization through secularization in Western societies. The values of the church doctrines and ethos have been watered down in the course of time. Many churches have been emptied of their congregations. Great cathedrals in Europe have become the relics of a golden religious age.[33] As a consequence, the doctrinal issues that separated the churches and caused a great deal of interest in some periods of history are viewed with great indifference. As the once great churches become empty as a result of increasing secularization, the doctrines that once reigned supreme are considered from a different perspective, at best as no longer binding, and at worst as detrimental to people's life together. The overall effect is that many of the churches, especially the so-called folk churches, find themselves with a constituency that does not have its heart in doctrines. The overall membership of the churches is not important in the light of the fact that "secularization has very much affected our churches at various levels."[34] It is further acknowledged that "the Christian heritage shapes also Europe. But secularization has edged out this heritage. . . . A distant relationship with institutionalized religion also belongs to the characteristics of the radically modern. Many people have left the Church."[35]

According to Aloys Klein, this situation has contributed to the diminution of the commitment of church members to church doctrines, distance from the church as an institution, and indifference with regard to it and to its teachings "where the official teachings of the churches have lost their meaning."[36] As one observer has put it: "A number of practitioners have tried to explain what is wrong with our theology in the West. Roger Edrington (*Everyday Men: Living in a Climate of Unbelief, Studies in the Intercultural History of Christianity* [Berne: Lang, 1988]) shows that our normal Christological confessions ('true man and true God') are at best meaningless for the great majority of the population of Western Europe."[37] Since there is a general feeling that Western Christianity in its traditional expressions is becoming exhausted, there is a widespread feeling that it has not much to say to its constituencies. "In the estimation of some, Christianity, in its Western captivity, is running dry; perhaps because it clings too tightly to its past cultural heritage of creed, code and cult, perhaps because Western culture itself, in its superiority complex and isolation, is breaking down. Whatever the reason, traditional Western Christianity is losing its ability to speak to the hearts and minds of many contemporaries."[38]

According to Wolfhart Pannenberg, the secularization that haunts the Christian churches in the West and has succeeded in marginalizing them in their societies is the direct consequence of their failure. In other words, secularization has been caused partly by the religious wars that were unleashed by the churches in the West and that consequently rendered the peaceful ordering of life impossible. "Here it must also be admitted that the division of the churches, together with their dogmatic antagonism and its destructive consequences for human community, has been the most important cause of the rise of modern secularism."[39] The churches were separated from each other as a result of intolerance towards one another and in this way accelerated the rate of secularization. "Mutual intolerance contributed decisively to the division of the church" and gave rise to devastating consequences for the place of the church in Western societies.[40]

As we had occasion to see, Pannenberg's argument, and that of those who share his ideas, is that overcoming the division of the churches will give Western secularized society a new lease on life and enable it to counteract the negative effects of secularization on the levels of both the Church and the society at large. In this view, the bilateral and multilateral dialogues are important instruments in this endeavor.[41] For, as a result of secularization and other related historical developments, the church has gradually become "a dying institution" which no longer attracts the multitude, and this has dire consequences even for the society.[42] The empty churches, whose decline in the West had started as far back as the 1760s, arouse the fear of "a dying Christianity" and a threat to the culture. If Christianity cannot hold its own in the face of the repeated assaults that weaken its place in society, the various confessional positions do not fare well and they cannot contribute to the well-being of society. As the French historian Delumeau expresses it, "For many of those who live around us, the Christian faith finds itself engaged in a process of decline which is expected to accelerate."[43] In such a situation, the place of doctrinal dialogues and their long-term effects on the life of the churches and congregations is a big question. For, as Ernst Lange observed, "the restriction of ecumenical consensus to ecumenical coteries and its lack of firm roots in the general outlook of ordinary church members has particularly serious effects on Faith and Order. For its concern is with *theological filigree work*. But the real problem is that it is theological work. For what real weight does theology, ecumenical theology especially, carry in the actual praxis of churches?"[44]

Dialogues and "Non-doctrinal Factors"

The interconfessional dialogues on the international level have often concentrated on the doctrinal issues that separate the churches. They have thus
not seen it necessary to attack other issues which separate both the churches
and the societies in which they live. They have taken it for granted that it is
doctrines that divided the churches in the first place and that the churches
have to apply themselves to solving them. Questions having to do with economics, politics, culture, race, sex, and other factors do not figure in the
discussions because they are often not viewed as "church-dividing issues"
and are sometimes seen as not proper for "theological" discourse.

In the course of the interconfessional dialogues, the multilateral ones have
from time to time recognized the importance of these factors as dividing
issues in the churches.[45] These were often known by the term "non-theological factors," a phrase which was gradually dropped in favor of "non-doctrinal factors." The reasoning is that no human factor can be closed out as
being "non-theological." No aspect of human life and activity can be judged
as being beyond the scope of theological discourse. The F&O Commission,
on its part, had recognized the importance of these factors and had authorized a study on them under the title of Institutionalism.[46]

The F&O World Conference in Montreal in 1963 had also recognized
the problems related to the transmission of the Gospel into other cultures.
"The problems raised by the transmission of the Tradition in different lands
and cultures, and by the diversities of traditions in which the one Tradition
has been transmitted, are common in varying ways to all Christians. They
are to be seen in an acute form in the life of the younger churches of Asia
and Africa today, and in a less obvious but not less real form in what was
formerly called Western Christendom."[47] Its implications for the unity and
division of the Church were not, however, drawn and discussed. Subsequently,
the topic was dropped from F&O studies.

But the fact that the so-called non-doctrinal factors have a more important role to play in the creation and preservation of church divisions is increasingly being acknowledged by many. "Often non-doctrinal factors become decisive when it comes to the breaking of communion as well as for its
restoration."[48] Some ardent supporters of the doctrinal dialogues are even
admitting that the churches must be called to recognize the necessity of discussing them. "It is necessary that the dialogues on the classical dogmatic
questions which have been conducted during the last twenty years be completed at present by dialogues on the more ethical or sociopolitical questions." In Andre Birmele's opinion, in calling for a worldwide Assembly on
the issues of justice, peace, and the integrity of creation (JPIC), the German
physicist Friedrich von Weizsaecker "poses a valid question."[49]

It is not necessarily doctrinal issues only that are uppermost in the per-
petuation of church divisions. There are also other factors that are equally, if

not more, decisive as well. But in many cases, the doctrinal discussions, the multilaterals and bilaterals, do not seem to recognize or come to terms with these issues, which become causes of separation even among Christian churches. "The things which divide people in general—conflicting economic interests, racial prejudice, nationalist feelings, class selfishness, thirst for power, rivalry for prestige, and so on—also divide Christians, which means that the particular social group (class, nation or race) is more important a factor in determining our behaviour than the Kingdom of Heaven to which we also belong."[50]

It is therefore necessary to note that the reasons which led to the sometimes violent ruptures between Christian churches and groups were not always determined by "doctrinal" matters strictly understood. There was a mixture of other "non-doctrinal" reasons which inflamed the spirits and contributed much to church divisions. This fact goes back to the time when some of the Western Christian traditions took their shape to become the West's orthodox expressions, lasting up to the present. In this case, it is worth listening seriously to the views of an Orthodox theologian: "Let us remember that dark pages were written undermining the unity of the faith in the one undivided Church during the two Ecumenical Councils of Ephesus (431) and Chalcedon (451). Except for the real Monophysites, all other conflicts appeared mostly because of terminology." Different factions held the same faith but a new language was being introduced which left some of them, particularly the oriental churches of Egypt and the Middle East, uneasy because of fear of being overruled by the Greeks. "Irresponsible people seized the case, however, and by politicizing the whole issue, manipulated it for nationalistic interests. The unity was broken because of these non-theological factors."[51]

But the havoc caused by these so-called "non-doctrinal factors" is not confined to seemingly minor divisions among the churches. Metropolitan Timiadis contends further that the rupture that transpired between the Catholics and the Orthodox in the eleventh century was not caused by purely "doctrinal" factors. On the contrary, there were many other factors that were far from being labeled doctrinal. Among these were cultural factors which played a significant role in the definition of the faith. These go back even to the New Testament era and to the first apostles. The heated debates between Paul, Peter, and James in the early church were about "socio-cultural" matters, namely, about the question of circumcision. There are many such examples in the history of the church where cultural and other factors played havoc on its unity. "Gradually, in addition to doctrinal differences, such human elements even entered into historic-dogmatic fields and, manipulated by certain fanatic extremists, prepared the way for the disastrous schism between the two ancient churches, Rome and Eastern Orthodox (1054)."[52] Even the Reformation period is not immune from such influences. Questions of power, politics, economics, and national feelings played a great role in determining the theological discourses of the actors, including, of course,

Luther. As Ernst Lange noted: "The problem of unity in the ancient church had always been a political problem, too; a problem of the Roman Empire. . . . The course of the Reformation had been influenced by political, economic and social factors."[53] An F&O study confirms this opinion when it states: "All the major divisions of the Church can be to some extent related to social and political lines of division in its secular environment."[54]

A Catholic theologian, Richard Schluetter, is led to weigh the reasons behind the stalling of church hierarchies before the doctrinal agreements so far amassed by the theologians. He ties this in with the new problem being pursued, whether there is a "basic difference" between Catholics and Protestants. His basic question is aimed at whether there are some interests other than theological which determine this sudden surge of preoccupation with the issue of "basic difference." Echoing the arguments of Mehl above, he is convinced that the ecumenical endeavors which aim at reaching agreement in the faith and the teaching of the church do not have only that aim in mind. Besides these "conscious intentions," there are "interests" and "needs" that go beyond them.[55] The author cites the opinions of foremost Catholic theologians, who assert that there is a "basic difference" between Catholics and Protestants. In the light of this assertion, all the statements made by dialogue groups to the effect that basic agreements have been reached on the fundamentals of the faith are put under a serious question mark. There is a basic contradiction here: there is agreement; there is no agreement. The author argues that the answer to this ambiguity is found only in some "interests and motives" that transcend the doctrinal statements. According to the views of some, there are even church institutions and officials who may appoint theologians to find differences in teaching at a time when they feel that the differences no longer explain the separation of the churches. These theologians would then use their acumen to come up with teachings which are designated church-dividing.[56]

But—it is here argued, reflecting once again the views of Mehl referred to above—there are hidden motives and interests for continuing to resist the acceptance of the agreements. The latter presuppose that the theological discussions which led to them were about finding the truth. As a consequence, they imply that, once they are received by the churches, they will certainly effect some necessary changes in the lives of the churches and their relationships to one another. But the need to preserve the social and institutional form of the churches becomes urgent, and this influences the debate on "basic difference." But so far, the debate seems not to have recognized this aspect of the problem. According to Schluetter, the debate is being used by some to preserve the already existing social profiles of the churches and to avoid any changes. "Just because the preservation of the confessional social profile proves to be of a very high importance indeed for the church, this motive will play—consciously or unconsciously, directly or indirectly—a very important role in the ecumenical dialogues."[57] Such desire for the preservation of what is believed to be one's own confessional heritage threatens in the long run to neutralize the current ecumenical endeavors. It will also have negative consequences on the bilateral dialogues. If the churches are not ready to recognize each other as sister churches in view of the agreements already reached

> then one is forced to draw the conclusion that the relationships among the confessional churches are not yet of such a quality which makes possible an ecclesial recognition of the convergences and consensuses in the issues of faith worked out in the bilateral dialogues. This would give the clue that, while progress in current ecumenism is in particular determined by the clarification of the relationships, it seems very much less dependent on a larger agreement in theological questions than on a real and deep ecclesial conversion.[58]

Increasingly, the question of reaching consensus on the basis of doctrines only becomes problematic. Any so-called doctrinal discussion that tries to deliberately shut off the many other issues which played and still play an important role in causing divisions among the churches needs to take them up at one time or another. There are of course obvious problems in expanding the discussion in order to include these issues. "The unity of the Church becomes a bit unmanageable when the grounds of division include what used to called 'non-theological factors,' such as culture, nationality, economic status, race, and (a late-comer to the list) sex."[59] But their discussion cannot, in the last analysis, be avoided for they are intrinsic to the division and unity of the church. As the late German ecumenist Ernst Lange avowed: "What divides the world also divides the Church. . . . It is also true that church divisions have always in fact been the result of conflicts about power. These conflicts were never purely religious in character. They have always been, in addition, robust expressions of social and political interests and church politics and therefore the pursuit of power by other means, which is only to be expected considering the role of organized religion in human society."[60] Any attempt to arrive at the unity of the churches without taking into utmost consideration all these factors that divide it is thus already bound to fail.

This insistence on the need to tackle the so-called non-doctrinal factors as essential elements in the search for the unity of the church is gaining increased importance. In a response to a view which argues that the agreements reached in the multilateral and bilateral dialogues will lead to unity, Melanie May retorts:

> He [Gassmann] trusts that the *products* of dialogue can and will resolve differences and achieve unity. However significant I believe such documents and agreements to be, I do not assume that, as such, they either can or will resolve differences or achieve unity. Therefore, I understand dialogue not primarily as a means by which we come up with

products that are then disseminated to the churches but as a way of life which we are called to incarnate, however variously, at every level and step in our movement toward unity.

May sees the serious problems that the many "non-doctrinal factors" pose to the quest for unity. These are issues that are not addressed or found in the agendas of the doctrinal dialogues. According to May, they are raised by women and youth and the Third World; these questions touch real issues of life, such as racism, gender, and economics: "As I reflect on the contribution of bilateral conversations to the ecumenical movement, I am impressed by the deep roots of diversity, roots not readily reached by statements of consensus or convergence."[61]

The effect of the "non-doctrinal factors" on the division of the church cannot be underestimated at all. In some societies, they have even gone as far as determining the lifestyles and professions of the people. This is to say that the adherence to Catholicism or Protestantism has had a very strong role to play in the division of societies themselves. All these configurations have an impact on the success or failure of the process towards unity. Berge, then, has a useful suggestion: "The political scientist Hans Meier accords these non-theological aspects first place as the grounds for the ecumenical disillusionment. Once a problem is pinpointed, it loses a greater part of its danger. One should not thus shy away from raising these issues openly and from including them in the brotherly dialogues among Christians of the various churches. This would certainly be useful to the *oikumene*."[62]

Dialogues and Women's Ordination

The interconfessional dialogues do not take place immune from historical vicissitudes. Hence, an unexpected incident may suddenly succeed in turning the smooth-running dialogues upside down. Let us take the issue of women's ordination and the Anglican Communion to illustrate this point. Tolerance towards women's ordination was affirmed at the 1988 Lambeth Conference of the communion. As a result, some of its dioceses started practicing women's ordination. Such a decision has completely put off balance the Anglican Communion's relationship with the RCC. As a result, the RCC expressed its opinion that such ordinations of women disturb the RCC/Anglican relations. In the words of Cardinal Willebrands: "The ordination of women, which has taken place in some dioceses of the Anglican communion, has set back the hopes for the restoration of fellowship with the Catholic Church. No less serious are the ecclesiological problems which these decisions entail within the Anglican communion itself."[63] The dialogues continue, but their future effectiveness is put into question and overshadowed by the total opposition of the RCC and the Orthodox churches to women's ordination. The seriousness of the matter can in no way be underestimated.

We cannot deal with this issue at length here because we shall make reference to it in a later chapter. But one is constrained at this juncture to take it one step further and make note of the view of women on this matter. The concerns of women and their role in the ecumenical movement have become issues of deep and lively discussion. On their part, some women have at various occasions expressed the opinion that the dialogues do not take their concerns into consideration. As Letty Russell put it: "Faith and Order discussions such as 'Baptism, Eucharist and Ministry' cannot deal with women's ordination using only the convergence method. The tendency of that method is to preserve unity at the expense of those who do not fit classical doctrinal formulations."[64] It appears from this view that the issue of women's concerns is far from being adequately dealt with by the dialogues.

The dialogues are also affected by the conflicts that arise within the same communion with regard to the question of women's ordination. The Anglicans themselves are divided over this very issue. While some of them are for it and have gone ahead in ordaining women, there are others who are strongly opposed to it. It has even become a cause for division among Anglicans themselves. Its seriousness is seen in the words of the Anglican Bishop of Ottawa, Canada, who declares that "an inclusive episcopate is a necessity for the *Koinonia* which is threatened by male exclusivity. This is as much a threat to the unity of the Church today as Arianism, for example, was in our past."[65]

As already indicated above, the Lambeth Conference of 1988 had resolved that each diocese make its own decision on this matter and that such a decision be respected by the other dioceses. But such a mediating resolution has not calmed some spirits, which have gone so far as to take radical steps in opposition to women's ordination. As Cardinal Willebrands has further stated, internal decisions within a communion will have far-reaching consequences beyond its borders. In his view, the future progress of RCC-Anglican relationships will also depend on the evolution of the inner-Anglican discussions.[66] Another Catholic has gone so far as to state that "the Christian world is, at the present time, undergoing a new kind of division. It is being split apart on the question of the ordination of women. Along the lines of this division, the Churches of the Reformation . . . are opposed to the older Churches, Catholic and Orthodox."[67] It may be seen very easily from such threats and counterthreats that the situation will be further exacerbated in view of the decision of the General Synod of the Church of England in November 1992 to ordain women priests.[68] Even though there are growing disaffections within the RCC regarding its position on the ordination of women,[69] such decisions on the part of one communion will certainly continue to seriously affect the relationships of the churches. They will also cast a big shadow over the capacity of the concerted efforts of the dialogues to make a difference in the churches' search for unity.

The Dialogues and Social Conflicts

There are also religious and national problems that come close to destroying the dialogues. For example, the relationships between Catholics and Orthodox in Eastern Europe have severely shaken the Catholic-Orthodox dialogue. These tensions have long histories and are not a thing of the present. They form part of what Dom Emmanuel Lanne calls "the unspoken issues" in the Catholic-Orthodox dialogue: "For reasons which history can explain there is sometimes in some Orthodox a distrust about the ultimate intentions of the Catholic Church, even in the Church's most generous gestures. And reciprocally, one meets with a similar distrust in some Catholics towards the Orthodox and their sincerity."[70] Some issues arise at some point to reanimate such suspicions. For example, the question of the Uniate churches, that is to say, the churches in the former Eastern bloc which are in union with RCC, has always been a thorny issue with the Orthodox.[71] They often see the presence of the Uniates as a case of flagrant proselytism by the RCC in what is seen as their area of influence. The participation of the Uniates on the side of the RCC in the dialogues, therefore, became an issue for heated debate. Some Orthodox have even characterized the Roman Catholic-related Uniate churches of the East as "an open wound in the body of the Orthodox Church and as a painful reality."[72] The Catholics, on their side, insist that the right of the existence of the Uniates after many years of persecution should not be questioned. The dialogues are certainly affected by such bursts of antagonism which have religious implications.

The dialogues are also, of course, hampered by inner conflicts. Even the Orthodox themselves have what they call "schismatic churches" with whom they do not have any relationship and by which the dialogues are disturbed. Any attempt or signal that the RCC, for example, might recognize these churches, such as the Macedonian Orthodox Church, is violently opposed by the greater number of Orthodox churches. Thus, some (Cypriot and Serbian Orthodox) show their protest by walking out of a dialogue meeting while others (the Greek and Jerusalem Orthodox) boycott it altogether.[73] Such incidences contribute to the complications that accompany the dialogues. These are not peculiar to the Orthodox. Sometimes the members of a team are united across confessional loyalties. That is, members of the same confession may disagree in their interpretation of their own tradition. In contrast, they would agree with the members who represent the other confession. There are cases where members representing the same confession in a dialogue group cannot see eye to eye on a variety of issues. This is reflected by cases where some members of the dialogue refuse to sign the final reports.

Basic Consensus—Basic Difference?

But there are theologians who take the reservations to accept the doctrinal dialogues on the part of the churches seriously. If the churches are not taking any significant steps towards unity after the compilation of so many agreed statements, would it be the case that there is what has been called a "basic difference" that stands between Catholics and Protestants? they ask. In what some see as a pursuit engaged by "primarily European theologians," (even though it is the case that the discussion goes beyond the European context, since quite a few American theologians are also involved in the discussion), the Strasbourg Institute had raised this very question.[74] It raises the question of whether there is a core difference which underlies all other differences among the confessions, one which might explain them all and, once resolved, would lead to a solution of all the other differences. Can it be localized and explained?[75] And if there is such a thing as a "basic difference," is it, in the last analysis, church-dividing or is it proof of the fact that the various confessions can live with their differences, which are consequences of their differing articulations of the faith? There are a variety of responses to this vexing question. Even though no definitive answer has been given, the posing of the question shows the intractable nature of the differences.

Even in the face of the many problems, it could still be said that the doctrinal dialogues have contributed to achieving some very interesting agreements. Two classic examples which can be cited to show how this has been done are the story of the BEM document and the discussion on the concept of justification by faith and its results.

Baptism, Eucharist, and Ministry

We have already had the occasion to note that the bilateral dialogues have contributed a great deal to the understanding of the Eucharist and ministry. The results of these discussions were also used in the multilateral dialogues. The accumulating agreements later led to one of the most important events in the history of F&O. The cumulative work on the issues of baptism, Eucharist, and ministry were brought together and finalized when the F&O Commission of the WCC adopted the document at its meeting in Lima, Peru, in 1982. It was then decided that the document be sent to the churches with the request that they respond to it through their "highest appropriate level of authority."[76]

Ever since, some 186 churches have sent in their responses to the Commission. These have been collected in six volumes under the title *Churches Respond to BEM.*[77] Even nonmembers of the WCC, such as the RCC, sent in their official responses for the first time to an ecumenical document. The latter has been translated into many languages. As a result, "this fruit of many years of ecumenical discussion has become the most widely distributed, translated and discussed ecumenical text in modern times."[78] Even though there are quite a few churches that have not responded—as we shall see later—and even though there were many questions that were raised regarding the churches' different views on the issues dealt with in BEM, the fact that it generated a fresh discussion on this scale was in itself a great achievement. Besides, there were many positive elements in the responses. Such a scale of unprecedented responses has thus led to dubbing the document "one of the outstanding ecumenical events of this decade, possibly the most important of all."[79]

The responses to BEM have given rise to other studies which are based on them and which will carry BEM's contributions forward. These studies concern some of the issues which were pointed out as problematic by the churches. Among these are found the questions of ecclesiology as well as others which called for further clarification of the issues. BEM has thus been one of the most successful products of the dialogues. What has been called "the Lima process" is still continuing.

Justification by Faith in the Dialogues

It is important to recall once again here the complementarity and the mutual concerns between the bilateral and multilateral dialogues. As we have pointed out earlier on a number of occasions, the topics dealt with in the BEM document are also discussed in the bilateral dialogues. The aims of both thus meet and reenforce each other. They draw from each other's resources and contribute to the furtherance of their pursuits. But there are also other topics which are dealt with in greater depth in the bilateral than in the multilateral dialogues. This is the case with the issue of "justification by faith."

It should be recalled that one of the main doctrinal reasons that lay behind the rupture between the RCC and the Reformers of the sixteenth century is said to be the conviction that salvation was attained only by grace through faith. This assertion was one of the basic doctrinal tenets that became the cause for the separation. The affirmation of this conviction led to a collision between Luther and the RCC.[80] The painful history which lay behind the division of the Church as a result of this doctrinal division has been amply referred to above.

But as the Malta Report observed, "after more than 400 years of separation" a joint Lutheran/RCC Commission was established with the aim of repairing the breach. Surprisingly enough, even in the first document produced by the commission, the representatives of the two confessions came to the agreement that "today a far-reaching consensus is developing in the interpretation of justification."[81] To the surprise of many, the agreement was reached without a long-drawn-out discussion. It was naturally expected that the discussions on such a central issue would consume a great deal of time.

But in the view of some, that was not the case.[82] Both sides expressed the opinion that an agreement has been reached. As Aloys Klein put it: "The conclusions show, *inter alia*, that as far as the interpretation of the doctrine of justification by faith is concerned—the subject of bitter theological controversy in the past—there is a fairly broad consensus today."[83] Furthermore, the agreement on one of the main doctrines that divided the RCC laid the ground for agreements on other issues. As a result of such an agreement, it was found that the relations thawed between the confessions to the extent that other bold measures could be proposed. This was proven by the fact that even such a "revolutionary idea" of an RCC "recognition of the Augsburg Confession (the main confessional document of Lutheranism) as an authentic expression of the common Christian faith" did arise and "thus turn an ecumenical obstacle into an ecumenical support."[84] It is true that such a formal recognition did not take place, in the last analysis. But the very fact that the issue of recognition was raised in the first place and that the discussions resulted in a very significant statement by the Lutheran/RCC Commission, which declared, among other things, that the joint study of the Confessio Augustana has led to "newly discovered agreements of the common [Christian] faith found in it," was a milestone in itself.[85]

The foregoing may give the impression that the doctrine of justification by faith has been dealt with by the Catholics and Lutherans only. By no means! It has been subject to a wider treatment by other communions as well. In fact, more than fourteen different dialogues have dealt with it.[86] Among these are the RCC and Anglican dialogues, to mention just one of many. In the document produced by the ARCIC II under the title *Salvation and the Church,* the dialogue teams also came to the conclusion that they had reached a substantial agreement on the issue of justification by faith. Here again, it is understood to be the "doctrine . . . which at the time of the Reformation was a particular cause of contention."[87] As a result of the discussion of this topic, the dialogue team concluded that "our two Communions are agreed on the essential aspects of the doctrine of salvation and the Church's role within it."[88]

On the whole, as has already been pointed out, the history of the relationships of many churches was often marred by mutual recriminations, condemnations, and "righteous wars." As the Lutherans and Roman Catholics admitted, "our ecclesial awareness has been traumatized by mutual condemnations."[89] The fact that people with such historical backgrounds can finally sit around the same table and reach "substantial agreements" on basic issues of faith should not be taken lightly. However much the historical conditions might have changed and however many secular factors may have influenced this turn of events, it cannot be denied that significant stages of change have been reached. In this connection, the view of one of the chairpersons of the commissions on the question of the agreement on justification by faith is revealing. In the words of George Lindbeck:

Here Roman Catholics and Lutherans officially recognized and sent by their churches declare together that only by grace through faith in the saving work of Christ and not on the basis of our merits are we accepted by God and receive the Holy Spirit who renews our hearts and enables us and calls us to do good works. . . . Luther would have been extremely happy. And I must say that for me, this sentence alone in view of its authority and weight is worth the hundreds of hours that we spent in our joint work.[90]

Disagreement in the Agreement?

In spite of these achievements, however, it is exactly here that one encounters one of the serious dilemmas of the interconfessional dialogues. Is there or is there not an agreement on the issue of justification by faith? We have seen so far that Catholic, Anglican, and Lutheran dialogue teams—to take just them as examples—have pronounced their agreement on the basic issue of justification by faith. Harding Meyer and Guenther Gassmann are categorical in their assertion that there is a substantial consensus which has been registered here. In the book they edited on this very topic, they state this conclusion in an unequivocal way: the foregoing analysis "must have shown that in these dialogues, even in the especially difficult and laborious Catholic/Lutheran dialogue, this understanding has been attained so that one can and must without timidity and hesitation speak of a 'genuine consensus in the doctrine of justification.' "[91] There are quite a few theologians from other confessions who share such an assessment and conclusion. This has also been corroborated by a distinguished German group composed of Catholic and Lutheran theologians.[92]

But the consensus is not universally recognized. On the RCC side, the reaction to a "substantial agreement" took special exception to this assertion by expressing its disagreement. It stated that "we are not, however, at the point of being able to ratify the final affirmation."[93] The RCC and the Anglican dialogue teams claimed to have agreed on the understanding of the issue of justification by faith. But the official RCC response shows that this was not the case. One finds oneself in the same situation concerning the RCC/Lutheran dialogue even though the RCC has as yet given no official response to the result of that dialogue, as it did with the Anglicans. This is corroborated by the fact that the dialogue between the RCC and Lutherans has picked up and is still dealing with this issue in its latest round of discussions.[94] Some point out further that even in the Malta Report, where the RCC/Lutheran agreement on justification by faith is announced, there is ambiguity with regard to the consensus. As Andre Birmele and Thomas Ruster acknowledge, it is only the Lutheran party to the conversation that states its opinion: "In the Malta Report, the question is raised but the response is given only from the side of the Lutherans. . . . The Catholic answer does not appear."[95]

This is further complicated when one listens to the opinion from the Catholic side. No less a person than Cardinal Ratzinger, the prefect for the Congregation of the Doctrine of the Faith, has declared that "there is a fundamental difference" in the understanding of the doctrine of justification by faith between the RCC and the followers of Luther.[96] This opinion is also shared by Cardinal Willebrands, prefect of the Vatican Council for Christian Unity, who himself writes that the said consensus must be assessed:

The third phase of dialogue began in 1986 and focuses on the themes of justification, ecclesiology and sacramentality. One task is to assess whether consensus can now be claimed between Lutherans and Catholics on the notion of justification, in light of statements made in the "Malta Report" (1972), in the important document *Justification by Faith* produced by the Catholic-Lutheran dialogue in the U.S.A. and in work done on justification by the mixed commission in Germany. In this regard the joint commission now has before it a working paper on "ascertaining the wide-ranging agreement on justification."[97]

It is no wonder, then, that a heated debate is raging regarding the extent of the consensus. The disagreements may be quickly summarized under two points. First, one agrees that, in the interpretation of the article, there is agreement. That is to say, Lutherans and Roman Catholics agree that a person is saved by grace through faith in Christ alone without any works on one's part. A person is declared righteous before God without any merits of one's own. But there is a further question here. As far as Lutherans are concerned, the article of justification by faith is accorded a prominent place. In fact, it is a hermeneutical principle with which one approaches the Scriptures; it is the key to their interpretation. All theological affirmations have to be related to this one article of faith. It is thus referred to as "the article by which the Church stands or falls." It therefore plays a prominent hermeneutical role in the Lutheran theological tradition.

The question that arises with regard to the agreements is whether the Catholic side has accepted the validity of such a position.[98] Opinions are divided here. The Malta Report, which is the basis for the agreement, indicates that there are questions that still remain unresolved. In its own words: "Although a far-reaching agreement in the understanding of justification appears possible, other questions arise here. What is the theological importance of this doctrine? Do both sides similarly evaluate its implications for the life and teaching of the church?"[99] The question remains open.

It is partly on the basis of these assertions that disagreements arise as to the level of agreement reached. There are those who point out that the said consensus is not as full as it is claimed to be.[100] Strong voices are also being raised on both sides that there is no such thing as a "substantial agreement" on the issue and that the Lutheran and Catholic positions are as far apart as they ever were before. It is the conviction of the proponents of this view that the differences in the interpretation of this article of faith remain unresolved, as they were in the time of the Reformation.[101] The discussion thus continues with no end in sight.

Agreements in Spite of Disagreements

With regard to other doctrinal issues, the proponents of the dialogues are convinced that many worthwhile agreements have been reached as direct results of the dialogues.[102] As a whole, one sees that, through their intensive discussions, the interconfessional dialogues have affected the ecumenical atmosphere as well as the interchurch relationships positively. The various confessional bodies have reached the point where they can sit down and calmly discuss issues which used to generate heated polemics. "Discussion is now possible in a dispassionate atmosphere. Confessions which until recently were unable to talk about the papacy with any kind of objectivity now take it into discussion."[103] There are still some issues which have not been discussed thoroughly. But the churches have now reached the stage where they can talk about their differences in a spirit of understanding which was not there before. The point of view expressed by the Lutheran/RCC Commission may therefore be taken as a correct assessment of the dialogical atmosphere: "Since the Second Vatican Council especially, our churches have been in dialogue in many countries and in many places. Striking convergences have been achieved and agreements reached on important controversial questions. . . . There are several differences between us which are also beginning to lose their divisive edge. . . . After centuries of deepening estrangement, there is a new sense among us that we are all 'under one Christ.' "[104]

Such changes in the ecumenical atmosphere between some churches are indeed astounding. This is also illustrated by the relationship between the RCC and the Orthodox churches. Before the Second Vatican Council, the RCC would neither mention the "Orthodox Church" nor would it accept an invitation to take part in a celebration organized by the Greek Orthodox Church, to take one example. But after the Council, Pope Paul VI, who earlier signed a letter declining the invitation, went against "the rules of protocol" to the Ecumenical Patriarchate of the Orthodox Church in Constantinople to meet Patriarch Athenagoras. Further steps were taken to heal the division. The mutual excommunications that had been valid since 1054 were lifted by both Rome and Constantinople. Visits were exchanged on a wider scale between RCC and Orthodox churches. It should be noted that the dialogue started in 1980 after "centuries of separation." It has been said that "this dialogue has modified the Catholic-Orthodox relationships, even if some areas of prejudices and fanaticism still persist."[105]

To sum up, we see that the dialogues face numerous problems. At one time or another, they have been confronted with the questions raised by the United and Uniting churches. The bilaterals were viewed as elements reenforcing the confessional consciousness which proves detrimental to the unity of the churches. The question of the relationship of the bilaterals to the multilaterals was also a problem in the first years. In the course of time, however, they strengthened each other. They contributed to the success of each other and thus became indispensable to one another. "BEM has integrated insights from bilateral dialogues between Christian World Communions. Now, in turn, BEM is used in several of these dialogues as a point of reference and framework of their common orientation. Reports from a number of dialogues refer to BEM when they formulate common affirmations. This is another indication of the complementary relationship between bilateral and multilateral dialogues."[106] Furthermore, a problem was raised with the question of the representative character of the dialogues. They were often related to the concerns of the Western world, in whose history arose the doctrinal problems dealt with in the dialogues.

More serious problems are raised by the issues of secularization and pluralism. Since these modern trends in the Western societies have become strong, they have made a dent in the influence of the traditional importance and hold of the doctrinal dialogues in the churches and their membership. The question arises as to how far the impact of the dialogues will effect a change in the membership of the churches which is increasingly indifferent and far removed from the concerns of the dialogues.

To this must be added the serious problem of the place of the "nondoctrinal factors" in the dialogues. To date, the dialogues have generally avoided them. The doctrinal issues are dealt with as if they are divorced from the historical, cultural, socioeconomic, and political contexts which gave rise to them and which continue also to influence them. Nevertheless, there is an increasing awareness that doctrines have to take these factors into consideration.

In the face of all these problems and difficulties, the dialogues have been able to make important and significant gains. The bilateral dialogues have made significant contributions through their conversations on the issues of baptism, Eucharist, and ministry. They have led to many agreements. This was carried further by the BEM document, which treated these very issues. It elicited numerous positive responses from many churches and contributed to extensive discussions on the doctrinal issues.

Positive agreements had also been reached with regard to the issue of justification by faith. This doctrine, which was at the heart of the separation of the churches in the sixteenth century, has been the object of significant consensus. Numerous dialogues have dealt with it and recorded agreements. But there are also those who contest these conclusions. These contestations have given rise to heated discussions both for and against the conclusions of the dialogues.

This brings us to the issue of reception—a process which follows upon the accumulation of the agreements and results of the dialogues.

— 3 —

Reception and the Dialogues

With their characteristic precision, a German group had succinctly described the process of interconfessional dialogues, their starting point, and their goals in the following words: "The starting point for doctrinal conversations is the respective *standpoint* of each confession. They discuss these standpoints in *dialogue* with the aim of reaching a *doctrinal consensus*. When the consensus is achieved, it is received in the still separated churches. When the *reception process* is completed, *communion* between the churches is restored and then the unity of the church has been achieved."[1] It does not of course work always exactly that way. As G. Gassmann has argued, it could also be said that "the ecumenical dialogue itself is already reception, it is characterized by reception."[2] Even so, the question of reception in the present context has arisen especially in view of the documents that have been worked out and prepared by dialogue commissions. It is the accumulation of the dialogue results that is calling attention to the urgency of their reception by the churches.[3] Therefore, the straining towards reception may be referred to as "a new phase of the ecumenical endeavor." It is a new development: "The notion of *reception* is now at the forefront of any serious reflection concerning Christian life and consequently Christian tradition. . . . It is certainly one of the most important theological discoveries of our century."[4] The work on the dialogues is certainly not terminated; it continues. And yet, they have reached a new stage.[5]

We have noted that in many cases, the first part of the work of the dialogues, namely, the presentation of the result in the form of a report or an agreed statement, has been accomplished on a number of issues. These statements have now accumulated over the years and have been presented to the churches. But the question of what one does with these results is not easy to answer. At first sight and as the dialogues would require, what should be done may seem obvious. That is, each church should take steps to make its own the results of the dialogues, by first studying them and then taking the necessary steps to implement them. But there is unclarity, to say the least, when it comes to dealing with the question of what to do next. Whatever steps should be taken, a term has come into vogue to epitomize what is needed: "reception." Many are of the opinion that the dialogues have now reached the stage where reception has to take place. In the words of Cardinal Willebrands: "We have come to a new point in the ecumenical movement [in 1982]. I would describe it as a transition towards a stage of decision. It is a period of transition, at several levels, from an ecumenical work involving chiefly conversations with theologians, experts and official delegates to the reception of the results of this work by the churches themselves."[6]

The year 1982 was also a decisive year in the "reception process." As pointed out above, it was the year when the BEM document was officially sent to the churches. This process has already been referred to as "reception," even by the preface to the text itself.[7] As is evident in the F&O Commission meeting in Stavanger, Norway, in 1985, the process of "receiving" the Lima document is on.[8] From what has been taking place already, the process may seem to consist in the decision of a church body, in this case the Commission, to present a convergence document to the churches. The latter pick it up, through processes specific to their polity, and study it. This step by the churches, of course, involves people—church leaders, theologians, church members, pastors, priests, etc.—and is done at numerous levels. The responses gathered through such a process are then sent back to the Commission. The latter uses the responses to open further discussions on the outstanding issues raised by the responses. It must be pointed out that sometimes differences between response and reception are drawn. But in most cases, they belong together and form phases of one another.[9]

A further element in this "receiving" process is the role the Lima document and its offshoots play in the process. This is to say that the document is also accompanied by a "Lima Liturgy" as well as by a number of study materials. By the use of such materials, and especially the liturgy, the doctrinal document, it is hoped, is translated into the life of the worshipping community. In this way, it starts its penetration into the living structures of the churches. "BEM, and the so-called 'Lima Liturgy' which has been used in churches and on many ecumenical occasions, have had an impact on the liturgical life, studies on worship and official revision of forms of worship in several churches."[10]

The Problem of the Definition of Reception

What we have referred to above are only a variety of elements of the process of a possible reception as they manifest themselves in relation to BEM as well as the other dialogue results. But as the numerous discussions on the issue make clear, the understanding of the term "reception" is not confined to such steps alone. As a matter of fact, there are many facets that witness to the width and the complexities evoked by the term. At the outset, in spite of the extensive use of the term, many of its users agree that there is some unclarity about its use, unclarity in that it may mean different things to different people. "There are different conceptions concerning the meaning and extended usage of the word in the separated Christian Churches."[11]

As we have noted above, in its classical understanding, it often refers back in church history to "the process through which the local churches receive the decisions of a council and thereby recognize its authority."[12] In this case, it has reference to the early councils which came together to resolve by means of common deliberations the particular problems—mainly faith issues—that faced the churches. These were councils composed of the bishops of local churches which were found scattered over a wide area or found in a particular region, as the case may be. The issues which brought together the council were discussed and a decision reached. It was not expected that the local churches automatically accepted the decision of the council. The decisions of the bishops who represented the local churches were not expected to be applied to the life of local churches immediately after the end of the council. Rather, these took time. The decisions of the council were incorporated by the local churches, often gradually and over a long period of time.

On the whole, the essential general features of the process which the term "reception" invokes may be summarized as follows. In the first place, it is a process which leads from one stage to another. It does not follow fixed procedures and time plan but takes place gradually. Second, it is related to a particular church event which is designated as applying to and important for the whole church. In the history of the church, the deliberations of councils and their decisions were such events. One often refers, for a good example, to the history of the early church and the gradual reception of the Scriptures as the canon of the church. This was a process that took time, accompanied as it was with aspects of selection, approval, and rejection. There were many books which were posed as candidates for inclusion in the canon. As time went by, some of them survived and others were rejected. This shows that not all decisions of councils are bound to be accepted. Some of them were also rejected. Third, discussions of specific problems facing a particular church in a region also formed part of the order of the day. This usually had to do with a false teaching, a heresy, that was understood to threaten the church. Such an event in one church and its decision would then be transmitted to others. They would accept or reject it on its merit. Fourth, especially after Constantine, in one form or another, the approval of the emperor also formed part of the reception process. He was instrumental in the calling of the council and saw to it that it concluded its deliberations in an orderly manner. After the conclusions were drawn, the imperial authority played an important role in giving the decision the necessary distribution and protection. Finally, under normal circumstances, it was up to the churches to accept or reject the decisions of the council. They were the ones who saw to it that the decisions were implemented in their everyday lives. They have the authority to measure the conciliar decision in view of its conformity or nonconformity to the received tradition.[13]

Since there are no ecumenical councils in the image of the early periods of the history of the church at present, it is understood that the current understanding of reception must be a little different. In the absence of such a classical situation, where the early churches could meet in councils, there is a great deal of reticence to say loud and clear whether the process of reception is taking place. It seems that one would only dare to go as far as saying that the process is in its initial stages. Even so, taking its clue from the conciliar events in church history, an attempt is being made to apply the reception process to the dialogues. Having recognized the importance of these dialogues and the fact that many results in the form of reports have accumulated over the years, many of their proponents are now convinced that they should lead to a further step. The positive nature of the fact of reaching agreements among the commissions appointed by the churches is often acknowledged. There are also some dialogue results, such as the Leuenberg agreement, which have been received by the churches. On the whole, however, these remain exceptions rather than the rule. In the greater majority of cases, the results still remain nothing more than commission reports. In the words of Harding Meyer: "But when one observes the countless consensus and convergence statements in which Lutheran, Catholic, Orthodox, as well as Anglican churches have taken part, the balance sheet is discouraging. In practically none of the consensuses reached in these dialogues would it be said that it has been received by the church and consequently has imposed an obligation on it or is embodied by it."[14] In such a light, the dialogue results cannot influence the lives of the churches to which they are destined and thereby contribute towards the realization of the unity sought. Now that the initial products are in their hands, the churches must be ready to integrate them into their lives and make them their own. But the crucial question is what one does in the absence of a council.[15] That is part of the reason why the concrete steps to be taken are not clear indeed. As Catholic theologian Peter Neuner admits: "There is great helplessness on all sides with regard to how reception is possible and what it means. This applies to the Lima document of the WCC as well."[16]

Many questions of a practical nature arise in this connection. Is it the decision of a hierarchy of the respective churches that should say the last word? Is it the authoritative body that decides whether the results reached conform to the teachings of the church? Or should the results be disseminated to the faithful for further discussion and reaction by them? But are the latter really equipped to pass judgements on results that have depended mostly on the discussion of the learned teachers of the church? In this regard, some are of the opinion that, for a variety of reasons, "these texts in their present form are fit to be received neither by the official authorities of the churches nor by the congregations."[17] Will it be other theologians, then, who will judge the fruits of the labors of their colleagues? That is why some see a number of stages of reception involving church authorities, theologians, the church members, etc.[18]

The best possible solution seems to combine a number of ways, as the case with the Lima process might show. The results are sent by the churches to be studied by groups of theologians, bishops, assemblies, or congregations, as the case may be. All these groups will be asked to give their opinions on the results. They will be asked to comment on them and say if these results are commensurate with the teaching of the church concerned. Their responses will then be directed to the authorities who will decide on the quality of the agreed statement. In the Catholic Church, this will be the "magisterial or the teaching authority."[19] If and when the results of the dialogues are judged not to contradict the official teachings of the church, the next step would consist in integrating the results of the dialogues into the teaching mechanisms of the churches and their liturgical life. Elements of the results of the dialogues would be gradually integrated into these church traditions and in this way bring in new elements that come from other traditions. In this manner, the riches of other churches are brought in. Some of the recommended ways would include "shared decisions at regional and national levels . . ., reception through liturgy and catechesis . . ., and lived communion."[20] This would then lead to the establishment of communion or church fellowship among the divided churches.

But one of the most serious problems in the process of reception is that there is a variety of churches which have different ways of weighing the importance of the results.[21] The churches go about in manifold ways in reacting to or in receiving them. There are no uniform ways of doing this, and this fact alone contributes to a great deal of misunderstanding. The churches have their own structural means of judging whether the results conform to their faith as they understand it. They have also their own procedures of deciding what the value of the reached agreements are. That is why the most painful question on the results of doctrinal dialogues may be, "What do the churches do with ecumenical agreements?"[22]

Even though the necessity of taking such a step is recognized by all, it is equally recognized that it has not fully taken place so far. A number of reasons are given for this state of affairs. In the case of bilateral dialogues, as the F&O Commission of the WCC admitted in 1981, "a major problem . . . is that the results of international bilateral dialogues are often not 'received' within the churches. . . . It was noted, however, that no bilateral documents have been produced which demand 'authoritative' reception."[23]

Furthermore, it must be reiterated that, even though the bilateral dialogues are officially sponsored by the churches, the results of the dialogues have not yet reached the point where they become authoritative enough to shape the lives of the churches. "The theological agreements reached have still no binding force for the churches. They largely remain in the field of theological opinions from which it is not yet possible to deduce any church decisions."[24] Some authors have gone so far as to state that "there is as yet comparatively little evidence of any tangible impact of bilaterals on the life and thought of the churches concerned."[25]

But the more one follows this series of steps, the more one observes the limitations of the method used. Raiser notes that even after the dialogues have ended—and he admits that they have produced a good amount of material—the hoped-for reception does not take place. "The transition from the dialogue stage to the reception stage does not really materialize. Rather, dialogues seem almost to reinforce confessional self-awareness."[26]

He observes further that, once agreements are reached on certain issues, some other challenges are discovered and dealt with. And so the work continues. Raiser wonders whether "the way from convergence to consensus is really accessible" and asks: "How much consensus is necessary as the basis for the unity of the Church . . .? Was there ever such a complete doctrinal consensus in the undivided early Church?"[27] Such questioning is echoed by Voss: "How far is it both necessary and possible to come to an agreement? How far should and ought the different positions perhaps coexist in order that the light of the full truth might shine in its liberating power?"[28]

Enough Agreements?

We have already had the occasion to see that, for some time now, there has been the growing conviction that so far as the doctrinal differences are concerned, enough agreements have been reached by church representatives to serve as sufficient bases for closer integration of the churches. On the whole, the differences on the doctrinal issues no longer pose themselves as church-dividing. There are no longer major obstacles to realizing the unity that was sought in the first place.

One finds that there are many who are confirmed in this conviction. As far back as 1973, a group of Roman Catholic and Lutheran university theologians representing ecumenical institutes in the then West Germany wrote a memorandum to their church leaders.[29] The main point of their message was that, in view of the progress already made in the understanding of the theological questions concerning the ministry, it was time that Catholics and Protestants recognized each other's ministries as valid. They were of the opinion that there were no longer any theological reasons for continuing to deny the validity of each other's ministries. They declared that "on the basis of the insights of ecumenical theology, a refusal to mutually recognize each other's offices cannot be justified, because these traditional differences must no longer be viewed as separating the churches. . . . Inasmuch as nothing theologically decisive continues to stand in the way of mutual recognition of the offices, a chief hindrance to altar fellowship is transcended."[30] They stated that they presented their work as a theological preparation to a possible official recognition that needs to be taken by the hierarchies of both churches. This idea was later picked up by Lutherans in another conference. In line with the above, it was there asked whether the differences that remain can be valid reasons for withholding the mutual recognition of ministries. The memorandum was of course rejected by the RCC German leadership as not contributing to the progress of ecumenism.[31] But it shows that the intense theological discussions have led to agreements which could serve as the basis for the restoration of the communion of the churches.

There are also many other theologians who support this assessment of the dialogues. During the celebration of fifty years of F&O in 1977, Juergen Moltmann summarized these opinions as follows:

> After fifty years of concerted theological effort we now have to say quite openly to Christians and church authorities that there are no longer any doctrinal differences which justify the divisions of our churches. To mention only the most important points, we have reached a common understanding of the Eucharist, baptism, the ministry of the church, the relationship of scripture and tradition, grace and justification, church and humanity. . . . If there is no longer any justification for our divisions, do they not then stand to be condemned?[32]

This is further confirmed with the observation of William Rusch when he writes: "The conviction of some ecumenical scholars is that the dialogues have already solved the major issues that have kept the churches apart for centuries. The challenge then is not to find solutions but to have those solutions become decisive in the churches."[33]

Building on such a conviction, there are those who have boldly come to the front to announce that the unity of the churches is possible on the basis of agreements registered so far. They even dare present an outline of the possible scenarios. One of the best examples of the boldness expressed in such a direction is the one undertaken by two Catholic theologians who have presented eight theses which, they believe, would lead to the concrete unity of the churches.[34] In believing this possible, the authors admit that they go against the opinion of many people who deny the possibility. They also acknowledge that the church authorities will not be so easily convinced to take the necessary steps.

Needless to say, such a plan has been received with mixed feelings. There have been various, sometimes harsh, reactions to the proposal. On the Catholic side, there have been critical as well as dismissive responses.[35] It was especially the dismissal by Cardinal Ratzinger, the prefect of the Vatican Congregation of the Faith (the body responsible for watching the correctness of the Catholic doctrine) that was caustic.[36] The cardinal dismissed such musings as being far from the truth and reality. On the Protestant side, there have been attempts to deal with it seriously in some quarters. These groups view the proposals as serious and worthy of discussion.[37] As expected, there is also some negative reaction to the thought of accepting the Pope as the head of the Christian church.[38]

Even so, at least in general terms, the conferences and the participation in them by the delegates of the churches, their reports, the studies of and the reactions to these reports by various levels of the church are parts of the reception process. So are the conversations in which the theologians take part. The change that the dialogue participants experience in the light of the meeting they have with members of other Christian confessions is also part and parcel of the ongoing process of reception. Even so, some definitive official receptions of agreed statements will even take years before they become part of the life of the church. It follows from this that reception is not a hasty process. It is one that stretches over a long period of time and which waits for its hour of official acceptance.

It is here that the difficulty arises aptly conveyed in the words of Slenczka:

> The step from the consensus of theological understanding to communion in the practical church fellowship constitutes the touchstone of the translation of the agreements reached, and consequently the goal of convergence. On the basis of many experiences—and this begins already in the churches committed to the Reformation tradition—it is in this step that the greatest difficulties arise. It is here that, in many cases, the whole theme of reception in the sense of concrete realization is concentrated. For at this very point, theological progress and the caution of church leaders face each other. It is here that factions emerge in the congregations. Last but not least, here also pile up the reservations which can be summarized once again under "non-theological factors," a concept which hails from the thirties.[39]

Slenczka argues further that it is often taken for granted that the main cause for the division of the churches was the disagreement between theologians. It is further thought that agreement between these very men would contribute towards healing the divisions. But would it not be the case that the communion itself would bypass the theological differences? It must be admitted that a theological understanding of any doctrinal issue "is not a sufficient means for the restoration of church fellowship."[40]

Slenczka is convinced about the need for the historical, exegetical, and theological research. But he puts the whole enterprise under a shadow and engages in a deep soul-searching when he continues to formulate his questions in the following manner: "But could it also be the case that, under some circumstances, very weighty theological and numerous other opposites may be compatible with one another in the context of an existing church fellowship without at the same time the need to break the fellowship? Couldn't it also be true that we need much less theological understanding for church fellowship than that which seems unavoidable on the basis of the methods adopted up to now?"[41] In the light of such questions, it is increasingly being recognized that "the ecumenism of consensus" has also its serious limits.[42]

Jensen also raises some important questions in this regard. He takes note of the fact that the dialogue partners begin with some understanding of the doctrines that separate their confessions. They list them carefully and according to a set program and apply themselves to solving them. In the course of time, it has become clear that dialogue partners reach "convergence" at the end of the dialogue. This fact has almost reached the stage where it is being taken for granted. That is to say that the dialogue partners claim to have reached a "substantial agreement." But all the convergences or consensuses reached do not add up to overcoming the divisions that still separate the churches. Once some divisive doctrinal elements are solved, the same elements seem to reappear in the garb of some others which take their place and which have in turn to be addressed. "As convergence is achieved on any matter of traditional controversy, so that remaining convergence is no longer sufficient to warrant church-division, the divisive power of the controversy seems merely to eject from its old and now inadequate habitation, and settle into some other topic of controversy. Nor does finishing the list squelch this movable divisiveness, since the process proves to be circular."[43]

We have seen how a great deal of effort is expended in the development of the agreements. This is a necessity which some do no want to avoid and do not think can be done without. In their view, it is indispensable.

> The hard slog of searching for agreement in faith, agreement which is "sufficient and required" to draw us together and hold us together, cannot be dispensed with. It is the price we pay for our lives of alienation, the price we pay for passing on and living the Christian Tradition in separation. We have to re-convince each other that we do, at the level of faith, believe and proclaim the same gospel and that those differences which once were the causes of wars, persecutions and martyrdoms, can be seen in a new light; they are no longer church-dividing issues. There is no way around the tedious, detailed and rigorous search.[44]

Still, the question that arises is whether the results of such a concentrated and serious work find the adequate responses that they are looking for and which they deserve from the churches. Some are not convinced that that is the case. A veteran of such dialogues, Bishop Lehmann writes:

> Many of the endeavours referred to, valuable though they may be, were initiated in a relatively arbitrary and haphazard way. There was no clear concept of the aim in view, and no strategy established between the various steps. This becomes most apparent when people asked just what concrete consequences followed from, for instance, bilateral discussions. The answer to the question is a profound embarrassment. Many who had worked for doctrinal consensus had the unwelcome experience of seeing their labouriously elaborated texts disappear into the files.[45]

In this connection, one should of course question the usually stated opinion that Western churches responded to BEM extensively. How does one confirm this attitude in the light of the weak participation of the faithful in the church? Is not the response rather the work of groups of experts who are familiar with their confessional backgrounds and the twists and turns of international doctrinal dialogues? How far are the rank-and-file church members involved in the formulation of the responses? How far can their voices and contributions be heard in them? Are they really concerned about, and up to the intricacies of, the concepts and practices of baptism, Eucharist, and ministry to formulate their responses theologically? In connection with the question of reception, for example, it is often stated that "any attempt to appraise the stage reached in creating unity between the Churches must be based on the acceptance by the faithful in the two Churches of the results of the work produced by the theological dialogue commissions."[46] But in the last analysis, do the ordinary church members really care about the direction and the results of these dialogues? Do they think that the dialogues actually matter after all? Discussing the importance of eucharistic fellowship and the longing that seizes the ordinary church member, Patrick G. Henry writes with regard to the situation in the USA: "There are, I know, profound theological arguments for delaying eucharistic sharing until other elements of division are worked out. But with a few bold acts of imagination those arguments could appear—what they are already in the considered judgement of millions of committed and thoughtful Christian laypersons—antiquated."[47] Taking his cue from such a situation, Raiser makes an interesting comment which can be applied to this point. He writes: "In the normal conduct of relations, 'church' means, however, in most cases the leadership of the churches."[48] In the last analysis, it is the latter who weigh the importance or otherwise of ecumenical activities of their churches; who relate the outside ecumenism to the internal mood and situation of the church; who sometimes refuse to accept radical ecumenical decisions, in the name of some church members who are prone to drag their feet on taking steps for change; who exercise the caution to fit ecumenical resolutions to the traditional practice and confessional heritage of the church.

The Authority of the Dialogues

The question of the reception of the dialogues is tied up with the level of authority they can muster. We have already seen that the members of the team are officially appointed by their respective churches or confessional families. It does not automatically follow from this, however, that the results of their dialogues constitute the official voice of their churches. The results reached by the dialogue teams, however groundbreaking they may be, have to be reviewed critically and meticulously by whatever authority the sponsoring church or confession possesses. As the ARCIC II document puts it in explaining the "status of the document" produced by the dialogue commission: "It is not an authoritative declaration by the Roman Catholic Church or by the Anglican Communion, who will evaluate the document in order to take a position on it in due time."[49] The authority of the dialogue results thus depends upon the instances that are competent enough to provide them with the kind of authority necessary for their reception. This is to say that a mechanism must exist or be created which gives them the necessary authority they are looking for. This proves to be one of the most difficult issues that the dialogues face. Let us look at one of the best examples in this case.

The Example of ARCIC I

The process of checking and ascertaining whether the agreed statements meet the criteria of the sponsoring body often takes a long time. To take the example of ARCIC I once again, one notes that the text was released in 1981.[50] This was initially greeted positively by the RCC as an important development in the dialogues.[51] On its part, the Vatican Congregation for the Doctrine of the Faith, which is other than the council that sponsors the dialogues, later studied the text and commented on it. In this text, the RCC had "issued a statement which indicated serious concern about certain areas of the Final Report."[52] But the official response came only after almost ten years of waiting.[53]

In a number of senses, this was a positive step. On the one hand, this was the first time that the RCC had given an official response to any result of a bilateral doctrinal dialogue in which it has been involved. It was a positive sign indeed that the Vatican took the necessary interest and effort to formulate a response to a bilateral dialogue. It gave the participants as well as other churches the chance to know the position of the RCC on the matters discussed in the dialogue. The response also enables the carrying out of further studies which will follow the agreement of the team. Furthermore, the response noted how much the dialogue report is appreciated by the RCC and referred to it as being a "milestone" which would not have been possible a few years ago. On the other hand, besides coming late, the document questioned the bases of the conclusions of the dialogue group. It raised serious objections to the so-called substantial agreement claimed to have been reached by the conversation group. In its own words: "The Catholic Church judges, however, that it is not yet possible to state that substantial agreement has been reached on all the questions studied by the Commission. There still remain between Anglicans and Catholics important differences regarding essential matters of Catholic doctrine."[54]

Some of the reactions to such a response from the Anglican side have been more than disappointed.[55] As one Anglican editorial put it: "If this tardiness is a scandal, its contents are a douche of cold water. No doubt ARCIC II will continue its deliberations, but the heart will go out of all the proceedings."[56] To some others, "further gloom has been shed on the hopeful travellers by the official Roman Response."[57] To still others, the response has missed the starting point of the dialogues. Instead of sticking to the original "rule of the game" agreed upon by the Commission, it demanded that the doctrine expressed in the report conform to that of the RCC. They accuse the response of going so far as to demand that the faith of the Anglican Communion be "identical" with that of the official teaching of the RCC. "Further misunderstanding is revealed in the concluding section of the response when 'consonance' with Catholic faith is interpreted as 'identity.' They are not the same."[58]

The positive aspect for the RCC is that it can at least give a coherent response to a dialogue document: it has a unique authority to judge the contents of such a statement through its magisterium. The procedure is more complicated with the CWCs. Whenever the results of the dialogues are ready, there is no competent authority at hand to judge them on behalf of the member churches. As a result, they are often presented at general assemblies which bring representatives of the member churches together. Resolutions are passed to the effect that the documents be sent to the churches for study and appropriate action. There rest the results often. For such assemblies have no authoritative means of taking any decision on behalf of the member churches that binds the latter. The member churches are free to take any step they feel is appropriate, commensurate with their particular legal status. This is illustrated by the situation of two different churches.

In the Anglican Communion, one admits that the church is in crisis due to the question of the ordination of women to the ministry and episcopacy. Anglicanism had often boasted of its comprehensiveness and its capacity to hold opposite theological views together. It did not adhere to any official theology which locked out some and affirmed others. But the question of the ordination of women has introduced a new element into the communion and seems to "threaten the disintegration of Anglicanism."[59] This also throws light on its relation to the results of the doctrinal dialogues and their appropriation and the authority which takes the necessary decision. There is therefore the RCC fear of Anglicanism as possessing "what sometimes looks like doctrinal incoherence."[60]

The autonomous status of the dioceses scattered all over the world also presents "the problems of authority."[61]

First, the twenty-seven provinces of the Anglican Communion are strictly autonomous.[62] There is the Lambeth Conference, which meets every ten years and brings them together for common deliberations, or the Anglican Consultative Council. But it must be pointed out that the decisions which are taken in these meetings "have no force of law until or unless they are given legislative shape by the Synods of the constituent Churches."[63] If any attempt is made to impose some sort of decision on the member churches, some of them have even gone so far as to boycott the meetings. There is therefore here a problem of authority.

The problem that the Anglican Communion faces with regard to the reception of the doctrinal dialogues in which it is engaged came into the open during the 1988 Lambeth Conference. As one Anglican writer put it, the partner churches of the communion were "distressed"

> by the fact that the Anglican Communion could not act as an ecclesial body with any real supra-national authority; it was this second revelation that seemed to put a serious question mark on all dialogues at the international level between Anglicans and other Christians. The question other Churches can no longer avoid asking is precisely what kind of ecclesial consistency the Anglican Communion has and what authority it has to implement any apparent agreement at the international level.[64]

This is also reflected in the opinion of Henry Chadwick: "More painful is the internal consequence that a substantial body of Anglican opinion shares the Catholic lack of confidence that there is sufficient authority for the change."[65]

Second, as is the case with the Anglican Communion, the Church of England, which is an important member of the communion, cannot take such important steps demanded by the interconfessional bilateral dialogues without the resolution of the British parliament. It must be recognized that the Church of England is a state church that is under the crown.[66] The archbishop, that is, the head of the church, is nominated by the prime minister and approved by the parliament. In this sense, he is a public servant. The church is so intimately tied to the crown that independent decisions cannot be taken without the decision of the parliament. This factor in the decision-making process of the Anglicans has been pointed out by no less a person than Cardinal Ratzinger. He has made reference to such concrete problems that stand in the way of taking an authoritative decision by the Anglican Communion even on the results of the dialogues. He raises the idea that the Anglican Communion cannot sometimes come to a decision without the resolution of the British parliament. He refers to the specific case of a new version of the Book of Common Prayer being rejected twice by the parliament in 1927. In other words, he puts a number of serious questions which compromise the claims of the dialogue group.[67]

This is an extremely frustrating aspect of the doctrinal dialogues. After a great deal of financial and other efforts were expended in coming up with a report, there are no mechanisms of authority in which to deal adequately with it. When one compares it with the original goal set by the parties to the dialogue—in the case of the Lutherans and Anglicans, full communion—and one sees the outcome hanging in the air, one cannot but raise the question,

Where does one go from here or what is the ultimate value of the whole exercise? Is the energy expended ever worth the outcome? This is exactly the sentiment expressed by J. M. R. Tillard in the face of the resolutions of the 1988 Lambeth Conference of the Anglican Communion. When the delegates voted, on the one hand, to accept the Final Report of ARCIC I and, on the other hand, to let each and every province decide on whether to ordain women to the priesthood, he wrote: "Poor members of ARCIC I! We have wasted our energy there. The term [the organic unity desired by the Malta agreement] is now hidden in the fog of Lambeth."[68]

The fact which is admitted with exceptional honesty by Anglicans is of course the case with all other CWCs except the RCC. "For the Catholic Church, decisions concerning the official reception of dialogue documents are made finally by the Holy See, and this is not being questioned in any way."[69] The weakness in receiving the results of the dialogues, admitted by the Anglicans, is repeated in all other communions that do not benefit from a centralized magisterium or teaching office such as is the case with the RCC. The non-RCC communions simply are not in a position to make authoritative declarations which are accepted without further questioning by their member churches. "World-wide confessional bodies (e.g., the executive committee of the Lutheran World Federation, the Anglican Consultative Council) can in a similar manner receive the results of the bilateral dialogues. But the fact is that such bodies cannot take any binding decisions on behalf of their member churches. For this reason, the prolongation, the continuation of the ecumenical reception process through and in the individual churches becomes necessary."[70]

The usual scenario regarding the interconfessional dialogues and the CWCs is as follows: Their leadership—mainly the general assemblies or executive committees—appoints the members who represent it in a dialogue commission. The dialogue teams conduct the discussions on behalf of the communion in a series of meetings. Once the results are ready, they are presented to the general assembly of the communion. The assembly passes a resolution to the effect that it "recommends it for study and appropriate action by the member churches."[71] The reference is always to the member churches, which are called to take steps individually and not together within the framework of the communion. In the last analysis, it is the churches which are in a position to take the necessary steps that are commensurate with their legal and ecclesial status. This means that they can either reject or accept the recommendation as well as the results of the dialogues. One is here faced with the contradiction that while it is the communion which took the step in the first place to engage in dialogue on behalf of the churches, once the work is over, it is utterly incapable of taking any concrete steps that contribute to the concrete realization of the goal that started the process of dialogue.

Making reference to the RCC/Lutheran document FACING UNITY, Anna Marie Aagaard reminds us of this very problem that arises regarding the status of the LWF to make a decision on the product of the dialogues. In such a conversation, the LWF is not speaking as a worldwide church. "Seen from the perspective of church law and church reality in most Lutheran state or folk churches, it is not possible to speak of two churches (i.e., Lutheran and Catholic), because the Lutheran Churches are not *a* Church."[72] The member churches are individual, autonomous churches which have their own structures of authority. There is no supranational body that takes decisions on their behalf and to whose decisions they submit. Picking up this problem with reference to the situation that exists in both the Anglican and Lutheran communions, Eugene L. Brand states: "In neither communion does the international expression of the communion exercise more than 'moral authority' over its members. . . . Neither global body can legislate for its members."[73] This state of affairs has grave implications for the reception of the results of the bilateral dialogues. There is an impressive accumulation of their kind over the years. But "as yet no such recommendation has been acted upon internationally."[74] This kind of situation certainly hampers the continuation of dialogues which would lead to any meaningful outcome. In order to be acted upon, the results have to wait for the establishment of an authority that would lead them to their goal.

The same problem faces the WARC and its member churches. There is imbalance between them with regard to their level of commitment even to the ecumenical movement. In his recent assessment of the ecumenical commitment of the World Alliance of Reformed Churches, Lukas Vischer emphasized rightly: "There is a striking discrepancy between official Reformed declarations and the real condition of the Reformed Churches. Even if the World Alliance of Reformed Churches leaves no room for doubt as to its ecumenical commitment, the fact remains that there is no clear consensus among the Reformed Churches in respect of the ecumenical movement. . . . The attitude of quite a few Reformed Churches is anything but an open one."[75]

The Equality of the Dialogue Partners?

This is further complicated when one considers the status of the bodies that are engaged in the dialogue. Do they consider themselves equals? Are the results of the discussions applicable equally to both? Do words like "church," for instance, mean the same to both of them? On the one hand, one would accept the fact that the two bodies have agreed to talk because they consider themselves to be in some ways equals. One would assume that they would not have sat together had they not agreed somehow on this matter in the first place. But this is not necessarily obvious.

One sees the problem even when one deals with the churches of the Reformation tradition. These churches have, for example, in the Leuenberg Concord of 1973, explicitly stated that they recognize each other as churches.[76]

This agreement, which was hailed as a model agreement which would be exported to other places when it was ratified by the Europeans, has now been signed by more than eighty churches.[77] But problems still remain even among such a seemingly homogenous group.[78] There are a number of complaints that are still heard with regard to this concord.[79]

First, the signatory churches are accused of mainly addressing issues that have their place in the past. In so doing, they avoid facing the challenges of the present, which are different. Second, in spite of the initial hopes they entertained for the overcoming of confessional differences in the future, this has not happened. Instead, the confessional differences have remained without being affected in any way by the agreement. The hoped-for "communion with a new identity" has not materialized.[80] Third, in spite of their agreement, they still lack any structured way of arriving at a common decision. "Because no common decision-making structures were envisaged, however, this endorsement by the Churches [of the Concord] has had only limited consequences. Except in a few places, it has not yet led to real common witness and service."[81]

But the mutual recognition of the churches that is seen among the signatories of the Leuenberg Concord is not apparent in the other relationships. When one considers the Orthodox and the Catholic Churches, for example, one finds out that they take themselves as the only true church of Jesus Christ. There are some Orthodox who are adamant in stating categorically that they are the only true and authentic church. The reason for their participation in the ecumenical movement is explained by what they see as their responsibility to call all the other churches to the true faith. The Orthodox Church "knows that she is the guardian of the apostolic faith and the Tradition in its integrality and fulness, and in this sense is the true Church."[82] It is the one church which has preserved the true apostolic faith from the start. The other churches, especially the Reformed, have to return to the Orthodox fold if they are to become the true church. It is true that there are some who argue otherwise. They affirm that they have no intention of demanding that other churches abandon their tradition and join the Orthodox. "The Orthodox Church does not expect that other Christians be converted to Orthodoxy in its historical and cultural reality of the past and the present and to become members of the Orthodox Church."[83] Even so, there are still other Orthodox voices which defend loud and clear the conviction that the Orthodox Church is the only true church. It has thus a unique "missionary task" to express the truth to the churches which participate in the ecumenical movement. This kind of attitude has been held by the Orthodox for many years. It has once again been reiterated at the occasion of the Third Panorthodox Preconciliar Meeting in 1986.[84] As a matter of fact, there is the assumption that the Orthodox Church alone remains the one and true church of Christ. Consequently, it follows that other churches are heretics.[85] In spite of such a self-understanding, the Orthodox continue to participate in the dialogues. Would this self-understanding ever lead to the reception of the dialogue results?

One is bound to raise the same question with regard to the RCC. It must be said that it had greatly modified its attitude towards the other churches during its Second Vatican Council.[86] Nevertheless, it still maintains that the true church "subsists in" the RCC. In the words of a Catholic theologian:

> Another statement of the Decree on Ecumenism that suggests the mind of the (Second Vatican) Council on our question is the assertion: 'It is through the Catholic Church alone that the whole fulness of the means of salvation can be obtained" (UR 3e).. . . But at the same time it is said, in general, of the separated communities, that "we believe they suffer from defects" in this regard. From this it follows that it is in the Catholic Church alone that the Church of Christ subsists with that fulness of the means of salvation which Christ entrusted to the apostolic college.[87]

As a consequence, the other churches are "separated brethren." Their churches are not recognized as full churches in the doctrinal sense of the term because they have theological deficiencies here and there. These deficiencies may be located sometimes in the understanding of the church which they adhere to, the teaching authority (lack of a pope), the ministry, etc. This defines or limits their place in the communion, which is claimed to be the term which defines the ecclesiology of Vatican II.

> To welcome the word of God by faith, to seal that welcome by baptism, to live in brotherhood, to be full of the will to witness to Jesus Christ, to celebrate the Eucharist, to remain in the communion of the episcopal college and of its head, these are steps inspired and supported by the Spirit of Christ and they create communion. To be sure, the latter does not possess all its essential characteristics except where an authentic Eucharist is celebrated and lacks its fullness except where the hierarchy is united around the bishop of Rome.[88]

These things add up to the fact that there is something lacking that puts the non-Catholic churches this side of the fullness of the true Church.[89] It is interesting to note how a Catholic further puts this:

> For Catholic tradition, an authentic ecclesial community is inconceivable without the deep fundamental *communion* of the Eucharist. Consequently, it affirms that where the Eucharist is celebrated by a group which explicitly and rigidly rejects the Eucharist celebrated by the group which—despite its need for conversion and reform—goes back, generation by generation, to the origins, then *sacramental* apostolic continuity is cut through, and a new "planting" is made. But is not this precisely what the Reformers did? Was not the Reformation, ecclesiologically, a *cutting off* from the eucharistic assembly of the

"traditional" community? It is in this profound sense that the Catholic tradition considers the Reformation as an *auto-excommunication*, not juridical but ecclesiological. According to it, the promoters of the Reformation *cut themselves off* from the eucharistic community and hence from sacramental apostolic continuity. The *cutting off* from the sacramental event in which Koinonia is manifested and nourished, the Reformation, in the eyes of the Catholic tradition, broke one of the essential links with the apostolic memory. It put itself outside the communion.[90]

This conviction on the part of the RCC has been strongly reenforced by the letter from the Congregation for the Doctrine of the Faith which came out in June 1992. It asserts that the Eucharist is at the center of the church understood as communion. But since the church is understood as a body, it implies that it has a head. This head is the church of Rome. It also follows that the Pope is "the perpetual and visible source and foundation . . . of the unity of the entire church." The churches which do not find themselves under the papacy are therefore outside the communion. This is meant to say that the churches which have no relationship to the Pope have no valid Eucharist and are therefore "wounded." This applies to the Orthodox as well as to other churches coming out of the Reformation. In the view of the RCC, the latter are in a much more serious situation. In the words of the letter: "The wound is even deeper in those ecclesial communities which have not retained the apostolic succession and a valid Eucharist."[91] As a result, they do not have the valid authority to celebrate a genuine Eucharist. Since the latter is the one element that gives authenticity to the church, and since the church is true only because it is under the Petrine office, any group that is outside this communion is not a church in the true sense of the word.[92]

There is no doubt, then, that both the RCC and the Orthodox churches claim that they are the true church of Jesus Christ. Consequently, even though it is not said openly and clearly for church political reasons, it is the return of other churches to their fold that is often expected if unity of the churches is to become a reality. Anything short of this step is condemned as unacceptable. It is easy to draw the conclusion of what this kind of understanding would ultimately mean for the reception of the results of the dialogues. It makes it crystal clear that the churches are not equal in status and the dialogues mean different things to them all.

Reformation Reticences

Even on the part of Lutherans and other "evangelical" wings, there is also a strong opposition to the rapprochement with the RCC. Some of them are opposed even to the dialogues. Their main reason for opposition is on theological grounds. They are of the opinion that discussions with the RCC lead to the betrayal of the heritage of the Reformation.[93] They lead to a compromise of the way to salvation as advocated by the reformers. These groups are of the opinion that the Protestant principles of faith alone, grace alone, Christ alone, Scripture alone are somehow set aside in the search for an understanding with the RCC. The radical dependence on the grace of God for the salvation of man is compromised in the dialogues, the main concern being to appease the RCC. Instead, a sort of work righteousness, through the introduction of man's cooperation with God in the attainment of one's salvation, is introduced contrary to the Reformation principles. Kuehn observes that "more and more voices are raising very basic criticisms concerning the results and projects of the ecumenical dialogues from the point of view of the Reformation self-understanding and identity."[94] This all adds up, in that there are still suspicion and refusal in terms of receiving the results of the doctrinal dialogues. Echoing these sentiments from the Catholic side, a key person such as Cardinal Ratzinger is even quoted as saying that "for him, the results of the dialogues are only products of 'ecumenism of negotiations'; at best, they may say something about the diplomatic dexterity and capacity for compromise of the leaders of the negotiations. Consequently, they may have nothing to do with the witness to the mystery of Christ."[95]

The situation in which the churches find themselves as not being conducive to the reception of the results of the doctrinal dialogues is mentioned. Sometimes, the churches are too contented with their own situations. They have grown so used to their traditions and idiosyncrasies that they are not willing to consider opening up for other influences. Sometimes, the churches have neither the courage nor the capacity to take bold decisions. Their authorities have been gradually sapped, so that they would be ill at ease to demand the taking of new steps by their constituencies. As Michael Kinnamon observed: "The remarkable theological work of recent years signals a new moment of decision for the ecumenical movement; I suspect that the next decade will be ecumenically difficult as a result. Many of our churches have such uncertainty about their teaching authority and decision-making processes that they don't know how 'to receive' ecumenical documents."[96]

One often talks about searching for the truth when one engages in bilateral dialogues. It is not the common denominator that is sought but the doctrine that is true. In the course of time there arises the very important question: What measure of agreement is sufficient for church unity? What are the essential faith articles that one has to agree upon in order to reach the goal of unity? What criterion does one then use to separate the primary and the secondary elements of the faith which determine the hierarchy of the importance of the articles? Which are indispensable for agreement and which can be left as signs of diversity?[97] These and other similar questions are open ones which will remain unanswered to haunt the ecumenical search for the unity of the churches through the medium of the dialogues.

— 4 —

Third World Reactions to the Dialogues

When one begins to deal with the relationship of the Third World to the interconfessional doctrinal dialogues, one is astonished to find a remarkable measure of agreement on one judgement. This is the fact that, in the course of the history of these dialogues, it has been recognized openly that generally speaking, the interconfessional doctrinal dialogues do not meet the needs and do not reflect the concerns of the churches of the Third World. This much has been recognized even on the part of the sponsors and organizers of these dialogues. It is worth our while to follow these observations and pick up the reasons behind them. We shall first look at both dialogues one after the other and then turn our attention to the voices of Third World theologians.[1]

The Bilaterals and the Third World

The CWCs, who organize the Forums on Bilateral Conversations in co-operation with the F&O Secretariat, have admitted severally that the concerns of the dialogues and that of the churches of the Third World do not mesh. They were of the opinion that the dialogues dealt with "classical" doctrinal issues which raise little interest in the nonwestern churches. As a result, they express the opinion that when it comes to the reception of the results of the dialogues, these churches will not be in a position to play any significant role. In their own words: "This model [i.e., discussion of classical doctrines], however, may not be totally acceptable to other churches, including those of the Third World, where the primary concern is the relation of the Gospel to questions of social justice. This *division of perspective* will also affect the reception of the results of the dialogues."[2]

In the same Forum, the participants also acknowledge that the membership of the dialogue teams is heavily Western and that theological perspectives other than the Western do not have a hearing. They therefore point to the need of widening the participation to include "adequate representation from all parts of the world."[3] In the next Forum, they go further in admitting that the interest on the doctrinal dialogues was mostly confined to the churches of the Western world: "Bilateral as well as multilateral dialogues and their results meet with a wider interest in the churches of Europe, North America and Australasia than in the churches of Africa, Asia and Latin America."[4]

Multilaterals and the Third World

The above-expressed views are also confirmed in the context of the multilateral dialogues, especially in connection with the BEM document. Since 1982, the responses to this document coming from the churches of the Third World have been meager compared to those coming from the Western churches. In the words of Martin Seils, who studied the Lutheran responses to the BEM: "The silence of the Third World is striking." While Seils tries to find technical reasons for this silence, he nevertheless senses the gravity of the situation when he writes: "The fact remains . . . that the almost complete absence of these voices represents a serious weakness for the whole discussion of BEM with all its promise for the future."[5] While the membership of the churches of the Third World in the WCC is high, the number of responses from these churches is comparatively small. This observation is also confirmed by the onetime moderator of the F&O Commission: "It has been noticed that third-world responses to the BEM texts have not been numerous."[6]

The meagerness of these responses has been recognized on a wider scale within the F&O Commission reports and commentaries. These acknowledge that the majority of responses come from the churches of the Western world. There are of course attempts to give reasons for the scarcity of responses from the nonwestern world. Among them, one may mention the following: First, these churches lack the necessary technical facilities. This is to say that the nonwestern churches do not possess the adequate infrastructures to enable them to follow the process of the formulation of the response requested by the BEM process. They lack the staff, the expertise, the committees, the financial resources, and "the 'Western' methods to carry out the complicated process of preparing an official response to an ecumenical document like BEM."[7] Second, the existence of a far greater problem is acknowledged when it is said that the doctrinal issues dealt with in the BEM document do not have to do with the history of these nonwestern churches. Therefore, these churches are not very much enthused by these theological arguments and positions. Furthermore, "BEM is shaped by a conceptual framework and language that is often strange to them."[8] Whatever the reasons, the verdict is the same. As Irmgard Kind-Siegwalt, a former staff member of the WCC F&O Secretariat in Geneva put it in her evaluation: "The Secretariat has officially received the responses of about 50% of all the WCC member churches. A good three-quarters of these are from

Europe and North America and from churches definitely in the Western tradition. Barely a quarter are from the countries of Africa, Asia and Latin America."[9]

A closer look at the whole issue shows that the uneasiness with the dialogues as well as with BEM does not have to do with technical aspects and methods only. On the contrary, it goes far deeper. Before we attempt to find an answer to this anomaly from a wider area, let us continue to limit ourselves to the area of the doctrinal dialogues. Here again, one does find a clue to the answer.

A Discordant Voice at the Launching of BEM

If one goes back to the year when the F&O Commission officially resolved to send the BEM document to the churches, one hears even then and there a discordant note. It was there that Jose Miguez Bonino—a Latin American theologian from Argentina and a person involved for many years in the ecumenical movement as a member of the F&O Commission and as a WCC president—argued that the Third World perspective put the accent on ecumenism not on the doctrinal dialogues as such but on a wider scale going beyond the dialogues. Miguez Bonino argued that ecumenism from a Third World perspective can only be thought of in a context which takes seriously the plight of the oppressed, marginalized, and exploited of the world. He raised the question of dealing with the relationship of the Gospel to an *oikumene* of suffering. His leading question was: "How can the body of the Church within the body of humankind correspond to the nature of the Gospel rather than conform to the "structures of the world" of sin? . . . It is, it seems to me, the hope and crisis of the ecumenical movement today."[10]

Miguez Bonino argues that the modern ecumenical movement arose within the context of Western domination and colonialism. As the Western world moved out to other continents through its conquest of other lands and peoples, the churches followed suit in the form of missionary activities. The search for the unity of the churches in the ecumenical movement was closely related to the unity of the Western world. There were social, economic, and political questions which arose in the European societies to which the churches had to address themselves, especially in relation to the two world wars. The ecumenical movement was deeply occupied with responding to challenges which arose due to the specific historical contexts.

At the same time, the churches engaged in the missionary movement saw the need to integrate themselves in the face of "the mission fields." They recognized that their confessional differences were not a match for the world out there and that they needed to pull their energies and resources together. This was purely a case of "*the missionary integration of the West in the ecumenical expansion*" (p. 62). A "crisis" is now taking place in the ecumenical movement, since the Western presuppositions and contexts of this movement are changing, bringing heretofore unforeseen conflicts with them. This "crisis" results from "the increasing self-awareness and participation in the ecumenical movement of a new reality of the oikumene—a Christianity different from modern Western Christianity in a world which is struggling to overcome the oikumene controlled by the modern Western world. In brief: the so-called 'Third World' and the Christianity of the 'Third World' " (p. 63). The coming of this new element breeds conflicts, and it is these conflicts that have to be addressed "on the road towards an authentic ecumenism within an authentic oikumene" (p. 64). But the house in which we live is a divided house; it is one in which human beings are divided between the rich and the poor. Even though Western ecumenism fails to address this issue, "it is in this perspective that we can debate the ecumenical question" (p. 65).

The nutshell of the argument of Miguez Bonino is that ecumenism has to deal with the *oikumene*, the one inhabited world. It has to challenge the structures of the church which have assimilated into themselves the sinful distortions of the structures of the world. It has to fight the divisions that rack society—divisions in which the church is deeply implicated. It has to oppose through its praxis the oppression that holds a majority of the human family at the bottom of the ladder. "Ecumenism . . . means the struggle for the creation of a new oikumene in justice to replace 'the Western modern oikumene' which is a structure of domination" (p. 67). It is interesting to note that at a moment when the BEM document was celebrating the consensus of Christians on the basis of doctrines, a strong announcement of a different perspective on the ecumenical movement was being made from "another quarter," namely, the Third World.

Such intimations of the feeling that the ecumenical endeavor was fissured between its "Western" and "Third World" components have already been enunciated by others as well. The longtime librarian of the WCC, Ans van der Bent, had noted such a fissure in his observation of the ecumenical movement as a result of his survey of numerous documents of the WCC. With regard to the doctrinal dialogues, specifically BEM, and their relation to the Third World, he offers a very sharp criticism:

> The real crux is that BEM is a typical Western document, rooted in the old cultural traditions of Roman Catholicism, Orthodoxy and Protestantism of the European continent. It is in fact a rather stale, anachronistic, lopsided and introverted charter of unity of the Western hemisphere. Its language, its style of reasoning and its conclusions are based on theological argumentation, hardly understandable to many non-white Christians with minimal catechetical instruction. Not accidentally African and Asian theologians had little part in it and not surprisingly cannot identify with its reasoning.

Van der Bent closes his analysis of the ecumenical situation by noting that the fragmentation of the ecumenical movement is taking place because the tensions between those who push for unity on the basis of doctrine and those who see the importance of the church as an advocate of the poor are not resolved.[11] And Kind-Siegwalt sees a huge gap and delivers a severe judgement when she concludes: "It is of course true that the Lima document has not facilitated *rapprochement*, but has made it more difficult. A number of non-Western churches felt it to be too 'Western,' too concerned with typically Western problems that reached them through the missionaries but which they do not feel as their own."[12]

The rumblings in this direction were also heard in an earlier meeting of the F&O Commission. In Accra in 1974, the Africans expressed their views in a very sharp way:

> We feel that all the expressions of the Christian faith up to now, from whatever area of the Christian Church (Orthodox, Roman Catholic, Protestant) do not speak to us at the depth of our situation, past, present or future. . . . The sin of the Church in the past has been that each particular expression of the human understanding, made according to local histories and situations, has claimed to be the *One* and *Only.* To us, this is blasphemous self-idolatry. Hence our disgust with the so-called ecumenical dialogue. Hence also our frustration in the hope of bringing reason to this dialogue.[13]

The distance of the Africans from such an ecumenical endeavor is enunciated clearly here. The ecumenical enterprise of doctrinal dialogues is accused of being cocksure and aggressive in regard to the other cultures and thus incapable of engaging in real dialogue. In fact, the imposition of Western Christianity is seen as part of the general violence engendered by the contact of the West with Africa.

Disaffections similar to the foregoing surfaced once again at the meeting of the Commission held in Norway in 1985. Within the context of the discussion of the doctrinal dialogues, there was a clear disaffection that arose from the Third World side. Some of the points are worth recalling: First, the distance of the concerns of these dialogues from those of some churches of the Third World was pointed out. "It was observed that some churches, for example, in Africa, have much difficulty in making their own contributions and priorities heard in the dialogues at world level, and that some of the same churches are unduly affected by outside influences." Second, there was the incomplete discussion on the difference between "developed," that is, "classical (Western) theology," and a so-called "undeveloped" theology. There was the conviction expressed by some that the latter's concerns are not treated by the dialogues. Third, the specific concerns that arise in the contexts of the Third World are not handled by the dialogues. The latter only deal with "the more 'classical' problems in the history and theology of the churches in Europe and North America."[14] Finally, the question of inadequate representation of the Third World in the dialogues and the consequent absence of their views to influence the dialogues is once again mentioned. The overall judgement is summarized in the following words: "II.1. The priorities of some newer churches are not the same as those for the older churches. . . . The problems of the newer churches of the Third World deserve to be considered at the universal level just as much as the 'classical' problems in the history and theology of Europe and North America" (p. 233).

These different and contradictory assessments of the dialogues come up once again at the F&O Commission meeting in Budapest in 1989. It was there that the tension arose between those who support the continuation of the dialogues in their traditional form, concentrating on the solution of doctrinal differences, and those who pleaded for dealing with the questions of justice in the world. The tensions between the traditional emphases of F&O on the one hand and the need to move beyond them to that of unity and renewal of the human community with a focus on justice had sometimes "veered toward open conflict."[15] As our first chapter showed, the tensions are still there and will continue to manifest themselves.

On the whole, then, one observes that the relationship of the doctrinal dialogues and the Third World churches has been occupying quite a few minds which are engaged in the dialogues. While their proponents have often been aware of the fact that the two do not go together well, they have also been concerned about giving their own answers to the difference of perspectives. The majority of explanations given often lean on technical reasons, the absence of this or that capacity or facility, or methodological deficiency, etc. What do Third World theologians say about them? It is now time to turn our attention to this question and to hear additional voices from their ranks.

The Verdict of EATWOT

One of the significant ecumenical events in the recent history of theology and the Christian church has been the formation of the Ecumenical Association of Third World Theologians. Its establishment is one more sign of the rising consciousness of the "marginalized of history" to organize themselves in order to make their real voices heard, instead of being represented by others. We have seen earlier how the coming of these theologies is being recognized in some circles, which even speak of "the challenge" being faced by "European theology."[16] Therefore, the movement of theological reflection in the Third World, of which EATWOT is an important voice, has been rightly viewed as a historical landmark.[17] The influence of these theologies has been such that the work they have been engaged in and the line of argument they follow have been recognized as having exercised a strong impact even on the WCC.[18]

Taking consideration of the place of EATWOT, it is interesting to note its view on confessional differences and its work. After attending the first five meetings, stretching over a period of a number of years, of this group of theologians coming from a variety of confessional backgrounds, one writer comments with regard to the question of the place of confessional differences in their deliberations: "It is astonishing but true that in all of EATWOT's intense discussions, confessional divisions have never surfaced. . . . Dogmas and doctrines that separate denominations have never been a root of disagreement among EATWOT theologians."[19]

It is indeed astonishing that one of the leading preoccupations of the ecumenical movement, an issue which quite a few churches and theologians spend their time on and expend their energy to overcome, namely, confessional differences, becomes a nonissue to leading Third World theologians. Such a gap is all the more astounding because doctrinal discussion has constituted a significant current of the ecumenical movement for many years. Yet the confessional backgrounds from which the theologians of this ecumenical association come, even though varied and many, do not become decisive issues and simply fail to appear in their agendas. They neither become dividing issues nor appear important enough to stand as points for discussion. In spite of the differences that characterize their theologies, it is not different confessional backgrounds that mark them. This startling phenomenon is worth investigating in some detail for it gives us a glimpse into the ecumenical preoccupations of Third World churches and theologians and their reactions to interconfessional doctrinal dialogues.

The composition of the membership of the association is varied. They come from different confessional backgrounds. Yet confessional differences do not weigh heavily on them. This fact is recognized by both adversaries and friends alike. Even Cardinal Joseph Ratzinger notes: "The association of theologians of the Third World is strongly characterized by the amount of attention they give to themes that belong to the theology of liberation. . . . The theology of liberation goes beyond confessional boundaries. . . . Liberation theology seeks to create from its premises a new universality by which the classical separations of the churches should lose their importance."[20] This has also been recognized by another observer as an exemplary ecumenical achievement which has to be imitated by others. Norbert Greinacher writes: "Still to be lifted up as special is the ecumenical cooperation of Third World theologians. Here, understandably, all the confessional borders have been transcended because it simply does not appear responsible to go one's own separate way in the face of common problems and the equally common Christian faith. It could well be that the problem of the reconciliation of the Christian churches receives in this manner a completely fresh and hopeful dimension."[21]

One of the striking new factors in this association, then, is that the theologians work together without in any way being hindered by their different confessional adherences.[22] These theologians are of the conviction that there are greater issues that demand their attention than the denominational differences. The divisions of the world are of such an urgency for the Church that the confessional divisions lose their sharpness in the face of them. Since this is a significant development in the enterprise of theologizing,[23] it behooves us to take a closer look at the reasons that lay behind it. A number of them have been given for the reluctance of Third World theologians to take seriously the confessional differences that preoccupy some aspects of the ecumenical movement. Let us now attempt to see what these are.

The Conceptual Framework

One of the frequent criticisms hurled at the dogmatic emphasis of doctrinal discussions is that they are too conceptual. One of their primary aims is to picture and define God in his entity. They concentrate heavily on the philosophical description of the Godhead and his relationship to the world. "Dogma," it is accused, "dehistoricizes and fixes God into eternal and immutable concepts. The reification that cult accomplishes at the level of symbolic action, dogma accomplishes through conceptualization."[24] Such fascination with ideas and the philosophically pure and clean God that it portrays, however, is far removed from the dirt and filth of history. He is alienated from the struggles of the poor and the marginalized. At worst, he becomes an alibi of the status quo. He becomes a spokesman of the unjust world order in which people who need to overcome their oppression do not find him as their ally. "The Christ of dogma divides; Jesus of the Gospel unites."[25] In this connection, the declaration of EATWOT is significant: "We reject as irrelevant an academic type of theology that is divorced from action. We are prepared for a radical break in epistemology which makes commitment the first act of theology and engages in critical reflection on the praxis of the reality of the Third World."[26]

Living in and Reading the World

When one considers the place of the Church in the world, what counts is not agreement on dogmatic issues. On the contrary, work for social justice, advocacy on behalf of the oppressed, working for the Kingdom of God in solidarity with the poor and the marginalized become primary. This is based on a serious and realistic reading of the social situation from the perspective of the poor.[27] A project having such a direction frees believers from the constraints and straightjackets of dogma and enables them to sacrifice their differences at the altar of the poor.

A relevant theology is more likely to emerge from those groups of dissenting Christians who in loyalty to Jesus have inserted themselves in the life of the people and are partners in their struggle for justice. It is heartening to note that more and more of such groups are being formed, at least in India. They are able to forget all denominational differences and meet on the common basis of discipleship under Jesus and commitment to the new humanity he envisioned. They, in truth, anticipate the Jesus-community of the future which will transcend all human barriers.[28]

The accusations made against the speculative theology of dogma is that it has neglected people. It has put them aside and continued business as if their lives did not matter as it goes about in the pursuit and exposition of its "eternal truths." It has neglected the concrete situations of suffering in which human beings live and die. Instead, it has satisfied itself with ideas for their own sake. But "we need a theology that is more human-centered, and oriented towards justice in society. This requires an option in favor of the oppressed."[29] Involvement in the real and concrete life of the people in all their agonies, fears, and hopes is the mark of a true theology. "Dogmatic theological statements from a church that stands on the sidelines as spectator or even interpreter of what God is doing in Asia can carry no conviction."[30] The local churches cannot be satisfied with propounding mere copies of theologies that are produced in the West which hardly reflect the real-life situation of the Asian peoples. Their call is to live and breathe with the people and speak in tune with their heartbeats.

Jean-Marc Ela expresses the fear that concern with doctrinal matters may draw our attention away from the real-life issues that are threatening the present and future of the peoples of the Third World. He argues that the present duty of the Christian faith consists in facing the contemporary historical challenge of averting the death of peoples. After complaining that "we have inherited a church whose mental structures were shaped by a decadent scholasticism" (p. 163), Ela goes on to say:

Our faith can no longer be described simply and exclusively in terms of Roman setting. Rome risks marginalizing the problems of the Third World because it is caught up in its preoccupations with what we may aptly call a three-dimensional universe centered on the doctrine of sin, the sacraments and grace. The churches of the Third World have other concerns, other preoccupations, other objectives: to see their people free themselves from oppression, from slavery, poverty and hunger.[31]

The critical situation that faces the churches in Africa is this: People are dying of hunger; they are victims of malnutrition, diseases, and economic exploitation. National life is collapsing or on the verge of doing so. Their future is thus dark and uncertain. Consequently, the burning question for the churches and for Christians becomes: What is the role of the Christian faith in the face of this tragedy that is unfolding? Will the church limit itself to caritative services here and there as it used to do? Will it opt for supporting the situation as is, without doing anything for the liberation of the poor? In the face of such prospects of mass-scale deaths, the doctrinal concerns become marginal: "In our environment, our faith does not ask questions about the sex of the angels or the infallibility of the pope; instead we question the lack of any genuine application of the critical function inherent in the Christian faith. How can we show that the African church is blocked by an ecclesiastical praxis that is, in fact, a kind of museum of a narrow moralism, a ritualistic sacramentalism, a disembodied spirituality, and a withering dogmatics?"[32]

The Alien Historical Background of the Doctrines

The discussions with which the doctrinal dialogues are concerned reflect a certain particular history. They are bound with theological quarrels that arose in the course of Western church history. As such, they are specifically bound to Western philosophical, cultural, and political circumstances. Unfortunately, these same disagreements and divisions were exported to other Christians in other parts of the world through missionary movements. The fact still remains that these exported tensions remain foreign to the new converts to Christianity. If the new churches are to be true to themselves, they have to come to the recognition that

> many issues that have agitated the minds of Christians are not really our major concerns. They are peripheral to us; they are imports to Asia (as well as elsewhere). A clear example is the division of Christianity into denominations and sects. These have been largely fashioned by European history and American concerns. They are not central issues for us. Having first created problems for believers in Christ, Western Christians then present us with an ecumenical movement and guidelines for contact between Christians; e.g., Roman Catholics and Anglicans. This is an example of the irrelevancies passed on to us. Europeans fought their politico-religious battles in the sixteenth century, and we as a result are divided into separate Christian churches today; plus we need their permission for greater communion among us.[33]

This constant reference to the confessional battles fought elsewhere and at another time in history and their capacity to hinder positive developments towards church unity in Third World Churches is amply documented. It is often referred to as one of the clearest weaknesses of the missionary era. It is viewed as one of the unfortunate legacies inherited from the missionary movement. The coming of the Gospel to Asia, to refer to one example, was accompanied by "a view of the church distorted by the divided nature of Western Protestantism."[34] It is acknowledged that the inherited confessions had become a kind of barrier which could not be crossed. The new churches were, as it were, imprisoned by and unable to venture out of, such confessional cages. In the event, they were bound to confessional books which do not arise out of their context, and consequently their witness to their context was compromised if not hindered. "When we make absolute the written confessions of the churches of another culture or age, we become incapable of discovering the new depths of truth God can reveal to us in Christ amidst Asian life."[35]

One may refer to the Indonesian situation as a concrete example which reflects a situation not unfamiliar to other churches, arising out of missionary activities. Once a Christian council had been established, the efforts of its member churches towards unity were faced as one of the sticking points. The local efforts were paralyzed simply because they were constantly under the shadow of their foreign selves. Referring to this situation, Simatupang writes: "The unambiguous aim has been to foster the establishment of one church in Indonesia. It has been in the area of unity, however, that the [national Christian] Council has produced the fewest results and the least creative thinking. One reason for this is that thinking on the unity of the churches has been too much oriented to discussion among confessional groups in the West."[36] It is true that the Batak church had written a special confession in order to "be admitted to the LWF" (p. 107). At the same time, it resisted accepting the general standard formula which acknowledges the primacy of the Augsburg Confession in the interpretation of the Scriptures, in line with accepted Lutheran practice. The formulation of a general "Christian" confession as opposed to conformity to a specific "denominational" tradition was chosen. This is typical of the uneasiness and soul-searching that accompanies Third World churches and theologies trying to deal with their ambiguous "confessional heritage."

The apprehension with regard to pure and simple confessionalism as a danger to the local church was felt acutely in Asia. An uncritically received adherence to the specific confessions usually leads to the isolation of the church concerned from its specific milieu. Its attention is more or less drawn away from its immediate environment. Its points of reference are more often than not foreign concerns which are far removed from its concrete situation and priorities. These only succeed in alienating it from its context. Asian leaders meeting in Kandy, Sri Lanka, in 1965, addressed themselves to the dangers of confessionalism and explained their reason for opting for a confessing church. "A confessing theology, i.e., a theology that is a result of the wrestling of an Asian church with its Asian environment, will naturally not be specifically confessional even though it may be indebted to many confessional traditions. *A confessional* type of theology, inherited by an Asian church as a part of its tradition, is usually a source of division; while a confessing theology will undergird the movement toward unity and union in the church of Asia."[37] It is also admitted that such a stance requires independence and support especially from confessional families, which regroup churches on the basis of confessions and are sources of finances and other material benefits.

While acknowledging some of the positive aspects of belonging to confessional bodies, there is the warning that such steps may deflect the resources of the local church from attending to its ecumenical responsibilities at home. This is not always easy. As the African churchmen expressed in Accra in 1974: "Many church union negotiations—even *within* a confessional group—have been nipped in the bud by a threatened stoppage in the flow of assistance to those currently receiving it. In some cases, even after union has been consummated, finance from missionary-sending agencies has prevented the united church from sharing all things in common."[38]

Moreover, especially in such contexts as Asia, where the churches are a minority, the Christian community has been unnecessarily divided and weakened by concerns that were brought from outside. These concerns have often stood in the way to unity of the local churches and fragmented them. Many see the way of unity as well as efficacity in carrying out the mandate of the Gospel in "viewing the confessional differences as a peripheral question."[39] It is to such ambiguity arising from denominational heritage that Bishop Manas Buthelezi refers when he discusses the "relevancy and validity of the Lutheran confessional corpus" stated by a gathering of African churchpeople. He refers to the fact that, wherever unions of churches have taken place, the confessional basis of the union was, more often than not, defended and formulated by foreign missionaries. The national Christians were often helpless spectators of what seemed to appear as a reenactment of the original confessional battles which were fought in the respective countries of the missionaries. The end result is that the new local churches are burdened with traditions which, in the best sense of the word, are strangers to their understanding of the mission of the church as well as to their specific heritage. One wonders frightenedly how important such declarations, referring to specific confessional documents mainly buried in church constitutions, can be to the life and witness of the churches. In other words, they seldom, if ever, succeed in jumping out of their "constitutional captivity" and making a difference in the lives of the concerned churches. Their foreign nature is thus acknowledged by being forgotten altogether and remaining in the archives of the church.

But Buthelezi poses a further question which is raised in the minds of many Third World churchpeople discussing the questions of adhering to specific confessional traditions that are tied to specific cultural, political, and national history. He writes: "In our opinion, the category of the 'human' has been neglected as a theological motif for understanding the expression of ecumenical solidarity in the interest of the ideological, namely, confessions and doctrines."[40] In such instances, the burning human issues such as those of racism and social injustice remain buried under the debris of confessionalism. To the detriment of the human need, they are relegated to the secondary position. "Yet genuine oneness in Christ manifests itself best on the level of 'naked humanity,' where the masks of 'common faith' and 'common confessions' as the basis of fellowship are often removed" (p. 73). The emphasis on confessionalism, which comes from outside and has been uncritically swallowed up by Third World churches, beclouds the human aspect that should be in the center of the Christian reflection in the local context.

Even when one deals with ecumenism, there is the burden of the past which is weighing unduly heavily on it. The present ecumenical task is hampered because of ecumenism's entanglement in past concerns which have often little to do with the problems of the present. This is the case with confessions and theology.

What is true of confession is also true of theology in general. It is very tempting to talk glibly about "ecumenical theology" or the so-called "classical theology." By these phrases is often meant a set of broad theological concepts which have survived as minimal points of agreement in the historical disputes among theological schools of thought which have emerged from the Graeco-Roman cultural tradition. It is these broad concepts which are being imposed as sacred cows and points of departure in modern ecumenical dialogue. One is sometimes left with the impression that churches in Africa and Asia are expected to sacrifice their theological priorities in order to appear to be in accord with the "classical tradition" of theology.

Whatever were the concerns of Luther in his time should not hide the fact that they are tied to his time. They should not be an alibi for Third World theologians to engage themselves with them and thus lose their contact with and their responsibility to their concrete Third World historical problems. They should not allow themselves to be tied to alien concepts which are far removed from their present historical situations. "We must remember that what was 'ecumenical' theology during the time of Luther is no longer adequate to comprehend the totality of insights of the church that has grown and spread to Asia, Africa and Latin America."[41]

In contrast to the confessional divisions, the persistent human divisions which become the basic issues challenging the unity claimed by Christians become points of concern for Buthelezi. It is well and good to come with confessional statements and agreements in theologies, but if these go nowhere in affecting the human relationships, they do not accomplish their aim. Therefore, it is necessary to go further and to develop other confessions which challenge the older ones in order to create new communities which take their confessing seriously in order to affect their human relationship in a radical and meaningful way. "We need now to slit open our historical, denominational and confessional jumble bags so as to bring about a new church realignment in which those who truly want to belong together will be made and helped to belong together. In certain instances the confessional bonds of the past are failing to bind people together on a human level. This calls in question our whole concept of unity."[42]

Taking these ideas further, John Gatu argues that "beautiful" theological "phraseologies" may only succeed, after all, in hiding the way we should go, in making us get lost on the way. What is of great importance at present is not actually the confessional differences that seem to separate us from one another. The existential problems that societies face are so urgent that one has to go beyond confessional statements and declarations. The elements that hold us to one another are Jesus Christ and the concrete situation in which we find ourselves. "This is the way I would like to understand church unity—a new creation, starting a new life with all the denominational and confessional identities dead and buried, bringing about a Christian identity of love and faith in Jesus Christ."[43]

Inherited Denominationalism

In some cases, missionaries belonging to different denominations were involved in a great deal of antagonism to one another. Catholics and Protestants, for example, disagreed sharply in the mission field while trying to convert the same people. In this way, they contributed to the confusion of many of their converts, who had a hard time knowing where they belonged.[44] Sometimes, the missionaries even went so far as to fight it out violently in the battlefield in order to gain the souls of their potential converts. In some cases, the denominational differences led to violent political clashes and party spirit. According to some observers of such histories, this had a very negative effect in the life of some countries for a long period of time. In the case of Uganda, for example, "the two main [political] parties of the early 60s were perceived by most people as embodying the religious cleavage in Ugandan society between Catholic and Protestant. . . . Whenever political repression was the order of the day, the churches were incapable of acting together due to this inherited division."[45]

From this perspective, it was often hoped that the interconfessional dialogues on the international level, such as ARCIC, would have some impact on the inherited hostilities and that the agreements reached by Catholics and Anglicans on this level would prove beneficial on the local level. But the problem was that the results of the discussions were practically unknown. Furthermore, they were often confined to discussions among Westerners. "The ARCIC was overwhelmingly European and North American. In any future negotiations, it is very important that the Third World be represented more adequately."[46]

Buthelezi takes this line of reasoning further when he sees the church itself as dividing human beings along national lines. When this is the case, it is not church division as such that is the problem, but that the church itself serves as an agent, as an instrument of division. "For the blacks [of South Africa], the quest for church unity is, therefore, not first a matter of solving the European doctrinal disputes of the 16th century but basically of restoring religious integrity to a community whose religious wholeness was disintegrated by European Christianity." In addition, the divisions among Christians have little to do with their faith. They are mostly based on the race of the person. The tragedy is that the church was practicing racial separation before apartheid became a law in the society. "As a Lutheran, I belong to a Black church simply because Lutherans on their own decided to create racial churches. Even the so-called multi-racial churches like Anglicans and Methodists are now experiencing the superficiality of that image they undeservedly bear."[47]

There are theologians who decry the denominational heritage received from the European churches. They view the division of churches on denominational lines as ridiculous because it puts the credibility of the Christian faith into question. Its presence in the African situation, for example, is deplored. It is referred to "as the scandal of the divisions and competition within the church," as "original tribalism" is being replaced by Christian "tribes"—Anglicans, Methodists, Roman Catholics, Baptists. Many are inclined to reject adherence to such divisions as unnecessary. In contrast to allegiance to such divisions, it is asserted that "it is with the religion of Jesus that African theologians are concerned." There is the conviction that these theologies still remain in the possession of the denominations themselves. These theologies are foreign to the African cultures and institutions of social structure. It follows also that many of the religious practices and paraphernalia that the African denominational churches still hold to are foreign. In order to be authentic to the African situation, "their [i.e., Western churches, Anglicans, Methodists, and Presbyterians] adopted denominational theologies, church practices, vestments, discipline, preaching and rites" should "all be subjected to the touchstone of the religion of Jesus of Nazareth."[48]

One laments the denominationalism that had been introduced to new believers as a result of missionary activities. The inheritance of the fruits of foreign battles, with the damages they cause in the planting of the Christian faith in other parts of the world, is experienced as a painful heritage. It is swallowed by people who cannot digest it all. Without their knowing, they become partisans in a struggle that drastically diminishes their capacity to address the challenges of their specific context. They inherit a confessional war they hardly understand. This introduces serious defects in the churches which have far-reaching consequences. Samuel Rayan admits that, in the Indian context, together with the caste system, "the denominational divisions it has inherited from the West" have become "additional reasons for the church's marginalization and limited credibility."[49] Worse still, their minds concentrate on issues that had nothing to do with them in the first place. "Many of the concerns that preoccupied Western theologians over the centuries were irrelevant to Third World peoples or even detrimental," writes

Tissa Balasuriya. "Instance divisions of North Atlantic Christians solidified into Catholic and Protestant positions on rather marginal issues and exported to rural villages in Bolivia, Sierra Leone, or the Philippines."[50] The solution to such problems lies in not according them importance. "The road to unity and reconciliation is not preoccupation with institutional elements, doctrinal formulations, and balance of power."[51]

One great handicap the newcomer has with regard to confessional groupings is not only lack of knowledge but the difficulty in penetrating the spirit behind the divisions. For, like it or not, they had to do with issues that concerned their time and specific circumstances. They certainly had as their points of reference and background the philosophical and cultural milieu (not to speak of the economic and political) of their era. In order to understand all the differences and nuances contained in the confessions and the doctrinal discussions aimed at reconciling them, one has to delve into all this foreign material. Can one really succeed? In terms of purely intellectual endeavor, one can perhaps do it and succeed. But how about the questions of interest, relevance, being on fire with this foreign material to the end that it justifies once preoccupation with it to the exclusion of preoccupation with people? As Buthelezi stated it:

> It seems as if, when the phrase "ecumenical dialogue" is used in the context of the quest for Church unity, what is assumed is the need to resolve certain historical and theological disputes as they are currently perceived in the light of European cultural experience. Hence there is a certain orbit of theological debate, emotion and style which is difficult to enter for those who lack the appropriate cultural inbreeding and a firm grip on the whole network of subtle presuppositions which underlie current ecumenical dialogue.[52]

Imported as they are by foreign missions and theologies, and since they do not belong to the indigenous scene, the new denominational divisions must be overcome by Western theology. It is this theological tradition itself which has to be responsible for healing the division which it brought about in the first place. "The witness of the churches in other parts of the world has been impaired by the legacy of the splits. In this respect, European theology has a special responsibility. It belongs to its homework, to clear up the theological differences that stand behind the divisions and hinder the manifestation of full communion."[53] This view is shared by Wainright:

> Christians from the Third World, and particularly from Africa, often express impatience with Western dialogues and debates. It is a double tragedy of Christian history that the historic, continuing, and perhaps new divisions which originated in old Christendom should have been exported with our missions to other parts of the globe. Collaboration and communion among converts to Christ are impeded there also. We

of the northern hemisphere need to set our house in order, not only for the sake of our fidelity to the gospel, but for the sake of the inheritance transmitted to the Church in Africa, Asia and the Pacific. And for that, we need the help of our "children of the Gospel."[54]

In this way, European theology would render a great service to the other theologians and churches. By doing so, it will free their energies for the very important tasks that lay before them and not tie them to the past and to differences that are alien to them.

Rethinking the Reformation Heritage

It is here that the importance or otherwise of the heritage of the Reformation becomes a burning issue. There are a number of elements that are raised with regard to the relevance and importance of its heritage to Third World Christians. First, the argument is made that the Reformation was tied to a specific culture and even population. C. S. Song picks up the observation made by Seeberg that "the Reformation represents 'Christianity in the understanding of the German spirit,' " and writes: "He was right. The faith of the Reformation is the faith seen through German eyes." If one accepts this premise, then one is led to further conclusions which are self-evident. Song continues: "However definitive, influential, and far-reaching the Reformation faith may have been, there is no reason why Christians who are not heirs to the German spirit must see and interpret Christian faith through German eyes. Those who are not endowed with German eyes should not be prevented from seeing Christ differently. They must train themselves to see Christ through Chinese eyes, Japanese eyes, Asian eyes, African eyes, Latin American eyes."[55]

This argument is corroborated by James Cone, the noted proponent of black theology. In his assessment of Third World theologies and the common elements that tie them together with black theology, he sees that all of them have been characterized by the experience of being told and taught that their own cultures were not good enough to express Christianity. Instead, they were blindly led to believe that Western Christianity, having its base in Western culture, alone was valid. This denies the validity of indigenous cultures. "Europeans and white North Americans taught us that the Western theological tradition, as defined by Augustine, Aquinas, Luther, Calvin and Wesley, is the essential source for a knowledge of the Christian past."[56] Cone goes on to argue that each cultural entity and people has the right and the duty to interpret and understand the Gospel from its own particular perspective.

Second, there is another serious challenge that arises when one focuses on the Reformation, as one must when one deals with interconfessional doctrinal dialogues. The Reformation is seen through different eyes. In other words, the accepted tradition of viewing the winning wing of the Reformation as the norm is seriously questioned. In the usual interpretation of the Reformation, Luther and the other reformers, as well as the documents which reflect their positions, are seen as the sources in which a true explication of the faith is found. The aims of the present doctrine-oriented discussions thus consist in attempts to preserve or revive the purity of the doctrine held and advocated by the reformers. But such a lofty view is the one perpetuated and held by the winners only. Viewed from the side of the poor and the marginalized, however, things have a totally different picture. Read from the "underside of history," it is not the winners but those condemned as losers who become the reference points. Those whose rights were rejected, their hopes dashed by military and religious forces, sometimes in collusion with the reformers, spring to life. They become the forerunners of the contemporary poor and oppressed. The oppressed of today thus trace their "historical ancestry" to movements of social and political changes aimed at obtaining the rights of peoples to human dignity. In the view of Gutierrez, "the great landmarks" of the struggles of the poor in Christian history, which are often forgotten, must be revived. In such history belong "the German peasant wars and the figure of Thomas Munzer in the sixteenth century."[57]

The Social Concerns

The reasons for such distance from purely dogmatic and doctrinal concerns are many. There are, however, two main reasons: first, the concern with social problems is growing. The understanding of the Gospel that is taking root in these upcoming theologies is that they are concerned with people more so than correct conceptual systems. Ecumenism thus undergoes a radical facelift. As Elizondo argues, it is no longer concerned with settling the doctrinal disagreements that separate different Christian churches, as is the case "in the West, [where] until recently, ecumenical dialogue usually centered around doctrinal questions." Elizondo refers to the experience of the Hispanic-American communities composed of Catholics and a variety of Protestants and says: "There is a tremendous unity among the members of various Christian denominations who are committed to working for the well-being of Hispanics." The main concern and driving force towards unity and the overcoming of denominational differences becomes the suffering person. Working together to change the situation of the poor, to defend those whose rights are violated, to protect and fight on the side of those threatened by unjust social orders leads to the discovery of Christian unity. "In this, denominational labels peel off and we catch sight of a profoundly Christian and unified people. This is a beautiful experience of a unity which is already in effect. It is a unity in action."[58]

This line of direction is confirmed again from another side, this time from Asia. Chandran states: "We affirm with joy that through solidarity with the cause of the poor, through participation in the just struggles, in their sufferings, and in their persecution, the first great barrier that for so long has divided our different churches is being broken down. In this option for the poor and in the practice of justice, we have deepened the roots of our faith in the one Lord, the one church, the one God and Father."[59]

This line of thinking is also confirmed in the practice of the base ecclesial communities in Latin America. "In a growing number of these communities a new form of ecumenism based on common praxis and a new synthesis of faith and political action are developing."[60] As Gustavo Gutierrez puts it, such an ecumenism replaces that which is based on theological academic discussions: "Meetings of Christians of different confessions but of the same political option are becoming more frequent. This gives rise to ecumenical groups, often marginal to their ecclesiastical authorities in which Christians share their faith and struggle to create a more just society. The common struggle makes the *traditional* ecumenical programs seem obsolete ('a marriage between senior citizens' as someone has said) and impels them to look for new paths toward unity."[61] This leads us to consider the question of unity and division, which must be understood in a different way.

Rethinking the Concepts of Division and Unity

Such reflections on the tasks and presuppositions of the ecumenical movement have far-reaching consequences for the understanding of the questions of division and unity.[62] We have seen time and again that for the interconfessional dialogues, the division of the churches is painful. But this division concerns those that took place as a result of the theological and doctrinal disagreements that arose in the course of the history of the Church. The aim of the dialogues consists, then, in reestablishing the "lost" unity of the church by first reaching agreements on the doctrinal issues that divide them.[63] On the part of the Third World theologians, however, there is a different understanding of division and unity of the churches that is being espoused. The churches are divided indeed, and this is scandalous. But the division which this group refers to is not on the denominational but on another level. The churches are divided on a human level. They are divided according to whether they support the forces of life which fight on the side of the poor, or on the side of the rich to oppress the poor. The poor are the battleground where the division of Christians is being fought. The basic difference consists in this: there is the "development of a Christian theology that sides with the poor and the oppressed and the development of a Christian theology that sides with the oppressor." It follows that there is "conflict and division among Christians" which should be addressed.[64]

In this perspective, there is a type of Christianity that is heretical and apostate. It has given itself wholly to supporting economic and political systems that are opposed to the liberation of the poor, to the just distribution of wealth in the world, and to the salvation of the greater part of the human community which is under the threat of death. This type of Christianity is concerned more with gain than with human life. It supports the mechanisms that promote the strengthening of the oppressive forces in the world. It blesses the efforts of those who accumulate riches through the exploitation of the poor and at their expense.

There is also another type of Christianity that is committed to the poor. In this type, first, it is the poor themselves who become the subjects of their own history and who stand up to oppose any system that oppresses them and denies them the attainment of their human dignity. On the basis of their understanding of the Bible, they believe that God is the God of the poor and is on their side. Therefore, they fight for their liberation. Second, Christians who believe that the God of Jesus Christ is the God who sides with the poor become committed to the cause of the poor. They throw themselves on the side of the poor and make their cause their own. Christianity is thus divided as to where it stands with regard to the poor. Likewise, its unity will come through the poor: "The poor are the mediation of God in ongoing history, a mediation of the Lord who is present in those who are crucified, the ultimate criterion of the faith around which all the confessions must be united."[65]

Such an understanding of the division and unity of the churches is epitomized in the situation that obtains in South Africa. A group of Christians acknowledge that the Church is divided into two. "What the present crisis shows up . . . is that the Church is divided. More and more people are now saying that there are in fact two churches in South Africa—a white Church and a black Church. Even within the same denomination there are in fact two churches."[66] Christians belong to different and opposing camps. But their differences are not denominational. On the contrary, it goes across denominational lines. It is not the old doctrinal differences that divide them into Catholic, Lutheran, Anglican, etc. Rather their division consists in where they stand with regard to the question of apartheid "and the situation of death" that it perpetrates in South Africa.

"The Church is divided against itself and its day of judgement has come" (p. 27). Christians are divided in life as well as in faith. In real life, they sit in different camps: Some are denied their basic human rights because they have a different color. They attend inferior schools, they are slaves to a small minority that maintains power over the majority; they are subjected to all kinds of harassment by the police of an "illegitimate state." They are imprisoned, tortured, even killed, and become strangers in their own land. All this is done in the name of the Christian faith. All such policies of oppression and segregation are enforced in the name of Christianity. Under it live the majority of the people who suffer daily humiliation by a system that does not represent them. They are marginalized and their basic rights trampled daily. Just like their oppressors, they also claim to be Christians and pray to the Christian God. The two concepts of God which are espoused by the two types of Christians do not mesh; they are in opposition to one another. Christians are thus divided on where they stand with regard to the inhuman system of apartheid. Their allegiance to the Christian faith is judged as to how they react to this system. The division of Christians is based on whether they are oppressors or the oppressed. "The true source—the scandalous true source—of division within the church lies . . . not fundamentally in denominational disunity, but in the moral scandal of the conflict between the oppressor and oppressed within the same church, even within the same denomination."[67]

For the South Africans, the Christians who are divided on racial lines share many religious things in common: they have been baptized in the name of God, they go to churches which bear the same denominational name, they share in the body and blood of the Lord and they confess the same confession of faith. Still they are divided! Therefore, the division that counts for these Christians is that which has to do with life. Any Christianity worth its name that does not have to do with the unity of Christians in their life is a heresy. Any Christianity that unites Christians in the confession of the faith but leaves their lives disunited is a heresy. Any Christianity that does not bring reconciliation among Christians on the basis of justice is a heretical version of Christianity. As Gutierrez said: "From now on it is impossible not to face the problems which arise from this division between Christians, which has reached such dramatic proportions. Clarion calls to Christian unity which do not take into account the deep causes of present conditions and real prerequisites for building a just society are merely escapist. We are moving towards a new idea of unity and communion in the Church."[68]

Jon Sobrino has related this to the classical ecumenical search for Christian unity and the attempt to overcome church division. Christians are agreed that division is scandalous. There is a consensus among most Christians that their disunity is not to be accepted as normal. Yet it is not the confessional division that should be the main element in the disunity of Christians. As a matter of fact, the different expressions of the Christian faith could be said to enrich one another. This can be the case especially when Christians accept one another in charity.

According to Sobrino, it is not the division on confessional grounds that should be addressed by the ecumenical movement. Rather, there is a far more serious division to which the movement should turn its eyes.[69]

This is the fact that Christians are divided more seriously in terms of their relationship to the world of the poor. The South African Kairos Document concurs in such an analysis: "The division that is most striking and scandalous is the division between the poor and the opulent, between oppressed and oppressors." This division "in itself is sin, and fundamental sin. . . . The fundamental division in humankind is that between life and death, between those who die because of oppression and those who live because of it."[70]

There is a "fundamental scandal," even a blasphemy, that operates in Christianity. This takes place when the Christian Church ignores the state of the world, the misery of humankind. Shutting one's eyes from the world of suffering in the name of concern for the confessional unity of the Churches is blasphemy. Blasphemy is there when the churches ignore the conditions of humankind and even stand on the side of the rich and powerful against the poor and the weak. "Today the name of God is blasphemed . . . when churches of any confession whatsoever ignore the problems of humankind, or relativize them in God's name or, worse yet, actually stand on the side of those who oppress the poor."[71]

Once it is understood that the division of which the Third World speaks is different from that of the classical interconfessional dialogues, what then is the road to unity? Here also a fundamentally different solution is proposed. From the Third World point of view, the unity of the churches will not be achieved when the various churches reach the point where they can say that they have overcome their differences in doctrine. It is not agreement on this or that doctrinal disagreement that will enable the churches to establish the unity of the Church. Unity is achieved only on one condition. This is made clear by the Kairos Document in no uncertain terms: "As far as the present crisis is concerned, there is only one way forward to Church unity and that is for the Christians who find themselves on the side of the oppressor, or sitting on the fence, to cross over to the other side to be united in faith with those who are oppressed. Unity and reconciliation within the Church itself is only possible around God and Jesus Christ, who are to be found on the side of the poor and the oppressed."[72]

The point being made here is that the question of confession is intimately tied up with life and action. The authenticity of Christianity and the Church is not seen and proved on the level of confessions. The scandal of Christianity does not ultimately consist in the multiplicity of Christian denominations which do not agree on how they perform liturgy, or on the concept of ministry or Eucharist for that matter. The real scandal of Christianity will be revealed only in the measure that it opens itself up to the divisions that wreck the human community. The unity of the Churches will be effected only when they meet in the poor. It is only when they affirm their solidarity with the poor that the Churches can finally say that they are on their way to unity. As Bonino said: "The question of the true unity of the Church is authentic only when it is at the same time the question of the true separation, when it gathers separate Christians in the conflict of confession—a confession which is a concrete historical praxis. The true quest for unity is not therefore to be found in the negotiations of ecclesiastical bodies . . . but in the conflict and encounter which takes place within and across them."[73]

This is also said in another way. The way to unity is through conversion.[74] Only when the Church converts to the true God of Jesus Christ who is the God of the poor and oppressed will she find her true unity. Repentance and conversion to the Other is imperative. Without such a drastic measure on the part of the Church, unity will always remain elusive. Unity of Christians and the Church is "set in motion by basic solidarity with the poor."[75] In this way, "a new form of unity has emerged from below—a unity of praxis and struggle. . . . Christians of all denominations . . . have found themselves united in resistance struggle and political actions."[76]

Following this line, many ecumenical manifestations which transcend denominational fences are witnessed in Latin America. These ecumenical expressions which opt for liberation are closely related to the poor. They are part and parcel of the base ecclesial communities. These ecumenical expressions bring together the oppressed majorities of both Catholics and Protestants. They come together on the basis of practical issues which unite them. It is not so much the settling of confessional differences that characterizes their ecumenism. It is rather the bearing of the everyday burdens of one another that ties them into one strong bond of fellowship and action.[77] It is solidarity with the poorest that becomes the measure of their ecumenical commitment. It brings together those who are engaged in the struggle to be free. "The most important ecumenical achievements of our time have come about through groups who undertake a concrete struggle on behalf of the oppressed. Once more it has been confirmed that a greater and more important struggle lessens the superficial differences in creeds and concepts."[78]

It was Jesus' will that his followers be one and united. Without unity, Christianity is bound not to be credible. But the unity which is according to the will of Jesus must not underplay the material issues that divide Christians. The recovery of unity has to face the divisive social, economic, and political issues. Instead of turning our attention to the purely theological issues, we have to attack squarely the social problems which stand in the way to unity. Daily life plays a greater role in the division of Christians. It is the daily life where Jesus encountered his enemies and friends. "The search for the restoration of the unity of the faithful follows upon the will of the community to create an equal, just and free society."[79] Without such concrete human relationships, the discussions between confessions are characterized by diplomatic and bureaucratic relationships.

The real aim of ecumenism consists, then, in the search for a new society which accords with the will of Jesus. This is a society which is made up of people who seek together justice, equality, and freedom. In this sense, "liberation theology is a profoundly ecumenical theology. It seems that the Christian's concern to collaborate in the process of liberating mankind unites him more effectively and surely with other Christians than does any attempt to resolve age-old theoretical problems."[80] It is only in the realization of these Christian values that Christianity becomes credible and the true spirit and message of Jesus is made alive. Such an ecumenism is no longer the privilege of the churches. It goes beyond them because it embraces the poor wherever they may be found, even outside the walls of the churches. It is a fact that the Christians who belong to the same social class and are marked by poverty exercise an ecumenism which aims at overcoming their oppression. "Before having to do with ideological concepts and doctrines, oikumene is in the first place a question of socio-economic and political action, an engagement, and finally, a historical project."[81]

The unity which is based on the participation of the poor in the search for liberation is one that is tied up with their daily lives. Even so, it is a unity that is impregnated with hope and love. It is inspired and made alive through faith in Jesus Christ, who himself is bent against all forms of oppression and marginalization. "This ecumenism is however lived beyond the confessional boundaries. But it is true that there is an essential interconnection between this ecumenical praxis of liberation and the renewal of the churches: this renewal begins with the decision in favour of the poor and their just cause. This decision is not subject to debate at all, it is rather the sign and the guarantee of the faithfulness to Jesus and his message" (p. 317). Any form of ecumenism that does not put in its center the goal of creating a just society, namely, "a true community of life of all peoples and the participation of all in the use of all available goods and resources, is false. In Latin America, the ecumenism which springs forth out of the liberation struggle of the poor and is lived within it is the only bearer of the Gospel, the good news, out of which the Kingdom of God comes" (p. 318).

The authenticity of such a line of ecumenical engagement and its contribution to unity is also recognized by the F&O Commission itself. In one of its meetings, it stated as follows:

> Through such "prophetic" ministry (i.e., "solidarity with the poor and oppressed," moving into sensitive areas of racial conflict, etc.), the churches have regained credibility in many parts of the world, especially in the third world. This has brought about an organic change in the concept and reality of church unity. As churches and Christians become engaged in human problems and issues in particular socio-political and cultural-historical contexts, they find themselves in unity that transcends confessional backgrounds and ecclesiastical barriers. By force of circumstances and in exercising "prophetic" ministry, many Christians have come to regard theological and ecclesiological issues that have divided the churches as irrelevant.[82]

Expanding the Field of Ecumenism

It is here that a further aspect of the call for expanding the understanding of ecumenism becomes urgent. The understanding of ecumenism as a call to Christian unity becomes too narrow for this understanding.[83] The ecumenism which calls for the unity of the churches, the healing of their divisions is, first of all, an "intramural" activity. It is only concerned with the churches. Second, it is concerned only with the doctrines of the church. It is therefore confined to the churches in the West, which have to do with the divisions based on doctrinal differences. This demands a particular charisma which the Western churches have. Churches outside this sphere, for example in Asia, have to benefit from their efforts and not repeat them. For to be involved in such a dialogue is a luxury for the Asian churches. "The churches of Asia do not have the time to confront each other following the classical model; they should rather *confront the world together.* Church to church ecumenism could truly be *the spontaneous result of the communal endeavour to discover the Asian face of the Christ.*"[84] The churches have now opted for a suprachurch ecumenism. This new form of ecumenism is open to the world.[85] It is the coming together of the churches, but some of them tend to be split once again. This new type of ecumenism has a potential to renew the churches. It has four elements: evangelism, dialogue, spirituality, and activism. The ecumenism which is based on these elements is open to the "pagan" world, which includes both East and West. It goes beyond the confines of the church in a communicative and cooperative effort with those anywhere who search for the meaning of life. For, as M. M. Thomas put it, "the politics of human community is not a 'deviation' or a disruption, but an integral part of genuine ecumenism." [86]

— 5 —

Common Emerging Themes

In the course of an attempt to deal with the "common emerging themes," one may be rightly tempted to raise a series of questions objecting to such an attempt. Aren't these two concerns—liberation and doctrinal orthodoxy—different? Don't they have contradictory approaches to theology itself? Are not their starting points, their aims, and their contents far removed one from the other? Besides, have they not been locked in bitter controversy on a number of levels? How can one speak of commonality of themes in theologies that seem to openly contradict each other on many counts? Furthermore, have they not been engaged in conflicts which are no less than bloody, mutual condemnations and pronouncements of heresy one against the other?[1]

In order not to lose sight of and to sharpen the legitimacy of such questions and not to minimize the confrontational situation, it is good to recall some of the critical engagements of these concerns. The best examples are already given to us in the discussions between doctrinal orthodoxy and liberation theologies unleashed in the middle of the 1980s. It was both in 1984 and in 1986 that the Vatican Congregation for the Doctrine of the Faith promulgated two instructions on the theology of liberation: "Instruction on Certain Aspects of the 'Theology of Liberation' " of 1984 and "Instruction on Christian Freedom and Liberation" of 1986. To this may also be added an article by Cardinal Joseph Ratzinger, "Liberation Theology," of March 1984.[2]

The concern of the Vatican is very clear especially in the third article. Here, Cardinal Ratzinger asserts that liberation theology poses a "fundamental danger for the faith of the church." According to the Vatican, truth and error are mixed up sometimes. For the error is not absolutely devoid of the truth but can contain a measure of truth. The danger which liberation theology poses becomes all the more real because it also uses quite a few of the concepts of "traditional" theology.

There is one thing that must be noted, however. This is the fact that, in such a discussion of truth and error, one notices that there are concepts which are familiar to both sides of the antagonism. One mentions, for example, "the option for the poor" which can be attributed to Jesus even in the view of the Vatican statement. "The Sermon on the Mount is, in reality, a choice on the part of God in favor of the poor." Again, "the fundamental concept of the preaching of Jesus is the 'Kingdom of God.' " And one mentions the exodus. All such elements or ingredients of the faith are there and are recognized by both as essential. They are there to be interpreted. But, of course, the interpretations differ. And that is where the threat of liberation concerns lies. In the view of one of the Instructions: "If one thinks of how radical this interpretation of Christianity that derives from it [i.e., liberation theology] really is, the problem of what one can and must do about it becomes even more urgent."[3]

We need not go in depth into the cleavage between the Vatican Instructions' position and that of the Third World liberation theologians. Suffice it to say that they are not easily bridgeable. We certainly do see that the differences are big indeed and the stakes are high. For our purposes, however, taking the divergences and convergences into account, it is interesting to note some of the reactions to and readings of the two official Instructions, which contain some of the severest and sharpest allegations and accusations hurled at liberation theologies. One finds out that the reactions to them are different; there are both positive and negative ones. Let us, for the sake of simplicity, divide the reactions into three. These views will be referred to in connection with their authors.

The first attitude is that espoused by those who are bitter opponents of the liberation line and support that of the Vatican Instructions. They agree with the official position of the Congregation that liberation theologies are a distortion of the faith of the Christian Church. In this case, they are "another gospel."[4] They are not true to the true faith to which they claim to adhere and which the church proclaims, nor do they interpret the given sources of the Christian Church faithfully. They are nothing more than modern-day heretics, contemporary versions of "heretical Christianities" that were invariably condemned in the past history of the Church.[5] But the most interesting factor is that, even in the face of such harsh condemnations, the critics are led to admit that there is often a subtle cross-fertilization of ideas and concerns that takes place. Even in the context of a deadly struggle for the "true faith" between two opponents, borrowing takes place. In this specific situation, even if liberation theology harbors errors, it has nevertheless succeeded in influencing the very centers and defenders of "the true Christian faith." As Richard John Neuhaus, a bitter critic of liberation theology, admits: "He [Gregory Baum] is surely right in believing that some of the key themes of liberation theology are, if not entrenched, at least deeply insinuated into both official teaching and popular understandings of the Church in the modern world."[6] The contribution of liberation theology to Catholicism and its influence on the latter are recognized by another Catholic: "The texts and priorities of Liberation Theology have made an irreversible contribution not only to theological speculation but to the texts of Roman documents and the sensitivities of worldwide Catholicism."[7] The subtle and persistent influence and osmosis of liberation concerns even in the camp of the "custodians of the orthodox faith" is thus a fact.

The second attitude may be gathered from the reaction of Leonardo Boff. He maintained that the first Instruction reflected the mind set of European theology. This theology normally starts to analyze topics on the conceptual level. In this case, the Instruction studied the question of liberation in an intellectual way and described the ideal situation in which liberation has to be understood. Boff argued that, in sharp contrast to this approach, liberation theology would start with a reflection on praxis. It is involvement in the praxis of liberation that gives rise to the theology of liberation. It is in the course of the concrete participation in the liberative activities of and with the poor and the oppressed that the theology of liberation is born. Thus theology without the context of struggle is not a genuine theology of liberation. Consequently, the first Instruction misunderstands the theology of liberation.[8]

Another viewpoint which is slightly different but may be construed as a continuation of this reaction is a serious attempt to call to task the position of Instruction I itself vis-à-vis liberation theologies. The approach here is to examine the Instruction minutely by comparing its remarks to the writings of liberation theologians themselves. Of course, the Instruction does not give the names of the theologians it aims to attack. It makes a general criticism without mentioning anyone by name or by quoting any specific sources. Therefore, it may be said that it is aiming at all and at no one at the same time. In any case, by its very perspective, the Instruction has unleashed a great deal of debate even on the meaning and interpretation of the Christian faith itself. The criticisms leveled at liberation theology by the Vatican were not simply accepted at their face value. As there were favorable reactions, there were also unfavorable and critical ones. Whatever the reactions, however, the point that needs to be made here is that the Christian faith is subjected to a serious reevaluation on the basis of the new awareness of faith and the givens of the world. Such questioning will not be left without comment because it challenges profoundly the hitherto dominant understandings of the faith. Therefore, the arguments pro and con contribute to the sharpening of the issues and to the search for the truth. In this sense, they also contribute to a much-needed confrontation for the sake of the truth.[9]

Given the criticisms of the Congregation and the grave consequences attached to them, one cannot lose sight of the critical remarks of Boff and Balasuriya. But there is a third attitude which emphasizes the positive aspect of Instruction I. In this case, its appearance is viewed as contributing to "a dialogue on this delicate topic. . . . What is taking place is a serious discussion on liberation theology" which will lead to a better comprehension of the theology of liberation. This is the line of argument that is represented by Gustavo Gutierrez, for example. He picks up some aspects of the Instruction which he thinks are important. The fact that the Instruction issued by the Congregation stated, for example, that "the expression 'liberation theology' is a totally valid expression" is a positive step.[10] In another context, Leonardo Boff himself goes so far as to say that the second Instruction was "better received" in Latin America because "despite its internal limitations, it made a favourable impression on public opinion and Christian circles: Rome supports liberation theology!"[11]

This is the line of reaction that is also advocated by Hennelly. He goes so far as to designate Instruction I as "a theological event of profound importance with far-reaching implications for the Catholic Church in every part of the world."[12] In his opinion, Instruction I puts an official stamp on the use of the liberation motif in both the local Catholic churches and the social teaching of the church itself. "Besides, the text I have quoted above on the application of liberation themes by local churches seems to me to provide Latin American and other Third World theologians with the carte blanche they need to continue on the paths they have already chosen."[13] On the basis of such opinions, such Instructions, then, are subject to a number of interpretations. On the one hand, they may be interpreted in terms of opposition against that which they were written. On the other hand, they may be viewed as giving an unexpected boost to that which they oppose, suddenly and perhaps unintentionally giving it the exposure and the approval it needs. It may sound ironic, but in the case of the latter, the Instructions may have given the theologies of liberation the necessary legitimacy they needed from the Vatican.

It is some such confrontation/influence that forms the background of the attempt that we are aiming at in this endeavor. The latter is done in the conviction that the concerns for liberation and doctrinal orthodoxy, however far apart they may be, have many things in common in that they refer, above all else, to the same basic sources. This is to say that they are referring to the Scriptures and to the "traditions" of the Church. Basically, they are bound to the person of Jesus Christ, whom they see emerges from them. The differences arise and become acute with regard to the interpretations of the same person, the scriptural books, and the "traditions." There are very serious hermeneutical problems that arise. Here, the question of method becomes crucial. In the long run, however, they cannot go their own separate ways because they are dealing with the same phenomenon, namely, Christianity, and all that makes it what it is. However much they may pull in different directions as a result of their interpretations, it is no secret that they take seriously what the other is saying, and, admit it or recognize it or not, the understanding of Christianity is affected by them. In this, we may agree with the judgement of Witvliet when he writes about the ecumenical use of theology: "In the Faith and Order division, the method of academic theology rejected by EATWOT is still largely predominant. Although EATWOT and Faith and Order both seek to do ecumenical theology, there is a world of difference between them in style and method. We cannot escape the impression that both organizations are theologically miles apart, and that is sad. It seems to suggest that ecumenical theology and contextual theology are mutually exclusive. Which they are not."[14]

Mutual influence, one of the other, is done on many levels. Even on the level of the theologies of liberation themselves, the discussion is always alive as to not only where the commonalities lie but where the differences also lie. There is place here for "cross-fertilization" and the disposition "to stimulate dialogue and exchange, to allow ourselves to be reached and influenced by difference and otherness."[15] There is a constant pressure to explore the points both of agreement and of disagreement and thus sharpen the contents as well as the tools of the various theological perspectives. It is in this sense that the discussions between various theologies in the context of the Third World are engaged.[16] In the same context, women, on their part, also raise their specific voices to bring in their contributions which are not covered by the overall perspective.[17]

To widen the horizon further, it is in the spirit of extending the field of dialogue that proponents of traditional Western theologies are invited to "an encounter with Third World theology." It was for this very purpose that EATWOT "decided to call a dialogue with First World theologians."[18] This is based on the conviction that it is the nature or characteristic of the Christian tradition that it is made up of contradictory trends. "Looking back to the Christian tradition we observe, on one side, commandments of love, dogmas of faith, and procrastination; on the other there is faith that heals, faith that moves mountains."[19] The many sides of the tradition thus have to engage in confrontation constantly if the health of the truth that the "traditions" must declare is to be maintained. As one theological tradition gives a prod to the other, there is also the possibility that the reverse will take place. In some circles, this prodding and reaction to it are already on the way.[20] That is why the need for a thorough debate based on an attempt at an understanding of the other position is an urgent present and continuing task. In the present study, this is based on the conviction that there are very real differences but, at the same time, real elements of rapprochement. It is in this spirit that the following common emerging themes are presented in a very tentative and halting way. After some digression, which hopefully may lay some groundwork for the attempt, we now turn to the themes themselves.

When one observes the theological and ecumenical landscape closely, one sees that there are a number of leading ecumenical concepts that have emerged in the course of a number of years. It seems as if such theological thinking and reflection have led many to focus on common constellational elements that seem to epitomize the Christian faith. It is astounding to note that a variety of theologians and groups, from a variety of backgrounds, seem to be converging in the recognition of the importance and significance of these concepts for the Christian faith. However much they may disagree on many other points and even on their interpretations and emphases of these very concepts, there are agreements on the significance of these concepts, which may be called basic to the expression of the faith. In Christian history, strewn with fatal theological battles which stretch over many years, such elements can be likened to lighthouses which may perhaps point to greater hopes for continuing search. What is astonishing is that these truths of the faith are acknowledged by Third World liberation theologians from different countries as well as the traditional Faith and Order theologians from mainly Western countries. People who would otherwise disagree do point out the significance of these elements. Let us now pick them up one by one.

The Concept of Communion (Koinonia)

In the ecumenical movement in general, the concept of communion (Koinonia) has gradually emerged to become a very prominent one indeed. In both the bilateral and multilateral dialogues in particular, this concept has gradually assumed a prominent place with a great potential.[21] It has come to represent not only the image of the church and that of the Christian life but the goal of the ecumenical movement as well. In this case, it is a happy coincidence because it is a rich concept, full of a great deal of potential for the interpretation of the Christian faith. While it is orginally both a New Testament concept and one that was used extensively in the early fathers of the church, it brings both the faith and the life of the church and Christians together under the living Christ. It spawns a wide-ranging meaning with a singular depth for explicating the Christian faith under Christ. This is the basic reason why many theologians of a variety of backgrounds and convictions have seized on it and expounded its importance for expressing the Christian faith and life.

In the interconfessional dialogues, the concept of communion (Koinonia) has gradually emerged as an overarching concept. "The concept 'communion' has been of decisive significance for the modern ecumenical movement." It is now being used in almost all dialogues where confessions, ranging from the Catholics to the Pentecostals, are involved. The concept of communion (Koinonia) has become the ecclesiological magic word for Catholics, Anglicans, Orthodox, Lutherans, as well as other Protestants. As Oscar Cullmann has said: "The word community (communion), as a translation of the Greek word *Koinonia*, has the advantage of making full use of this biblical concept which is of special importance to ecumenism."[22] In Catholic circles, it has been gradually recognized that the term had gained special importance during the RCC's Second Vatican Council.[23] It was used there as a term to convey the idea of the church even though with certain ambiguity.[24] It was, however, picked up and fully developed in the extraordinary Synod of Bishops of the RCC in Rome in 1985.[25]

In the interconfessional dialogues, it was the RCC-Anglican dialogue which initially discovered the importance of the concept. As a result, the dialogue was hailed as a breakthrough in the understanding of the church. Ever since, the concept has been used by other dialogue groups as well. As the Fifth Forum on Bilateral Conversations noted: "It is striking that the notion of *koinonia* is central in the understanding of the nature of the church in almost all dialogues. . . . *Koinonia* is the fundamental understanding of the church emerging from the bilateral dialogues."[26] Consequently, in the words of Tavard, "the theme of the Church as Communion has emerged as the dominant theme of the post-Vatican II ecclesiology. . . . The communion-ecclesiology illustrates a shift in ecumenical awareness. I attribute this shift to the post-conciliar experience of bilateral dialogues."[27]

This trend can also be corroborated with reference to the work of the F&O Commission of the WCC. In the statement on unity prepared for consideration by the WCC Canberra Assembly and later adopted by it, the unity of the church is viewed in terms of communion (Koinonia).[28] Furthermore, in preparation for its fifth world conference in 1993, the Commission has picked up communion (Koinonia) as the concept guiding its work. As the title of the draft document shows, the tendency is to bring together faith, life, and witness under the umbrella of communion.[29] It is apparent here that there is a search within the whole ecumenical movement for transcending traditional categories which limit the ecumenical task. As Martin H. Cressey has put it: "Not only Faith and Order studies, but all the aspects of the ecumenical movement have drawn the churches into thinking together about the combining of faith, life, and witness. Yet what word is to be used to express the 'combining'? 'Communion' was the first choice."[30] The concept of "communion as a leitmotif" seems to serve well these various attempts at focusing or crystalizing the ecumenical calling and task.[31] As Mary Tanner, the moderator of the F&O Commission, further put it: "It is, as Archbishop Aram Keshishian in his moderator's address to the Central Committee of the WCC in August 1992 said, 'a pivotal concept' and it is the one most likely to breathe new life into the search for visible unity. In getting hold of the dimensions and richness of the concept of koinonia the work of Faith and Order, and indeed every part of the ecumenical movement, finds its proper context."[32]

The concept of communion lends itself readily because it brings together a variety of concerns. It means fellowship among believers under the headship of Christ. But this fellowship is not a static one. It is, rather, "a fellowship in *solidarity.* Solidarity is not optional. It impels a common participation in material and spiritual need, in material and spiritual resources." It is a "commitment throughout one's life and work." This fellowship is not confined to the believers' group but is "open in service and social action to the world."[33]

Such a focus on the term communion (Koinonia) does not at all mean that the various churches have not hastened to use the term to describe their own idiosyncrasies. Some churches, like the RCC, Anglicans, and Lutherans have adopted the term and used it in their own particular sense, which should not escape criticism ("The church understood as communion").[34] There is also the further danger that communion (Koinonia) as such becomes a purely theological or spiritual term. In this case, it assumes an idealistic air which has no bearing on life as it is lived. But the extra-ecclesial aspect is a very important element in the understanding of communion (Koinonia). In this connection, it is worthy to note that the Basel Document even goes so far as to say that communion (Koinonia) is a concept which points to the quality of community that the human community should have: "The human community is to be the image of the infinite love which links the three divine Persons of the Trinity; therefore it should be a KOINONIA (Communion) of love."[35]

There are a number of theologians of liberation who have also picked up the term. In Gutierrez's view, the concept arises out of the New Testament and has three elements. First, "it signifies the common ownership of goods necessary for earthly existence." Paul uses the term to designate the collection of money that he makes from other congregations to aid those in Jerusalem. The spiritual/material aspect is central to the concept. Second, it is tied to the union of the believer with Christ in the Eucharist. Third, it means the union of Christians with the Father.[36]

Oduyoye and Mbiti also pick up the importance of the concept of communion from their African background. Communion is not only very important but integral to the ordering of a full life. It defines the relationships that people have with one another and with the ancestors. It is what ties them together in one community. It embraces all the members of the community into a shared unity. Such a community is expressed by ordering life as much as possible to the end that it serves the good of all the members. When one suffers, all suffer and share in the suffering. They delve into the life of one another by making their contribution to the fulfillment of the life of each member. No pain that one member undergoes is left as an individual problem that has to be solved individually. Whenever any catastrophe hits the entire community or one or some of its members, all the members are touched. They bring all their resources to attack it. There is a living bond that holds the various members together.[37]

Taking into consideration such understandings leads the veteran Indian ecumenist M. M. Thomas to ask: "Will Koinonia emerge as a Vital Theological Theme?" His hope is, of course, that it will. In his opinion, it is the concept that can bring together the various emphases and concerns that characterize the ecumenical quest. According to Thomas, there are three important elements which characterize this quest at present. These are, first, the emergence of liberation theologies and grassroots movements struggling for justice "and their efforts to discover the meaning of koinonia-in-Christ." Second, there are "the insights about responsible world society" which are concentrating on Justice, Peace, and the Integrity of Creation. The third element is the dialogues with peoples of other faiths, which reflect the concern for a common search "for human community at local, national and global levels." To sum up his vision, M. M. Thomas says: "What I am trying to say is that probably koinonia (communion and community) may turn out to be a vital theological theme providing dynamic unity for the total agenda of the World Council of Churches in the years ahead."[38]

Even in the face of some possible distortions that may arise, therefore, the concept of communion (Koinonia) seems to offer a promise in the understanding of the faith and of the goal of the ecumenical movement. Its potential is so wide that it proves hard to confine it to particularistic or spiritualistic interpretations. In the latter case, it is so tied up with "materialistic" aspects that it is impossible to reduce it to any realm without violating its rich and comprehensive meaning. Therefore, a further exploration of this concept in the future is a promising ecumenical endeavor.

The Centrality of the Eucharist

Closely related to the prominence of the concept of communion (Koinonia), and finding itself in its center, is the Eucharist. There is an increasing agreement on the centrality of the Eucharist not only in the worship of the church understood as communion but also in its life. The Eucharist, it is increasingly being understood, is not peripheral to the Christian life and faith. On the contrary, it is in the center. It is the sacrament which throws its shadow on the entire life of the church and the Christian.

The Lima Document (BEM) consistently relates the Eucharist to the church and the world. In the Eucharist, the participants take part in communion. Those who share in this memorial act are united with Christ and with their fellow sharers. This has far-reaching implications in the lives of the church and the believers because it has worldwide implications. The Eucharist transcends the milieu of the Church. "It embraces all aspects of life." The entire spectrum of life is subsumed under it. For those who take part in it are called to live in opposition to all forms of injustice, racism, and political and economic oppression. "The Eucharist involves the believer in the central event of the world's history." The Eucharist links the believer to the world. In imitation of Christ, "Christians are called in the Eucharist to be in solidarity with the outcast."[39]

The conclusions of BEM are also reflected in a number of bilateral conversations. As mentioned above, ARCIC I, which focused early on communion (Koinonia) as an expression of the church, also saw the centrality of the Eucharist in it.[40] Communion is a relational term which cannot be fully translated into individualistic terms. It finds its full expression in the sharing of bread and wine together with all the company under one Christ. But the sharing of bread in the community is done in view of the world and points beyond itself to the world. "When we gather around the same table in this communal meal at the invitation of the same Lord and when we 'partake of the loaf,' we are one in commitment not only to Christ and one another, but also to the mission of the church in the world."[41] In the Eucharist, therefore, there is an "inseparable link that binds together eucharist and diakonia, the sacrament of the altar and the sacrament of the brother and the sister."[42] In this light, the Eucharist in the context of communion (Koinonia) becomes a fertile ground for developing the deeper meanings of faith and life.

The importance of the Eucharist is also emphasized by Third World theologians. Here, there is a greater emphasis on the exigencies of the eucharistic meal and its relationship to the world of the poor and the needy.

In the establishment and strengthening of communities, bread and blood play significant and even central roles. These elements are taken extremely seriously in the building up and fortifying of relationships even among traditional societies. Those who take part in common meals transcend their hostilities and confirm and seal friendships.[43] Eating meals together is sign and symbol of friendship, love, unity, and the removal of any hatred that one harbored against the other. "Communion through shared meals takes place among people who are, or who wish to be, on peaceful and friendly terms. . . . To eat from the same dish is to enter into vital relationship with the other. . . . Shared meals conclude most social and ritual events."[44]

The Eucharist here is not simply a liturgical act; it is not a matter of Christian worship alone. But it goes beyond the circle of the church to embrace the world. Reflecting some of the points in the Lima Document, Gutierrez says that "communion with God and others presupposes the abolition of all injustice and exploitation."[45] The Eucharist has thus intrinsically to do with human fellowship. But there are conditions which call for the right celebration of the Eucharist. In the words of Gutierrez again: "Without a real commitment against exploitation and alienation and for a society of solidarity and justice, the Eucharistic celebration is an empty action, lacking any genuine endorsement by those who participate in it."[46]

In the light of such statements, there are serious social questions which are increasingly posed in connection with the Eucharist, questions regarding the quality of commitment in the life of the participants to the poor in the world.[47] This questioning is first addressed to those who are inside the church. Do all "Christians" participate in the Eucharist irrespective of their social status? What is the place of discernment with regard to one's relationship to one's neighbor in everyday life? Related to a question which he says is raised "by some of us during church unity talks of altar and pulpit fellowship," Buthelezi therefore poses the question: "Can poor people really belong to the same church as those who have made them poor? Can we truly share the blood and body of Christ if, by deliberate economic planning, there is injustice in the distribution of the material gifts of God?"[48] Ulrich Duchrow takes this further in introducing a question that ties the celebration of the Eucharist with the everyday life of the believers and their responsibilities: "Do thieves, profiteers, and the victims of their depredations, all of whom call themselves Christians, continue to share together in the eucharist even if the thieves and profiteers blatantly go on thieving and profiteering and disguising or denying its reality and extent?"[49]

To Third World theologians, the Eucharist is no longer dissociated from the concrete everyday life. It is not simply a religious act which has to do with the liturgical life of the church alone. If it is to be related to the life and death of Jesus Christ, as well it should, then it has profound repercussions for the life of Christians as well. "The Eucharist celebrates and anticipates the relationship of communion among human beings willed by God. It calls us to question radically all structures of injustice throughout the world."[50]

This is also the tone carried by BEM when it declares: "The eucharistic celebration demands reconciliation and sharing among all those regarded as brothers and sisters in the one family of God and is a constant challenge in the search for appropriate relationships in social, economic and political life."[51] "The commitment to the cause of the justice of the kingdom which is present in the struggle for justice for the poor . . . requires that the churches recover a practice of discipleship which expresses the *koinonia* of the Eucharist."[52]

Unity and Renewal

A third common theme where the concerns of F&O and the Third World coincide is in the issue of unity and renewal. It is to be recalled that F&O has usually concentrated its work on the unity of the Church. The divisions of the churches on confessional grounds has been the scandal that it has always held before its eyes. It has thus concentrated on solving them. But from time to time, the question of the relation of the unity of the church to that of humankind or, specifically, the place of the church in the world, has forced itself upon the consciousness of the Commission. From time to time, the need to tackle this issue squarely dawns upon it.[53]

This need to tackle this problem has been felt from time to time in the course of the history of the F&O movement. The difficulties that have to do with such an undertaking are clearly noted by Handspicker when he writes: "There is a threat of a 'horizontal schism' threatening all our Churches. The reasons for this are many, but perhaps a key one is seen in different attitudes to the world." He saw that there are those in the Churches who witness the work of the Spirit in the emergence of "free nations, international groupings, and in projects where Christians and non-Christians seek together for peace and justice in the new social structures created by the technological revolution overtaking all societies." There are tensions which arise because of the fact that there were equally other Christians who mainly saw "the Church as the ark of salvation, as a means of escape from the ambiguities and negativities of the world in which they live." He foresaw, then, an "increasing polarization" between these "two poles" which would pose as a serious challenge to the work of the F&O movement.[54]

The F&O movement has not been able to escape or avoid these tensions within itself. It had periodically reacted to them in a variety of ways. Most of the time, it accepted the need to deal with these tensions on account of pressures from outside itself, "under the pressure of recent ecumenical history."[55] There is therefore the impression that the F&O ecumenical current is somehow forced to deal with the relationship of the church to the world against its own will. Dealing with the relationship of the church and the world seems to have been often seen as a task which is not covered by the strict ecclesiastical mandate of the Commission. Since it is understood that the main problem facing the churches is the confessional division among them, and since the divisions are mainly caused by doctrinal disagreements, the focus of the work of the commission was concentrated on solving these differences. The achievement of the unity of the Church was attainable through this road.

In the course of the history of the movement, what Deschner calls "interdenominational or classical ecumenism" was gradually pressured to open up its doors for other concerns. Beginning with the WCC Assembly in New Delhi (1961), the pressure to widen the horizon within which the question of unity must be considered was raised. In this case, "the rise of the Third World" and its entry into the ecumenical scene were crucial in effecting such a "shift."[56] This pressure was intensified at Uppsala (1968) in which the study on the "Unity of the Church—Unity of Humankind" was launched. It was then recognized that this was "a new direction" for F&O. At Louvain (1971), which dealt specifically with this study, the Commission concentrated on the discussion of issues designated "areas of social conflict," such as justice, racism, culture, politics, religious pluralism, the handicapped, and their relation to the unity of the Church. The study was followed in Accra (1974). It is interesting to note here that the question of "liberation"—a Third World theme—was handled with seriousness, and participation in it was highly recommended. It seemed that F&O had at long last learned that "Christians engaged in the struggle for liberation in fact often find themselves closer to others who share the struggle with them, Christians or not, than to other Christians who are not committed to it." It was further noted that oppression could be perpetuated under the guise of unity.[57]

A second factor is that, even if a study on the relationship of the church to the world was undertaken, it did not often lead to any substantial or concrete conclusions. It was as if the studies were done in a halfhearted or haphazard way. Since dealing with the world as such was generally believed to fall outside the mandate of the Commission, the studies which concentrated on this very particular issue often ended up inconclusively, as some of the evaluations state. "Still, the two trends—the Church's solidarity with the world and Church unity—have not become interrelated." "Other speakers argued that previous Faith and Order work in the area had often failed to interrelate the concern for church unity with divisive factors in the world."[58] The general conclusion, then, is that this study "came to a standstill, unfinished. . . . The theme remains an unfinished task."[59]

After the apparent failure of the first phase of this study (1968-1974), there were critical voices which once again called on F&O to relate its work to the world.[60] "From the beginning, Faith and Order has been asked too often: Why are you so abstract? What is the relevance of your work?" Deschner stated at the Commission meeting in Lima (1982). He also noted that, once again, the pressure from women and the Third World was instrumental in the undertaking of a new study on this very theme.[61] It was in an attempt to address these and similar criticisms and concerns that the Commission launched another study, "The Unity of the Church and the Renewal of Human Community."[62] In doing so, the F&O was trying to combine its original concern for the unity of the Church with the Church's place in the world and thus responding to Third World concerns. This study program "seeks to relate two classical ecumenical concerns: the search for the visible unity of the Church, and work towards the renewal of the Church, and the whole human community."[63] There are of course strong voices within the Commission who regret that any attempt to shift away from the original task of the F&O to include "non-church" issues in response to the Third World would lead to politicizing the movement. Here again, F&O has retained an air of irreality with regard to this aspect of the work because it found it difficult to relate it to what it always understands as "its first and specific concern . . . this Church unity concern remains our first and constitutive vocation."[64] The questions of what method to use, how not to mix the two without separating them, how to preserve their distinctiveness without dividing them, were paramount questions.

The Vancouver Assembly (1983) gave agreement for the continuation of this study. It was later referred to by the Commission "as of strategic significance for the orientation of the whole work of the WCC" and as "bringing rich and profound resources to the quest for visible unity."[65] There was also the growing conviction from many sides that the two cannot be divided one from the other; they belong intrinsically together. "We have learned in the ecumenical movement that unity *and* renewal of the church go together, one is the condition as well as the consequence of the other."[66]

This view was also reflected and emphasized by others. "The problem of Christian unity cannot be separated from that of the unity of humankind."[67] The first result of the study was made available and sent to the churches in 1990.[68] This in no way hides the fact that increasing tension became a regular element of this study. As Konrad Raiser had observed: "The discussion has taken place in a controversial way, and it still continues."[69] One of the important working methods of this study is to meet with those who have a different perspective in the understanding of the Gospel. Moving out of its traditional theoretical engagement with doctrines, the Commission went out to encounter Christians and churches who live the Gospel in a variety of contexts. The recognition of the need to bring in the contributions of these groups which were not part of the F&O areas of concern in the past broke new ground. These groups, which had so far been marginalized and did not figure in the F&O programs, had the opportunity to bring in their contributions and their criticisms. There is nevertheless the fear, as Manas Buthelezi put it, that "the Singapore and the Porto Alegre documents are likely to be seen as footnotes to the main 'Church as Mystery and Prophetic Sign' text." His plea is that the important points raised in these reports be incorporated into the main text. "Otherwise, the theological concerns of Singapore and Porto Alegre are regarded only as elements of a case study and extraneous to the normative theological agenda."[70]

The novel approach is that the groups brought their experience of the Church to bear on the study. This was not the traditional F&O method. It mainly focused on theological expositions which do not often touch life as it is lived and often suffered. In this context, groups such as the African-Americans pointed out to the Church their exclusion from its active support in real life because of the color of their skins. On this basis, they offer a shattering critique of the study program when they state:

> African-American Christians who, in the midst of their enslavement and oppression, came to know God in Christ and to participate in a divine plan of salvation learned to associate mystery not with God's presence within the Church, but with God's ability to work outside the Church and in the world. The concept enabled African-American Christians to see the Church as a sinful institution, largely devoid of God's presence, and the world as a primary locus for God's activity. The "mystery" was God's absence in the Church and God's presence in the world.[71]

In its Singapore meeting (1986), F&O concentrated on "the ecclesiological significance of the church's involvement in issues of justice" in order to look at the issue from the Asian perspective. These reflections contribute to the growing conviction that "the quest for visible unity, and the involvement in issues of justice, are not accidental or optional for the church but are expressions of its very nature." The liberating Gospel of Jesus Christ, and the Eucharist, central to the church's life and a powerful source of proclamation and prophetic witness, mean that "if the church neglects to confront oppression, the church denies its own nature." Others noted that the church loses its credibility "when it calls unity around creeds, sacraments and ministerial offices but ignores the pain of the poor and oppressed."[72]

The next stop was in Brazil (Porto Alegre), where the F&O held another consultation on the same topic, viewed from the Latin American perspective. One finds that the particular emphases from those in the Latin American context were not well received by the staff, which was critical. The report of the group was not accepted as official.[73] But the significant fact is that even F&O no longer avoids the issues but tries to integrate them into its own program. This will certainly affect the traditional concerns of the Commission.

In this connection, it is interesting to note that, as far back as 1971, the onetime moderator of the F&O Commission, John Deschner, wrote in connection with the predecessor to this study:

I suspect it will not be wrong, one day, in retrospect to call this study (i.e., Unity of the Church—Unity of Humankind) something of a turning point in the history of the Faith and Order movement: from a classical ecumenism which considered traditional denominational divisions as the central issue of the church unity problem to a more contemporary focus which also takes into account the human divisions which invade and divide the church. The two approaches are not alternatives but complementary.[74]

He repeated his view later in saying that there is a promise in a continuation of this study because it deals with one of the themes which "has been, more than most of us realize, a means of deepening the relation of Faith and Order to other units in the WCC and to the Council as a whole."[75] Making a direct reference to the former observation, Paul Crow, a veteran of the Commission, wrote in 1989 as follows: "Surely our experience from Lima to Budapest has proved that this theme is one of the most emotional but also one of the most promising processes in Faith and Order and the whole WCC."[76] There is the need for continuing study of this issue, which is full of promise indeed.

The Preferential Option for the Poor

This concept has swept some sections of Christianity for some time now. Liberation theology especially has put it in the center of its explication of the Christian faith. The words of Hennelly aptly summarize the centrality of the issue in the current ecumenical situation:

> For the first time in history, liberation theology has created an opportunity for the voice of the poor—the mute invisible four-fifths of the world—to be heard clearly and loudly in every corner of the planet. It is a voice of intense urgency and a powerful challenge, especially to the Christian Churches of the First World, and also to its theologians, who have not made it a priority over the past five centuries, despite that it is a central concern of the Bible. For these four billion human beings represent starkly and unambiguously the poor, the orphan, the widow, and the stranger who were identified time and again by the prophets of Israel as the place to encounter and to know Yahweh. The four billion also clearly epitomize the "least of my brothers and sisters," to whose suffering Jesus of Nazareth called his followers to respond as the ultimate test of their commitment and eternal destiny (Matt. 25).[77]

The expression "preferential option for the poor" has become a hermeneutical key in the expounding of the faith. It is interesting to note that a great variety of Christian ecumenical groups have picked it up and made it their own.[78] As a matter of fact, "in the view of many, the approach adopted here by the ecumenical movement, that of 'the church in solidarity with the poor,' represents a significant breakthrough in the history of the church."[79]

There has been a growing awareness in the ecumenical movement that the poor are in the center of the church. In a sense, the poor have of course always been with the church. It could be said that the poor were not absent from the consciousness of the Church. They were always present in one way or another. But in the past, to take just one example, the references to the poor in the Sermon on the Mount (Matt. 5-7) were interpreted in individual terms. They were understood as referring to the ethical standards of individual Christians vis-à-vis the poor as individuals. The common and dominant understanding was that the poor should have patience with their condition and accept it because it was given them by God. For the rich, their wealth was a gift of God and they should remember the poor in accordance with their generosity of heart.[80]

On the basis of such an understanding of "the ordering of creation," the church has often tried to keep the poor at arms length. This is the case especially during the Industrial Revolution.[81] There is ample evidence to show that the poor—in this case, the industrial workers with their filthy outfits and dirty bodies—were not welcome in the church, at least not in the company of the rich and clean. They had to be content with separate early morning worship services.[82] In the light of such historical precedents, the apprehension still persists that the Church might continue to deal with the poor in its age-old traditional way. Referring to the "Word from Darmstadt" released by the Brotherhood (Bruderrat) of the Evangelical Church in Germany in 1947, Schweitzer, for one, stated such a possibility as follows: "It should thus be made known before God and humanity that, since the Industrial Revolution, the greater majority of Christians in our land have failed to give enough support to the demands of the workers for more justice. The few pioneers were satisfied with the customary alleviation of extreme needs." And Schweitzer adds a threatening note: "It is to be feared that such a comportment will repeat itself with regard to the Third World."[83]

Ample references could of course be made to some protestors in the course of the history of the church against such stereotyping of the "proper place" of the rich and the poor in both church and society. There were those few who came up with radical solutions which questioned the ordering of church and society and the place of the poor in them. One remembers the arguments of Ambrose and Chrysostom, who viewed all property as God-given capital legally belonging to the poor as well; Origen had even maintained that the income of the church should be divided equally among the poor and servants in the church; people such as Thomas Muntzer had advocated a community life where everything was shared in imitation of the life of Christ.[84] But such movements and protests were peripheral and did not radically affect the overall comportment of the church towards the poor. In recent years, however, there has been a growing conviction that "the poor are a clue to the understanding of the Church. The Christ of healing and suffering love, dramatically symbolized in the cross, teaches that the poor belong to the very nature of the Church. Churches which are not in solidarity, in loving presence, with the poor will not be able to witness to Christ in the world."[85] In various degrees, the conviction has thus grown that the poor are and should be in the center of the life and mind of the Church.[86] Consequently, the poor have become a serious ecumenical issue. "Churches are now experiencing the kind of renewal that the Holy Spirit can bring to them through the poor: in many parts of the world a new type of church is emerging from the poor."[87] In such a church, Christians are breaking the human barriers that separate them from one another and are struggling together to overcome their poverty. In this struggle, their faith in Jesus Christ is viewed in a renewed perspective: Jesus Christ is rightly viewed as being one of them.

As a result, in the last thirty years, the discussion on the shape of the poor's presence in church and society has been transformed. It has moved to the center of attention and will remain there.

> Today there is a new challenge. In this time of new reformation the question [of salvation] has been reformulated very forcefully by feminist theologians and Third World theologians. If one finds the presence of Christ among the poor and marginalized of church and society, is not this an important locus, not only of renewal, but of salvation? Or to put it the other way around, if the poor and the oppressed are a sign of the coming kingdom where all are welcome, is there salvation for the non-poor, the oppressors of every nation who cut themselves off from this particular locus (Matt. 25:31-46)?[88]

In this light, there is no doubt that the question of the relationship of the poor to the church or their role in defining the church has become a thorny one. The least that can be said is that "this option in favour of the poor and the oppressed sometimes creates tensions because it questions not only the structures of society but also that of many churches themselves."[89] And when the question of the church's relationship to the poor arises, as has been done by the CCPD studies, their role in defining the church becomes thorny.[90] Some want to lead the discussion away from the main issue and leave it there in confusion. In such an attempt, the main question as to what the church should do with the poor and how it should relate to them becomes a secondary issue. The best strategy for doing this has been to talk about the presuppositions that underlie the discussion on the poor and the church: Is a Marxist social analysis being used? Does the idea of "class struggle" lay behind talk about the poor? Who are the poor, and who are the rich, after all? Are there not different ways of defining them? Are there not myriad sources and causes of poverty? What does it mean for the church to be in solidarity with the poor?[91] The end result is that the poor are forgotten in the process. And the church is lost, swimming in confusion, and paralyzed, but finally absolved of its responsibility. And one wonders whether this, after all, is the task of theology. But as an F&O study makes it clear, the Christ and the poor go together: "Christ's movement towards men was one of kenosis and poverty. The Church only follows this movement, therefore, when it is ready to be poor for the sake of community—a requirement which is particularly hard to grasp today. What is poverty in the modern age?"[92]

Whatever the questions, the theme of the church and the poor has become a burning issue in the ecumenical movement today. "The challenge of the poor for theology and the church is in fact a burning issue for the oikumene, an issue which Mission cannot ignore."[93]

This is no less the case with the F&O Commission. From the side of the Third World have come to it "the growing urgency of two liberation motifs: the notions of the Church of the poor" as a way of thematizing how the Third World views the ecclesial issue, and of "the community of women and men in the Church" as a no less clamant theme, "especially but not exclusively, in the West."[94]

Anticipating such a pressure, the F&O Commission had already recognized a decade ago the close connection that obtains between Jesus Christ, the Eucharist, and the poor. "The Christ of the Eucharist is the Christ of the poor. If social justice is not proclaimed, the sacraments lose significance, although their 'sign' character remains. And thus the question is posed: Have we seriously examined the implicit claim here that the uniting power of the sacraments is inseparable from the principle of social justice?"[95] In stating the issue in such an explicit manner, it is recognized time and again that the poor are in the center of the worship and life of the church.

F&O has thus rightly been increasingly preoccupied with this very issue. It has tried to tackle it in a number of its studies. It has been aware of the fact that it cannot ignore it: "Our discussion of the *struggle for human justice* . . . also raised sharply one issue that Faith and Order cannot avoid: the relation between eucharistic fellowship and the principle of social justice. For, as was pointedly said, the Christ of the eucharist is the Christ of the poor. Does our consensus statement on the eucharist yet face this challenge?"[96]

Following such questioning within the Commission, some of its statements have put the poor in the center of Christianity, namely, with Christ. "There are newly-emerging dimensions to the theme (The Unity of the Church and the Renewal of Human Community), e.g. the focus on the poor."[97] The pressure from the Third World is persistent here. There are groups who continue to urge F&O to deal with it as a serious element of the Christian faith. It was especially the Porto Alegre consultation which drove home the point within F&O when it stated: "Fundamental ecclesiological consequences follow from making the poor the starting-point for a renewed understanding of our faith."[98] In this connection, the question posed by Konrad Raiser in light of the importance of the poor for the faith is worth taking seriously with the serious consequences it implies: "Is not then the Christ of the Eucharist also the Christ of the poor? Does not a practice of the Lord's Supper which divides the unity-creating power of the sacrament from the demand for concrete reconciliation and justice in the body of the church fall under the judgement of God? Can there be a Christian fellowship (communion) without a church discipline, without the readiness to condemn apostasy (fall from the faith), i.e., to condemn heresy in a concrete way?"[99] The question that is increasingly being asked is pointedly phrased by Duchrow: "*Where* do we expect, *where* are we ready for, the encounter with Jesus Christ?" Connecting this question to that raised by Bonhoeffer, he faults the church for failing to raise the obvious question: "Who and where is Jesus Christ, the crucified, for us today?" Taking his clue from Matt. 25:31-46, Duchrow arrives at the following conclusion: "What Jesus is saying here, therefore, is no more and no less than that *our very salvation itself, and not just our ethical status, is decided by our behaviour in respect of the basic needs of our fellow human beings.*"[100]

It is the very meaning of the Gospel that is at stake here. The increasing conviction is that the Gospel has to be interpreted from the side of the poor. It is only then that it becomes the true and authentic Gospel. Any interpretation of the Gospel that leaves out the poor is a heresy. "We may be preaching perfectly orthodox doctrine but it is not the gospel for us today." The Gospel of God preached by Jesus was distinguished by the fact that it proclaimed the liberation of the poor from the yoke that held them captive. It announced the destruction of the powers that held the poor in their tutelage. It affirmed that God has let a new day break, a day which sets free those who are suffering under the oppression that is imposed on them by others.

More than this, God is on the side of the poor. He takes their cause as his very own and fights against their oppressors on the poor's behalf. God takes sides here; God is not neutral. God makes the decision in favor of the poor and leads them to liberation. It is a point of view which challenges the "accepted" understanding of the Gospel. As Bonhoeffer put it: "There remains an experience of incomparable value. We have for once learnt to see the great events of world history from below, from the perspective of the outcast, the suspects, the maltreated, the powerless, the oppressed, the reviled."[101] It is a painful discovery which the ecumenical movement can no longer do without.

Justice, Peace, and the Integrity of Creation (JPIC)

Divisions among the various currents that constitute the ecumenical movement have often been felt very sharply. This was visible even as late as at Canberra.[102] The most intractable separations in the movement have been in the relationships beween faith and life, confession and action, dogmatics and ethics. While for many such divisions have seemed artificial, they have always persisted in the ecumenical movement under the influence of "classical" theology. In the same breath, there have always been attempts to unite these currents. One of the major such attempts was made at the Vancouver Assembly of the WCC (1983). It was then decided that "to engage member churches in a conciliar process of mutual *commitment (covenant) to justice, peace and the integrity of all creation* should be a programme priority for World Council programmes."[103] That the call here was based on the attempt to tie faith and life is clear. One could not fail to notice the big concepts that have guided and have been dear to the work of F&O, words and terms such as "conciliar process," "confessing Christ," as well as "ecclesiology." In this way, there was the hope that faith and life would not be set apart but joined in the confessing and living of an authentic Christian life.[104] The so-called political issues would be tied up to the ecclesiological ones, which often belonged to the realm of F&O.[105] It was as a result of such an attempt that JPIC was dubbed "a novel phenomenon in the history of the ecumenical movement. Never before have the churches joined together to such an extent and in such a form in order to give a common witness to their faith." The fact that the churches have taken this upon themselves was hailed as "an ecumenical event."[106] It is even amazing to note that JPIC played a role in the redefinition of the concept of unity sought by the ecumenical movement. The WCC Central Committee asked the F&O Commission to come up with a new statement on the unity of the Church to be presented to the Canberra WCC Assembly, in part due to JPIC and the "Unity and Renewal" study. The latter had opened up new vistas which went beyond the declarations on the unity of the church formulated in New Delhi (1961) and Nairobi (1975).[107] In Canberra, a new element was introduced in the statement on the church as Koinonia. Here the churches were called to relate closely the movement towards church unity and JPIC.[108]

The JPIC process has traversed promising as well as difficult roads.[109] In one of its high points, it had succeeded in bringing the European churches into an assembly which was hailed as one of its kind.[110] For the first time since the Reformation, these different churches came together to deliberate on the issues of JPIC. The message of the Assembly, made up of Catholics, Orthodox, and Protestants, was received with an overwhelming majority. In this light, this Assembly was hailed as an "almost ecumenical miracle"[111] and a "church-historical turning-point since the Reformation."[112]

We have no time here to dwell on the difficulties faced by the JPIC process, especially in Seoul.[113] In this connection, one cannot pass on without mentioning the serious confrontation that arose between the Third World and the West at the convocation.[114] Even so, one needs to point out that, even in the face of the many difficulties experienced by the process, there were further calls to continue it. The Canberra Assembly, on its part, came out strongly on this score when it resolved that JPIC constitutes "the central vision of the WCC" in the coming years.[115] In addition, the statement on "the Unity of the Church as Koinonia," prepared by the F&O Commission and later adopted by the Assembly, also states as follows: "To call all churches to recommit themselves to work for justice, peace and the integrity of creation, linking more closely the search for the sacramental communion of the church with the struggles for justice and peace."[116]

The interconnection between faith and life aimed at by JPIC is a noble task. Yet the rough road traversed by JPIC and F&O cannot be hidden. On the one hand, it cannot be denied that justice has become a central element in the expression of the faith of the Christian church. "So there exists today wide ecumenical agreement that commitment to justice is a direct consequence of Christian belief."[117] This concerns the New Testament as well:

> To the entire New Testament, not only to the apostle of the gentiles, the practice of justice constitutes a self-understood and unconditional part of the Christian faith commitment (Glaubensvollzugs). . . . In their prayers and work for "the unity which is at the same time God's will and gift to his Church," the Christian churches ought not to lose sight of the fact that unity in faith in the Gospel and in the eucharistic fellowship in the table of the Lord is closely tied to the call to the churches to a common action in the service of justice.[118]

This does not hide the fact that it has also become a key obstacle, in the eyes of many.

On the other hand, the question of the unity of faith and life, faith and justice, confession and praxis is an ecumenical line which has to be pursued in the future.[119] The question of the relationship of justice to the faith which the church professes was often controversial. Some admitted that the two belong together. The issue of justice is not peripheral to the faith. It forms a central part of it. As the (former) German Democratic Republic reflections on JPIC have put it:

> The conciliar process for JPIC should not be considered to be an ethical endeavour of the Church in the first place, but must be seen as a reality belonging to the source of its mission, from where the Church takes its very existence. It is not primarily a moral and political effort . . . but precisely the inner core and authentic heart of the being of the Church, even before it comes to action. Thus it is clear, that the Church, when acting for JPIC, is dealing with its proper concern.[120]

But the issue of justice, with which JPIC is partly concerned, will face difficulties on the question of power. This element comes often to the fore in the discussion of justice. In the last analysis, justice demands the sharing of power of the strong with the weak, of the rich with the poor. This is the stumbling block: "It became apparent that the creation of more just structures was primarily a question of power-sharing: redistribution of power, not technical solutions to the problem."[121] Raiser further claims that his question of power has become acute especially in connection with the JPIC process.[122]

There is a further promising road taken up recently by the WCC in this direction. This is the attempt to address directly the tensions that have characterized the various currents of the ecumenical movement, especially regarding F&O and Life and Work. The direction taken is to relate the concept of Koinonia (communion) with that of JPIC. It is here admitted that "the ecumenical movement suffers damage so long as it is unable to bring the justice, peace and the integrity of creation (JPIC) and the unity discussion into fruitful interaction."[123]

The healing of this rift is to be sought in the implications of the term Koinonia: "*Koinonia* is the term proposed as a description for that unity sought by Faith and Order and the conciliar process of Justice, Peace and the Integrity of Creation" (p. 11).

The key uniting term is once again communion (Koinonia). This has to do with the nature of the church as well as with its commitment to justice. Any unity that is not ready to make sacrifices in the attainment of its goal is cheap unity. The costly unity that is called for by the nature of the church and the Gospel it preaches must be intimately tied to the moral struggles for a just society. Confirming what has been said earlier, in this struggle the sacraments have a central place: "Questions of faith and moral and social questions are inseparable from the act of Christian witness that baptism mandates. Eucharist as a sacrament of communion, to cite a second example, is real food for a scattered people in their moral struggle, to heal the brokenness of human beings and community" (p. 10).

As we saw earlier, communion (Koinonia) is, then, related to the New Testament as well as to an array of important concepts which have been operative in the ecumenical movement. Among these figure the concepts of covenant, ecclesiology, conciliar fellowship, diversity, and unity. The overall conviction is that "such interaction" between the search for unity and JPIC "is possible and promising" (p. 22). The further effort is to challenge the F&O Commission, which is commended for having taken seriously the reflections on JPIC, to think anew its direction, taking such possibility and promise into consideration. There are concrete suggestions presented to facilitate this reconsideration. The way is thus open for a fruitful interaction and mutual challenge, edification, and exploration.

Women in Church and World

The "Unity and Renewal" study consists of numerous branches, so to speak. To be exact, it has four components. In all four, there are elements which are pertinent to our line of pursuit here. The question of justice has already been treated in connection with JPIC. But we concentrate on one more aspect of this specifically because it has very much to do with the common themes that we are exploring. This promising issue, which was related initially to this very topic of unity and renewal and which has invaded the ecumenical movement, is that related to the forceful coming of women into the movement. This again is a new development that has shaken the ecumenical movement. With the coming of women into it, the ecumenical exercise, often limited to the domain of men, is seriously put into question. This is the case because women question in a very forceful way the traditional stereotypes that have characterized not only the world but the church as well. But in spite of the problems and conflicts that may have been instigated by this entry, the issue of women in the movement will remain one of the promising ecumenical issues in the future.

It is no wonder, then, that, at the instigation of the WCC Central Committee initially, the F&O has dealt with it in its studies. For, as we have had the occasion to notice from time to time, besides the Third World, the pressure that comes from women has gradually shaped the ecumenical agenda in a profound way because it also raises the issues of "church unity, justice and human liberation" and the difficulties that are tied to them.[124] This is promising because it tries to combine the two concerns together in an innovative way. In its method, it follows the contextual approach which has been dear to liberation theologies. Furthermore, it was intended as an opportunity to study the whole gamut of faith questions and the sources of the faith in a new way, namely, from the hitherto unheard perspective of women. Therefore, it was expected not to be content with traditional responses. At the same time, one observes that both the ecumenical movement in general and the concerns for liberation in particular have also been rightly pushed to come to terms with this issue. We cannot go into the details of the studies in this regard, but it is appropriate that some of them be mentioned.

One of the serious questions raised by the entry of women is the contradiction between the fact that they are a majority in the church while at the same time they are marginalized by not being represented in the positions of authority and leadership. This fact reflects an ordering and identity of society which is distorted against women. On such a basis, their concerns and priorities are often relegated to the back seat. This includes the sexual discrimination that goes with it, their prevention from being ordained, the biblical views on the place of women in the church, their search for equality in work and life, lack of their fair share of influencing the policies of the church. In this light, it is obvious that "the question of women" will also have serious implications for the understanding of theology and the traditional interpretations of the Bible.[125]

One of the positive methods that was used in this study was relating it to people at the grassroots level. It did not begin with theological issues in the abstract but approached people concretely in their local contexts. This enabled people to look at the place and role of women from specific perspectives. The origins of this program, entitled "The Community of Women and Men in the Church," go as far back as 1952. But it did not pick up to the extent of becoming a study program until 1975, when the proposal was presented to the WCC Nairobi Assembly (1975). From here on, it continued to gain momentum in F&O Commission meetings. The major steps to be taken to carry it out were made at the Commission meeting in Bangalore.[126] This was followed by the first meeting, in Sheffield (1981), which dealt with the issues.

Sheffield was viewed as something special in the history of the churches. It was assessed as being the first of its kind to discuss the issues which concerned the community of women and men in the church. It was also a conference where conflicts arose with regard to a number of issues related to the theme. Among these were the questions of the equal representation of women, the false conceptions of sexuality, the ministry of women in the church, and the interconnection of race, class, and gender. This whole net of ideas led to the questioning of "the authority and interpretation of scripture within the ecumenical movement."[127] As a search for "a community of equals," it remains a study that will always have something to offer in the future of the ecumenical movement, for it deals with the ecclesiological issue of "an inclusive community."

— 6 —

Concluding Remarks

In the preceding pages, we have tried to cover a wide area of ecumenical activity. We have tried to define the problem that an encounter between the Third World and the interconfessional dialogues may mean for the ecumenical endeavor. To enable us to grasp the issues at stake, we have attempted to describe the concerns of the dialogues, their visions of the unity of the Church, the various perspectives related to them, the problems that the dialogues face in their reception, etc. We also undertook the task of presenting some Third World reactions to the dialogues. Finally, we zeroed in on some of the themes which have become concentration points for the various perspectives, however different from and polemical towards each other they may be. In the next-to-the-last chapter, we delineated the salient features of an ecumenism that succeeded in being drawn to central themes that will play a very important role in its continuity.

In this chapter we shall bring together the various arguments and draw some of the conclusions which seem, in our view, indispensable in the present state of ecumenism. In view of the confrontation between liberation and doctrinal orthodoxy, there are a number of elements that have to be taken seriously for the future of the ecumenical movement and, it seems, for the future of Christianity as well. We have already made references to some of these elements in the previous chapter, but they need to be evoked and sharpened once again. These concern especially the profound changes that have transpired in the worldwide Christian church and, consequently, in the ecumenical movement. These changes need to be taken to heart seriously and corresponding steps be introduced commensurate with the changes. For, as Barry Till observed in 1972: "Unless the World Council can reform itself [and I would add the ecumenical movement], streamline itself and move significantly in the direction of a Christianity that is non-white and non-middle-class it may not survive to be the *World* Council which so far it has only been in an embryonic form."[1] We observe that, ever since, the rate of change has been accelerating, and this call has become more urgent.

The Big Change

In the course of the discussion so far, we have drawn attention to the fact that there is a big change going on in the texture of the worldwide Christian church. We have seen this happening in the numerical aspect. This is to say that since the beginning of the 1980s, the majority of the membership of the Christian Church no longer resides in the North, as it used to be for hundreds of years, but has moved to the South. As the Christendom of the past which operated in the West gradually collapsed, it has given way to a minority status for Christianity in the West. Such a change has given rise to what Johann Baptist Metz has called the "polycentric world-church."[2] This worldwide Church is no longer taking it for granted that it has to be under the religious-cultural tutelage of the West. It is, rather, struggling to move away from it and assert its right and duty to understand the Gospel in the context of its own varied cultures, which do not often mesh with that of the West. In some circles, this tremendous change is received with great enthusiasm. It is even considered to constitute a possible "coup-d'etat of the Holy Spirit."[3]

In addition to this numerical weight, there is also the theological outburst which has characterized this change. Liberation theologies from the Third World have become decisively important in the exposition of the Christian faith within and without the ecumenical movement. Not only have they become a challenge to it; they have also reached the stage where they play an important role in the definition of the ecumenical agenda. Once again, in some circles, such an ascendancy of this theological development has been viewed with great alarm. The alleged "triumph of liberation theology" in the WCC has been not only vilified but has also been seen as a betrayal of the ecumenical task and goal as set out by the founding fathers, as well the betrayal of the principles of the Christian faith. The argument was often put forward that these theologies only succeeded in deviating the ecumenical movement from its specific calling. They implicated it in areas which do not belong to its specific ecclesiastical mandate. There were therefore harsh criticisms hurled at the ecumenical movement, and especially the WCC, as well as consistent calls to subject the ecumenical movement to the radical rethinking of its goals and to rid it from its captivity to these new theologies.[4] These echoes were also echoed from within the F&O itself.[5]

Whatever the uneasiness and the disturbance introduced by these changes may be, however, it cannot be denied that a shift of great significance is taking place in the world Christian Church ecclesiastically and theologically.[6] The landscape has changed radically and become a source of crisis. With it have also changed the priorities and the concerns of the world church. The role of the Third World in bringing this about is clearly acknowledged. As Norman Goodall observed in 1972: "In the great matter of the nature of the Church, its ministry, its unity and the form of it, these once called 'younger churches' provide an increasingly persistent challenge not only to the disunity of the West but *to the assumption that the historic grounds for that disunity possess any contemporary relevance over large parts of the Christian world.* Even though Goodall could not at that time see anywhere the emergence of local theologies in Africa and Asia, he nevertheless stated: "There is much in the contribution of these lands which raises for the West new questions about the meaning of history, the patterns of church life and the priorities in thought and action which would characterize a truly Christian community. As a result of the two factors here touched upon, *the centre of gravity, so to speak, of the World Council of Churches has markedly shifted.*"[7]

This does not of course deny that there are various traditional forces and movements within the Christian church which continue as if no changes have taken place. There are those who live and act by making modifications to the old (dis)proven practices. One of the outstanding anachronisms in this area is the continuing myth that the West is still Christian and that it has the duty to continue to be engaged in missionary activities to evangelize the non-Christian, i.e., nonwestern, world. This myth was not true even in the nineteenth century, when "it was no longer realistic to think of Western countries as 'Christian,' and non-western as the 'mission field.'" Such views die hard, and many missionary enterprises as well as the bases of their support are still living and acting under the banner of such perspectives.[8]

But the fact is that a change of tremendous consequences has taken place within the shape of the worldwide Christian Church as a result of the coming of the Third World. Under normal circumstances, the overwhelming balance in favor of the churches of the Third World would have led to commensurate changes in the administration and the setting of priorities of the world Church. But appropriate steps reflecting these changes have not yet been put in place. This is reflected in the comportment of the biggest Christian church in the world, the RCC, with regards to its constituencies in the continents of Africa and Latin America.[9] The stories of the preparations for the Synod of Africa, held at the Vatican in 1994,[10] and the Latin American bishops conferences, held in 1992 in connection with the celebrations of the discovery/conquest of the "New World," are typical examples.[11]

Such exercises seem to be attempts to hold back the clock of change that has already invaded the worldwide Christian Church. They are forms of resistance to new developments. But there are persistent assertions emanating from the Third World which even insist that the time is ripe to envisage radical changes in the administration of the Church. "One African theologian has already suggested that it is time for the election of an African pope and for the World Council of Churches to move its central headquarters from Geneva to Nairobi."[12] The tremendous changes have serious repercussions for a number of givens that have been taken for granted in the past and on which the ecumenical movement has been nourished.

The Questioning of Western Identity

There is a growing awareness that shifts of far-reaching consequences are taking place. These shifts are accompanied by shocks that somehow put a question mark not only in the whole "Christian enterprise" of the Western world but also on its very identity. The two are intricately tied together. And this is what renders the ecumenical task extremely complicated. Ludwig Ruetti has succinctly put this problematic in the following way:

> In modern times, the identity of the West, that is to say, the existence and the self-understanding of the West, was (and is) characterized essentially by its conduct of conquest and domination in diverse forms—direct or indirect, open or hidden. It follows that the questioning of Western domination does not touch only *one*—at best secondary—aspect of the West but the kernel of the identity of the West itself. The churches, theology, and mission, as well as the so-called younger churches which resulted from it, are also implicated in this problematic nature of the West.[13]

Such an identity crisis touches also the entire Christian Church, which had its center in the Church in the West. To this identity, the religious-theological and the cultural-political-economic elements were intimately tied.

It follows, then, that the rise of the Third World puts the hitherto alleg-edly Christian identity of the West into the witness box to be subjected to critical questioning. In this case, the identity of the Christian faith in the West and all the activities that were carried forth in its name in the direction of the Third World are examined critically.[14] Even the missionary activities, which were viewed innocently in the past as being "the proclamation of the Gospel to the heathens," are viewed in a new light.[15] They are suspected and even accused of being the handmaidens of the colonial expansion of the West, accomplices of its interests, and the means to destroy the cultures of peoples, leading inevitably to their subjugation.[16] As a result, in the coming of the Third World, every aspect of the life of the church in the West as well as Western civilization and society themselves are subjected to a critical scru-tiny.[17] As a matter of fact, the radical interpretation implied by this change of cultural and philosophical presuppositions in the interpretation of the Chris-tian faith brings about a serious soul-searching about the ultimate authentic-ity, integrity, and truth of the Christian tradition as bequeathed by the West.

The ecumenical movement itself is not free from such a scrutiny because it was intimately tied up with the history of the West. Even in its center, the very problem of the redefinition of the ecumenical goal made necessary by the "irruption of the Third World," to use the pregnant terminology of

EATWOT, cannot be escaped. A series of shock treatments, which began to be applied to the Western bases of the movement beginning in the early fifties, pushed it to reconsider the bases of its foundational concepts, which ultimately affect the goal. This began with the triumph of communism and the emergence of what was then understood as a "New China."[18] There were two important things that happened as a result. On the one hand, this sudden emergence of a system believed to be anti-Christian was viewed as a very serious challenge to the Christian faith and church. It forced the Christian missions into a serious soul searching. The sudden expulsion of all Western missionaries from the mainland was viewed as a serious "debacle" of the missionary enterprise.[19]

On the other hand, the success of Red China to feed what amounted to one-third of the world's population and to organize it in a new way staggered Western analysis and expectations. As one writer put it: "That a revolution as radical as China's could happen is to this writer an historical enigma."[20] This new event, which escaped Western control and comprehension, coupled with a series of others which originated from the Third World, was viewed as a new threat to the supremacy of Western civilization and its claim to be Christian and in accord with the principles of the Gospel. The ecumenical movement, on its part, was shaken profoundly as a result of a series of events having to do with China. As Raiser put it: "The decisive shock for the ecumenical movement came, it must be said, only with the victory of the communist revolution in China, which put an end to the most ambitious missionary enterprise in modern Christian missionary history, and with the Korean war. Together with the successful liberation struggles in India and Indonesia, these events signalled the end of the long period of Western (Christian) world domination." The "China experience," "the catastrophic end of the missionary work in China," led to a "profound crisis in the self-understanding of the ecumenical movement."[21]

In the corridors of the ecumenical movement as manifested in the WCC, there was another specter that was rising. This was the Programme to Combat Racism (PCR), a program which "aroused so much controversy in the churches, and evoked so much interest in the mass-media."[22] This program was launched in view of the changed situation of the world, in which the white-dominated world was encountering its alter ego, the other, till then dominated by it. The churches of the West were then challenged to contribute to the fight against racism by lending concrete support to those who were struggling to liberate themselves from the shackles of white racist supremacy. Eventually, many Christians and churches were shocked to see that Christian churches were involved in the support of groups who stood up to fight the evil of racism by all means necessary.

It is interesting to note that, at the same time, this was an issue that raised questions not only concerning the identity of the churches "which were more a part of the racist system than they had ever thought"[23] but also of the identity of the West as a whole. The program became unsettling because it brought a different view of the history of the West with regard to the countries of the South and the blacks in the USA. It challenged the assumptions which whites had of themselves. The identity of the white man and the understanding of Christianity tied with it was thus put into question. As Roger Williamson put it: "Heated discussions between the big churches of the West and the WCC have their nucleus in the threat to our identity as white, Western, well-armed nations with a specific Christian identity. The PCR could and can thus be understood as a threat to our wellbeing, our white-ness."[24] No wonder, then, that the impact of PCR was so strong that some went as far as expressing "the hope that it will not break the back of the ecumenical movement."[25]

The pressure on the West applied from the hitherto marginalized peoples and churches of the Third World is not something that may be viewed without serious consideration. It has indeed serious repercussions with regard to the assumptions and presuppositions that have so far been taken for granted in the Eurocentric understanding of the world. Such a commonly held Weltanschauung is profoundly put in question; it is no longer taken for granted.[26] This becomes a painful experience in the Western world. The questionings that arose as a result of the coming of the Third World did not remain without having any impact on the Western psyche.

The challenge of the Third World has contributed to a radical questioning of life in the industrialized countries, and has unnerved the confidence of many Western Christians, both in secular and religious matters. Western secular history and church history are so inter-twined that it is impossible for Western culture and institutions to be challenged without challenging the church as well—at the level of theology, ethics and institutions. Increasingly, Christians in the North Atlantic community of nations feel threatened and unsure of themselves. Their way of life seems vulnerable and under attack. Yet what is at stake is not their affluence, or even their moral capacity to respond to physical need at a "sacrificial level," but the fundamental assumptions of "success," the "good life" and the meaning of the Gospel in a world of limits. That is a tougher challenge, a more unnerving challenge, than most people in the West imagined as recently as six years ago. *It is a confrontation which sends shock waves upon the institutional Church as well as on all central social institutions of Western society.*[27]

In the theological and ecclesiastical arena, this translates by shifting the former givens in a profound way. Henceforth, the centers of Christian vitality and theological fecundity have moved away from the West. The traditions that were taken for granted in the explication of the Christian faith are viewed from a different perspective. They do not serve as points of reference in the understanding of the Christian faith as they used to be but are interpreted from a new perspective. As Harvey Cox pointed out:

The whole of Christianity is undergoing "de-europeanization," a jarring demographic metamorphosis that is dismantling the thousand-years-old idea of "Christendom" and undermining a millennium long style of theology. The church of Charlemagne and Innocent II, of Luther and Wesley and Pius XII, is already gone. In its place there is now appearing a Christian movement of black and brown and yellow people, the majority of whom—if current trends continue—will be forced to live their lives in the crowded, hungry megacities of the southern hemisphere. In nearly every Christian church in the world today whites are a shrinking minority.[28]

As Dorothee Soelle also expressed it, the promise coming out of these churches for the future of Christianity is important: "The hour of the reformation is the hour of the poor churches in our world. The fundamental reformational situation is being defined by the emergent churches of the poor countries. The second reformation will come from neither Wittenberg nor Geneva nor Rome but from the poor churches in the Third World."[29]

Moving the Foundations

This has far-reaching ecumenical consequences. Following this major change, even the term "ecumenical" is understood in a much wider way. In this understanding, it recaptures its original meaning. It no longer refers to the narrow church unity goal but is concerned "with the whole inhabited world."[30] As James Cone has contended, the argument in favor of this meaning was the work of Third World theologians. These "began to insist on a definition of ecumenism that moved beyond the traditional interconfessional issues to the problems of poverty and the struggle for social and economic justice in a global context. In their attempt to connect ecumenism with the economic and political struggle for a fuller human life for all, Third World theologians also began to uncover the original and more comprehensive meaning of the term *oikumene*."[31] This leads once more to the questioning of the ecumenical sources and foundations.

We have seen how the initial ecumenical shocks were administered by the events of China and further by the PCR. A no less important shock of the movement arises when one takes consideration of the fact that the beginnings of the ecumenical movement go back to a thoroughly Western comprehension of the social, political, and religious situation of the world. The ecumenical movement—which arose out of the missionary movement—was the child of its time. The missionary movement was buoyed by the inevitable triumph of the Western world. The West had then succeeded in dominating the world, and it was regarded as imposing willy-nilly its will on all other peoples. It was straining to create an integrated world through the mechanism of the philosophical, cultural, scientific, and religious resources of the

West. The task of embarking the rest of humanity onto the sea of progress was alimented by "its widespread belief in the divinity of man and in limitless progress."[32] It was then understood that the further task of the West was to expand this domination for the good of the world and to share its "civilizing mission" to all the peoples who were deprived of it.

The churches and missionary agencies also breathed this atmosphere. They formed an integral part of this milieu. They constituted part and parcel of this grandiose scheme. They served as the arm of Western expansion, for they saw their religious role as converting the whole world to the Christian faith. This was then understood to be the calling of the white, Western world. "The Western Christian man saw himself called to guide the destiny of the world, and the Western colonial powers were viewed as leading actors in the plan of divine Providence."[33] The leaders of the ecumenical movement themselves were part of the well-educated bourgeoisie which shared this zeitgeist. In their opinions and worldviews, the imperatives of the Western world and that of the Christian Church went hand in hand. Differences that obtained between them were not visible in their eyes. It was the forward movement of the (Christian) Western worldview and ethos that was uppermost in their activities. The ecumenical movement was thus clothed in such a Western garb and had its foundations in such a milieu.[34]

It is true that there were some historical events that gravely disturbed such assumptions. The two world wars, for example, were such occasions. Wars that pitched allegedly Christian nations against each other were not easily comprehensible. They therefore became causes for deep soul-searching among Christians. It was even this atmosphere of self-doubt and questioning that gave birth to some currents of the ecumenical movement. As Melanie May appropriately reminds us, the beginnings of F&O were not innocent, in the sense of being totally devoid of nontheological ulterior motives. As she aptly put it:

> It is important to consider how the work of Faith and Order on church unity may have been influenced by memories of, and hopes for, a restoration of "the Christian West." The least that we can do is to admit honestly that the perception of Faith and Order as the preserve of traditionalists is not altogether unfounded. The work of Faith and Order has predominantly been conceived by, and carried out in the language of, ordained Euro-American men from North-Atlantic churches.[35]

But the crisis to which the war gave rise and which such attempts tried to address was not triggered from the outside. It was, rather, an inner-western discussion. It could thus be contained.

But the questioning that was brought about by the rise of the Third World beginning from the fifties was of a different nature. It came from outside the West. It was a critical questioning that arose from the peoples who were allegedly civilized by the West. Instead of expressing their gratitude for the civilization as was expected, the former began not only to pose critical questions but to reject the assumptions that characterized their relationship with the West. This goes to show that "the WCC [and the ecumenical movement, I would add] . . . has been conditioned by the historical circumstances in which it was born and has grown to maturity. But those circumstances have now changed."[36] As we tried to point out above, this "shaking of the foundations" has far-reaching implications for the ecumenical movement itself.

The Changing Ecumenical Vision

This process of questioning the basic building blocks of the ecumenical movement gradually extends to the questioning of the very goal of the ecumenical movement itself. Gradually but consistently, the very goal of the ecumenical movement has entered the process of being interrogated (cf. chapter five above). The common description of the ecumenical goal as the unity of the divided churches began to appear limited. This traditional vision was understood to concern itself only with issues which have to do with the history of the Western churches which underwent church divisions in the course of their history. But as the number of nonwestern churches increased in the ecumenical movement, the question was asked whether such a definition could easily be assimilated by them or whether the goal would not be too narrow and restrictive. There was the argument that there were additional issues that separated the churches which needed to be taken into consideration. Questions that have to do with racism that separated churches on the basis of the color of their skin—to take just one issue as an example—went right down to the definition of the goal of the ecumenical movement itself. As a group report of a 1980 consultation on racism put it: "In fact, the remarkable extent to which there is now a consensus within the WCC on the evil of racism goes to the very heart of the ecumenical movement. . . . The unity of the Church is inseparable from the unity of mankind. . . . Our experience shows that denominationalism and racism have destroyed the unity of the Church."[37]

There is an increasing awareness of the fact that there is a significant shift in the understanding of the ecumenical goal due to the coming of the Third World in the ecumenical movement. In this light, a serious challenge is hurled at the movement.

Towards the end of the twentieth century we are caught in the din and confusion of the struggle for a new organization of human life and society. The churches, sociologically and ideologically shaped, united and divided by previous systems, are also in crisis as new forms of articulation of Christian life, of the Christian message, of theology and organization begin to emerge. Shall we persist in abstracting the quest for unity from this situation and continue to proceed as if the lines of unity and division of a previous time were still relevant?[38]

Such a call coming from the Third World, which urged taking the divisive issues of the world into consideration, unleashed a great deal of uneasiness. It was recognized as being a new, unsettling voice. As Knutson said in 1972: "For many years we did not speak of that in the World Council; the unity of the church was our main theme and when we spoke of fellowship we meant the fellowship among Christians. But now the question of the division of the world and the unity of mankind have come before us with tremendous force." The result can only be described in sharp terms: there is "confrontation," "polarization," "breaking of fellowship," etc.[39]

It is one of the heartening signs that even a onetime moderator of the Commission of F&O recognizes this pressure for a shift in the agenda of the ecumenical movement, resulting from the shrill voice of the Third World churches. He writes: "One impression is that the new Christian majority [namely, the Third World churches] is asking . . . for a profounder view of what church unity can mean for justice and peace in human community and for the integrity of creation itself, as the churches enter the twenty-first century. *And that, historically considered, is a momentous agenda shift for the ecumenical movement.*"[40] He continues to strengthen his argument by declaring further: "The third-world majority in the Christian church signals a historic shift in how the ecumenical movement can understand the problematics of church unity. *Something truly new for the communion of Christ and for the human community is taking place.*"[41] In this connection, Deschner repeatedly speaks of a "coming North-South ecumenical encounter" which is deepening and which will characterize the ecumenical movement of the future.[42]

We have seen above how Deschner welcomed the study on the "Unity of the Church—Unity of Humankind" in 1971, declaring that it had broken a new path in the program of the F&O Commission. More than two decades later, he continues to advocate that there is a need for change in the vision of the ecumenical movement: "There is no question that church unity has been the focal issue in the modern ecumenical movement. But there is growing ambivalence about that today. Many insist that the ecumenical movement must turn to other issues if it is to have a future."[43] The main reason behind such a need for a review of the goal of the ecumenical movement is precisely the coming of the Third World. With regard to the concept of Christian unity, Deschner argues that it has to be reviewed in the light of the new "challenges of South-North ecumenism."[44] He argues that in the reconceptualizing exercise, some of the "elements," such as pluralism, intercontextual understanding, ecumenism under the cross, convergence, and Koinonia, have to be taken into account. His main thrust is that it is no longer sufficient for the ecumenical movement to be satisfied with the earlier definitions of unity. There is the need to go beyond them.

This all goes to strengthen the argument that the agenda of the ecumenical movement will have to change. The givens have simply changed. The pressure from the Third World for this transformation is on, and this will have to have a greater role to play in the future of the movement. For as Hollenweger put it: "The main ecumenical problem of the future is not—as we think in the West—the dialogue between Catholics and Protestants or the dialogue between free and established churches, but much more whether or not we can inspire a viable dialogue between the oral Christians of the South and the literary Christians of the North."[45] This view is corroborated by yet another writer. In the light of the fact that many of the churches which participate in the ecumenical movement are now nonwestern and that they are moving in a different direction than their "mother churches" by avoiding the relationships of tutelage, John May writes: "The task of not letting the ecumenical communication with these non-european variants of Christianity break off may well prove to be the decisive ecumenical task of the future."[46] The future of the movement will greatly depend upon whether the eyes of those who concretize the agendas of the movement will have the necessary courage to look this reality in the face and adjust accordingly. Whether money and power will thwart this spirit, like many other such efforts have been thwarted, will have to be seen. If that be the case, it will be one more tragedy among those which have characterized the history of the Christian church throughout the centuries.

The Church of the Poor

We mention once again an element which we have already dealt with but which we need to look at once again, albeit briefly. The reason is that it is one of the astounding phenomena of the twentieth century that a significant part of the worldwide church has literally become part and parcel of the three-fourths poor of the world; it has become "the church of the poor." As David Barrett wrote in 1982: "Altogether, some 1.5 billion human beings on earth are malnourished. Christians suffer along with others in this predicament. In all developing countries, Christians living in absolute poverty number 190 million. This is 'the Church of the poor.' By the world's standards, they have nothing."[47] For this church, the issue of poverty thus no longer serves as an issue to be discussed from a distance but is an issue to be lived and confronted existentially. While part of the worldwide church lives in abject poverty, another part is engulfed by what Galbraith calls a "culture of contentment," asking more of the same while a greater part of the world goes hungry.[48] In the long run, the gap between the two unequal parts of the Church grows and becomes a potential source of separation. As Harvey Cox observed with regard to the RCC: "Today, the leaders of the Catholic church are confronted by a whole congeries of incipient schisms and potential reformations. This time, however, the fault lines, marking where fissures could heave open, run not so much along doctrinal lines, but between North and South, between the traditional center of Christianity and the Third World, and between the parts of the church that are relatively comfortable and the parts that are desperately poor."[49] This state of abject poverty not only is being increasingly questioned on the basis of the faith but has become an issue of faith. It inevitably sends one back to the sources of Christianity to explore anew the nature of the faith and its relation to this situation of inhuman poverty. That is exactly what has been happening in the last three decades in Third World circles.[50]

As the issue of poverty invaded the church, a fresh return to the sources led to the discovery that poverty was at the heart of the Christian faith.[51] Poverty was no longer a "social" or "political" issue; it was, rather, a deeply religious one. The person in whom God appeared, Jesus Christ himself, was indeed poor. In choosing to manifest himself in Jesus Christ, the God of Christians demonstrated his preference for and solidarity with the poor.[52] Consequently, the questions having to do with the Christianity of "rich Christians in an age of hunger,"[53] "A World Broken by Unshared Bread,"[54] the meaning of communion (Koinonia), baptism, and Eucharist have to be seen in a different light. Henceforth, these concern the very questions of faithfulness to or betrayal of the very Gospel that constitutes the Church. The question of heresy, which Visser't Hooft invoked,[55] hangs like the sword of Damocles over the Church. As Brian Wren put it: "There is no reason to suppose, for example, that the present prosperity of the rich North of the globe, or the culture or institutions of Western democracies, are of permanent or absolute value in the sight of God. If our way of life turns out to be founded on the impoverishment of others, we should not be surprised if those foundations are shaken."[56]

Such a situation demands a new reorientation of the ecumenical task. The start and the goal of ecumenism have to be thought through anew. The earlier presuppositions that gave rise and impetus to the ecumenical movement have changed. Ecumenism has thus to take into consideration this change. The Western sources that alimented the ecumenical movement have now been superseded by new developments. New situations and priorities are shaping the ecumenical agenda. The future of the ecumenical movement will thus depend to a great extent on its ability to take this new situation into account. As Pablo Richard puts it:

> Christians also began to think of the church from this angle. They began to build a church that could be the spiritual power of the poor in the Third World as they struggle against the centers of death. They rejected a church conceived of basically as a Western spiritual power, struggling against so-called non-Christian countries. It was the North-South contradiction—not the East-West contradiction—that provided the basic criterion for the church of the future. We are rediscovering all the

cultural and religious treasure of the Third World and we see that the future of Christianity lies in its ability to dialogue with the great cultures and religions of the Third World.[57]

The Entry of Women

We have seen above how the entry of women into the ecumenical movement has contributed to opening up a new vista. Even though it does become an issue of conflict, the issue of women in the church has also succeeded in becoming a source of new thinking and commitment in the church. Whatever problems it might have given rise to on the traditional understanding of the place of women in the church, it has nevertheless given new life to ecumenical endeavors. "The Community study showed that 'women's issues' touch the identity and life of the whole church."[58] With the coming of the concerns of women in the ecumenical agenda, the ecumenical vision has been enlarged. New and hitherto unconsidered possibilities were opened up for the ecumenical movement.[59] We have already seen how the coming of women into the movement put serious question marks beside the many theological concepts that characterized the history of Christianity.

The influence of women on the question of the goal of the ecumenical movement cannot be underestimated. It was also strong because it was tied with the concern for liberation.[60] Feminist theology was thus increasingly becoming an integral part of a wider theological movement which saw its central concern in the attainment of liberation. There were many basic correspondences in the methods used by feminist theologians and those from the Third World, such as the need to read "the Bible from the perspective of the oppressed . . . the dominated victims of society."[61] The importance of the context for theological reflection, the emphasis on the sociopolitical and economic factors in the history of the formation of the Christian tradition, the ecclesiological significance of oppression and marginalization were important for both.[62] It is no wonder, then, that the concerns of women and the Third World coincided and strengthened one another.

This is why the studies conducted by the F&O on the "Community of Women and Men" also broke new ground with regard to the definition of the ecumenical goal. These studies contributed once again their share in demanding further attempts to redefine the ecumenical goal. In doing so, they brought about new understandings which challenged the traditional understandings. The point here is that it is not the denominational divisions only that are understood as being the church-dividing issues: "The divisions of the world are, insofar as the church is a human institution, church-divisive issues." As such, it is not only they which have to be subjects of theological discussions or define the ecumenical goal. The divisions that split society into men and women, as well as racism, economic exploitation, etc., are also church-dividing issues. "The point is that the search for Christian unity, and the struggle to overcome the brokenness of the human community (a brokenness which leads to divisions within the church as human institution) are part of one and the same response to the Gospel of Jesus Christ."[63] In view of the history of the F&O, this is indeed a recognition with far-reaching consequences.

In this connection, the "Unity and Renewal" study, within which the "Community of Women and Men" was lodged, has made a substantial contribution to the rapprochement between liberation and doctrinal orthodoxy. It may be said that through this study, the concerns for liberation have made considerable headway into the realms of doctrinal orthodoxy. There are, of course, critical voices that are still abroad. But as Mary Tanner observed: "The recent history of Faith and Order suggests that the 'profile' of the Commission is changing in a way that gives recognition to the need for as broad and diverse a community as possible to reflect upon the Commission's classical agenda."[64] This new development has even been characterized as linking up with some elements which figured in the by-laws of F&O but which had been somehow neglected. Whatever the case, there is no doubt that the "Unity and Renewal" study and its component parts have forced the issues of liberation and its concerns into the circles of doctrinal orthodoxy. Whether the tensions and contradictions that arise due to such infiltrations will be tolerated and bear fruit or be vehemently opposed and rejected—as we saw in the first chapter—only the future will tell. But there is no question that a decisive and important step has been taken.[65]

Digging Further into the Ecumenical Memory

In this connection, and in the attempt to think seriously in terms of the relationship between the concerns for liberation and doctrinal orthodoxy, one has to go back and dig into the ecumenical memory. In doing so, it behooves one to refer to the concrete experiences of Christians during the world wars in Europe, which alimented the ecumenical vision and action. These experiences may give us a glimpse into the realities which have to be brought into play whenever one thinks about the beginnings and goals as well as about the continuity of the ecumenical movement. These experiences inform us that suffering caused by the wars, forced displacements, and refugees played a vital, an essential role in the deepening and consolidation of the ecumenical consciousness. As Lesslie Newbigin noted: "One could say that the WCC was born in the death throes of 'Christendom.' Life and Work and Faith and Order were dealing with people who were already Christians. But these Christians were slaughtering each other in bloody wars. They had failed to address the monstrous evils of their societies."[66] With such a situation as a background, the questions of love, peace, justice, international cooperation were concrete visions which characterized the fledgling ecumenical movement.

Strangely enough, the various aspects of suffering caused by wars were instrumental in bringing together Christians hopelessly divided in their teachings. The people who were engaged intimately with the ecumenical movement were also affected by the sufferings of their time.[67] They were subjected to their own sufferings as well as those of their fellow human beings, which had an impact on their goals. It might be said that sufferings fed and shaped the ecumenical movement in a profound way. In the opinion of Melanie May, this factor was decisive in the emergence of the F&O movement: "The formative work leading to the first world conference on Faith and Order in Lausanne, Switzerland, in 1927, was done during the years immediately following the first world war, the great war. That war severed the connective tissues of pre-war Europe. Faced with scenes of slaughter and the ruins of any notion that history represents progress, the originating context of Faith and Order was, in short, the crisis of Western civilization."[68]

When Christians of different denominations found themselves in the foxholes created by internecine wars, they rediscovered their unity in Christ in these very threatened situations.[69] Furthermore, it was the sharing of themselves and their resources with their suffering sisters and brothers that gave them a new vision of the unity of the Church and their unity in the same Lord. Even wars catalyzed the ecumenical spirit. As the late WCC general secretary observed:

> Instead of a period of stagnation the [second world] war proved to be a time of deepening and intensifying ecumenical fellowship. The struggle to be the Church . . ., the common suffering, the opportunity to serve prisoners of war and refugees from other nations—these proved more powerful factors in building ecumenical conviction than conferences, committees or journeys. . . . Churches and individual churchmen proved willing to pay a heavy price for their membership in the *Una Sancta*.

It was then claimed that it was people who were involved in such a task who earned the title of being "the real builders of the ecumenical fellowship."[70]

The experience of suffering was the catalyst that brought many Christians of different denominations together. It forced them to go beyond their alleged differences and bound them to a unity that they never tasted before. The suffering they underwent together made them transcend their confessional boundaries and threw them into the arms of one another. Suffering was the instrument that helped them find their way back into the unity of the faith. The participation in suffering opened up new ways of coming together which were never there before. "In the period between the two world wars and after, *the sense of a common heritage in peril* gave to Roman Catholic-Protestant relations in many countries a depth of fellowship in Christian witness which had never before existed. In Germany, Roman Catholics and Protestants suffered and died together in prisons and concentration camps." Not only did they suffer together and thus discover their unity but their suffering enabled them to serve others outside their circle of faith as well. "Together they sometimes served the suffering Jews or refugees; friendships were made which only death could unbind. . . . In France, similar suffering and similar friendships led to new depths of mutual understanding and respect. . . . The co-operation was often public and official to a degree unknown before or since."[71] There were unique relationships that were established due to the suffering that tied people together. Suffering was a powerful force that broke confessional specificities.

The churches and Christians which were united in suffering also were united in the service of those who were suffering. They stretched out their arms to share in the sufferings to which many were subjected. Refugees and displaced peoples from different backgrounds were surprised to find the churches looking after their needs in places where they did not expect them. Such encounters in strange places among Christians of different backgrounds were some of the strong and lasting memories that fed the ecumenical movement. Many of those who found themselves at the end of their tethers were received and cared for by the ecumenical body when they least expected it. "Many lonely men and women discovered in their camps what it means to belong to the world-wide fellowship in Christ which seeks its children wherever they are. For the World Council, which had so far moved too exclusively in the sphere of conferences, reports, and documents, it was a searching and salutary experience to enter into immediate contact with the stark needs of human beings." Contrary to expectations of disruption through the war, the ecumenical movement was "given more substance."[72]

Even after the end of World War II, the reality of suffering was not effaced from the ecumenical memory. It continued to play a significant role in the thinking of the ecumenical movement. In a study commissioned by F&O, to refer just to one example, this fact is once again evoked. It is there acknowledged that suffering played a role in the concentrating the attention of ecumenical participants. "A new situation was created" whereby Churches were brought together and led to think of one another due to the suffering to which they were subjected. "The persecution which the various Christian Churches suffered in common has brought the Churches together in a way which was hitherto unknown and has developed a new understanding and a real brotherhood between them."[73]

It is thus indispensable for the future of the ecumenical movement to remember that, unless Christians refer to their soft sides of suffering and degradation which are due to their particular situation caused by wars, famines, and other human tragedies, then they cannot be brought to contemplate realistically and sensitively the needs and cries of their fellow human beings. In order to find oneself on the path to a solution together with those who suffer, there must be the recognition that one is dealing with a human problem that strikes one or the other of the human family at different times. In this spirit, the Evanston Assembly was right on target when it declared: "Our calling lays upon us responsibilities for seeking a better social and political life. . . . Obedience to God's will must lead the believer into the heart of all the world's sorrow, pain and conflict. . . . The cry for help of the world's people for bread enough to sustain life in their bodies must be heard by the Christian as the cry of Christ."[74]

Hidden in the ecumenical memory and sustaining it, then, are the human tragedies that shake the human community from time to time. The ecumenical movement as it took place in Europe was thus enlivened and invigorated by the sufferings within which its people found themselves. As was mentioned already, even the F&O movement was not immune to the influence of these experiences of suffering that contributed to its establishment and continuity. As a program outline of the study on the "Unity of the Church and the Renewal of Human Community" rightly remembered:

> Already the founders of the Faith and Order movement envisaged the work for the unity of Christ's church as a necessary presupposition for a contribution to the need of a common witness and service of Christians and churches. Such common witness and service was called for after the First World War by a world divided by nationalistic and ideological power-structures and rich and poor nations and by humankind burdened with human social, political and economic problems and yearning for the essential elements—both material and spiritual—for the human life[75]

The experiences of war and deprivation had led Christians to rediscover not only one another but the meaning of the Gospel as well. The whole gamut of Christian faith and life was seen in a new light as a result of the particular situation of suffering. As the Lund Conference of the F&O stated: "God has brought us together in years of war and occupation, in prisons and camps, in areas of orphan missions, and for works of relief and reconstruction. In many quarters we have been brought nearer to each other by a rediscovery of the full message of the Gospel, of the Church, its worship and sacraments, and its service to the world."[76] Sharing in the suffering fate of others was a renewing element in the ecumenical movement.

On the whole, then, it is no wonder that one of the decisive factors which pushed the churches to embrace the ecumenical movement, making it pass from a movement of individuals to that of the churches, was "the conflict with the anti-Christian forces, particularly fascism in the 1930's" in Europe.[77] In like manner, no ecumenical movement worth its name that forgets this memory in the face of the "church of the poor" which forms part of the world-church will have any future indeed. Such suffering leads one back to the basis of the Christian faith itself. The Montreal Conference pertinently insisted that reference to this basis was indispensable.

In our particular times and places, the following are *some* of the ways this question *must* be put to ourselves: (a) If the Church is the body of the crucified Lord, can it ever expect to be more honoured than he? (b) If the glory and victory of the Lord is seen in his being exalted to the cross (John 12.28-33), can the Church attain a greater glory or exhibit a greater power than by following him gladly, even into suffering at the hands of men? (c) If the Church consists of followers of the Lord who spent his time with publicans and sinners, why does it look so much like a congregation of scribes and pharisees? (d) If the Lord of the Church was crucified outside the camp (Heb. 13.12), why is the Church so often comfortable within its walls and so hesitant to emigrate to new areas in order to risk bearing its witness within endeavours to establish justice and mercy, even where the powers of destruction are at work? (e) How can a Church which tolerated the barriers which separate men today, whether east and west or black and white, face its Lord who has broken down the wall of partition (Eph. 2:14)?[78]

These questions still remain pertinent especially in the face of "the church of the poor." They remain especially so to the heirs of the conference. Taking into consideration the attempts to take these points seriously through the "Unity and Renewal" studies of the F&O, Paul Crow has a judgement and a warning to give: "Faith and Order has hardly found the will or the methodology to confront these church dividing issues [i.e., the implications of genuine solidarity with the poor, the ministry of women in the church, and inclusive language], but any delay will only weaken and distort our efforts for unity and our hope for renewal."[79]

Ecumenism as a Social Movement

Again, in connection with "the church of the poor," it should not be forgotten that the ecumenical movement was indeed a social movement. At its best moments, it was often associated and in tune with the forces that were inclined towards the positive changes of society.[80] Inside it, there were those elements which, based on the understanding of the Christian faith, worked for the communal good and for the betterment of the human condition. The actors which were involved in it were carried through by a vision of the global society which transcended the present. In this sense, the ecumenical movement had "a social relevance."[81] In this connection, it is appropriate to recall the memorable words of Adolf Deissmann—who is said to have used the term "ecumenical movement" for the first time—uttered at the 1925 Stockholm Conference where he tied suffering and ecumenical solidarity together: "The ecumenical idea is born here in Uppsala out of deep suffering like a dawn out of the night of thunder and has united all . . . to a network of a sense of solidarity in the midst of hate and destruction."[82]

Arising from such a perspective, the ecumenical idea often denounced human sufferings that were based on the denial of the principles of Christian faith, such as racism, exploitation in one form or another, social injustices, oppressive political systems, etc. "One of the strongest roots of the WCC occupied itself with the social, economic and political problems of the world. The church's task of watchman seemed to have gained a new dimension in international circles."[83]

It follows that the ecumenical movement will never be true to itself if it ever sheds this aspect of its roots. Those who accuse the movement of "politicization" due to the influence of the Third World are thus unaware of the history of the movement. "Strangely enough, they did not seem to realize that the Council—and the churches that participated in it—had been politicized all along. In fact, even a cursory reading of the documents of the ecumenical movement of the last fifty years reflects all the tensions and conflicts of the Northern Hemisphere, from the aftermath of World War I to the Cold War and detente, not to mention World War II."[84] There are therefore those who rightly argue that the decline or crisis of the ecumenical movement is due largely to its abandonment of some of the noble principles that characterized it in the early days of its history.[85]

Instead of being on fire with the ideas that fed it as a movement early in its history, it became satisfied with its state as an institution. Many of the principles that prodded it to transcend itself were shed gradually to accommodate itself to certain trends. In other words, it settled down without being any longer attracted by the social dimensions that were intrinsically important in constituting it as a movement in the first place. The communion (Koinonia) towards which the movement strains must always inspire it. It must be also recognized that the implications of this communion (Koinonia) are far and wide indeed. In the words of Eberhard Juengel: "The situation in which someone is a person who is suffered for by God and his fellow-man points us towards that community of suffering which the apostle speaks about in Philippians 3:10. In this community one can become the mouth of another. One can open his mouth for the dumb (Prov. 3:18). He becomes ipso facto a politician whenever he does this. Speaking for the suffering is a political action which is essential to faith."[86]

Dragging in the "Non-Doctrinal Factors"

One has to inject here once again one of the points made earlier. The divisions that wrack the world are operative in the church. In view of the discussions even within F&O, this assertion has become a truism. Since the church does not escape these divisions that shatter the society in which it lives, these issues which divide it are a challenge to the church "not indeed only in her comportment but in the very center of her existence."[87]

This fact is also recognized here and there by the F&O Commission. In one of its standing commission meetings it stated: "The division of the Church points to and reflects the division of the world. Discussions of church union cannot be divorced from the social context of the churches since mankind is the inevitable context for the unity of the Church."[88] By its own admission, this is a late development in the workings of the Commission itself. "It was only after the Uppsala Assembly . . . that the Commission began to see that . . . the very issues which divide the human community are themselves primary obstacles to the unity of the church. In a real sense, the Commission now realized the world inter-relates with the church as much as the church provides a sign to the world."[89] It must be recognized that this is a move in the right direction. Doctrinal orthodoxy can no longer ignore or leave out of sight the many historical developments that challenge the faith. To this end, F&O has itself faced the need to develop a "holistic vision," recognizing all along "the creative tensions" and problems that will accompany it.[90] It was in this positive spirit that the recommendation was made that "the study should acknowledge, as Latin American theology has done, that theology cannot be undertaken from an apolitically neutral position and that the churches cannot be divorced from the ideologies of their social context."[91]

It is here that feminists point their finger at the wound which hurts. It has to do with the question of the use of power in the attempt to change unjust structures. Usually churches are not disposed to tamper with the structures in which they live. They find their modus vivendi and try to serve as reconcilers and mediators. This is tied in with what has been called "the double sin of the church: The first sin of the church is that it often resists engagement in the world, claiming God's sanction only for the abstract spiritual realm and saying that hunger and injustice are relative matters. The second sin is that it is structured according to social patterns of the world and yet refuses to be critical of this capacity."[92]

Notes

Introduction

1. World Council of Churches, SIGNS OF THE SPIRIT: Official Report Seventh Assembly. Canberra, Australia, 7–20 February 1991, edited by Michael Kinnamon (Geneva: WCC Publications, 1991), pp. 37-47.

2. Ibid., pp. 16-17, 281.

3. Helmut Kremers, "Das Gespenst des Synkretismus," LM 3/91, p. 129.

4. Herbert Schroer, "Gottes Geist ist nicht die Mutter Erde. Nochmals Canberra: Widerspruch gegen Frau Chung," LM 7/91, pp. 279ff.

5. Robert Paul Roth, "The Seventh Assembly of the WCC," AREOPAGUS, Easter 1991, p. 50.

6. K. C. Abraham, "Syncretism Is Not the Issue: A Response to Professor Chung Hyun Kyung," IRM 80, nos. 319/320, July/October 1991, p. 340.

7. Michael Kinnamon, "The WCC at Canberra," ET 2/1991, p. 20.

8. SIGNS OF THE SPIRIT, pp. 28-37.

9. Tissa Balasuriya, "Liberation and the Holy Spirit," ER 2/1991, p. 202.

10. Hermann Brandt, "Kontextuelle Theologie als Synkretismus? Der 'neue Synkretismus' der Befreiungstheologie und der Synkretismusverdacht gegenueber der Oekumene," OR 2/1986, pp. 144-159.

11. BREAKING BARRIERS: NAIROBI 1975, edited by David M. Paton (London: SPCK, 1976), pp. 64ff.

12. Konrad Raiser, "Beyond Tradition and Context: In Search of an Ecumenical Framework of Hermeneutics," IRM 80, nos. 319/320, October 1991, p. 349.

13. SIGNS OF THE SPIRIT, p. 125.

14. J. M. R. Tillard, "L'Esprit Saint etait-il à Canberra?," IRENIKON 2/1991, p. 176. English version "Was the Holy Spirit at Canberra?," OIC 1/1993, pp. 34-64.

15. J. M. R. Tillard, "Faith and Order after Canberra," OIC 1991-4, p. 381.

16. SIGNS OF THE SPIRIT, p. 16.

17. Margoth Kaessmann, DIE EUCHARISTISCHE VISION: Armut und Reichtum als Anfrage an die Einheit der Kirche in der Diskussion des oekumenischen Rates (Munich: Kaiser Verlag, 1992), pp. 13ff.

18. Konrad Raiser, "Growing into Ecumenical Covenant," in CATALYSING HOPE FOR JUSTICE, edited by Wolfgang R. Schmidt (Geneva: WCC, 1987), pp. 51ff.

19. Nils Ehrenstroem, "Movements for International Friendship and Life and Work, 1925-1948," in A HISTORY OF THE ECUMENICAL MOVEMENT, 1517-1948, vol. 1, edited by Ruth Rouse and Stephen Charles Neill (Geneva: WCC,

3rd ed., 1986), p. 573. Cf. also pp. 426, 567, 592ff, 700.

20. Walbert Buehlmann, THE COMING OF THE THIRD CHURCH: An Analysis of the Present and Future of the Church (Slough, England: St. Paul Publications, 1976), p. 20. Cf. also David B. Barrett, who writes: "By A.D. 2000 the centre of gravity of the Christian world will have shifted markedly southwards, from Europe and North America to the developing continents of Africa and South America" ("A.D. 2000: 350 Million Christians in Africa," IRM 59 [1970], p. 49f).

21. Josef Homeyer, "Die Kirche und Europa aus katholischer Sicht," US 4/89, p. 472.

22. JESUS CHRIST LIBERATOR: A Critical Christology for Our Time (London: SPCK, 1972), p. 44.

23. Per Frostin, "The Hermeneutics of the Poor—the Epistemological 'Break' in Third World Theologies," ST 39 (1985), p. 127.

24. David Barrett, WORLD CHRISTIAN ENCYCLOPAEDIA (Oxford: Oxford University Press, 1982), p. 5.

25. Johann Baptist Metz, "Erneuernde Impulse aus den Kirchen der dritten Welt," THEOLOGIE DER GEGENWART, 29, no. 1, 1986, pp. 171-174.

26. Deane William Ferm, THIRD WORLD LIBERATION THEOLOGY: A Reader (Maryknoll, NY: Orbis Books, 1985); THE CHALLENGE OF LIBERATION THEOLOGY: A First World Response, edited by Brian Mahan & L. Dale Richesin (Maryknoll, NY: Orbis Books, 1981), p. 1.

27. Theo Sundermeier, "Fremde Theologien," EvTh 50/1990, pp. 524-534.

28. KAIROS: Three Prophetic Challenges to the Church, edited by Robert McAfee Brown (Grand Rapids, Michigan: William B. Eerdmans, 1990), p. 2.

29. Juergen Moltmann, "Theologie im Uebergang—wohin?," in Hans Kueng/David Tracy (eds.), THEOLOGIE—WOHIN? Auf dem Weg zu einem neuen Paradigma (Zuerich: Benziger Verlag, 1984), p. 28; Johannes B. Metz, "Standing at the End of Eurocentric Era of Christianity: A Catholic View," in DOING THEOLOGY IN A DIVIDED WORLD: Papers from the Sixth International Conference of EATWOT, January 5-13, 1983, Geneva, Switzerland, edited by Virginia Fabella and Sergio Torres (Maryknoll, NY: Orbis Books, 1985), pp. 85-90; Claude Geffre, "La theologie europeenne a la fin de l'europeocentrisme," L&V 40, no. 201, May 1991, pp. 97-120.

30. LIBERATION THEOLOGY: A Documentary History, edited with introductions, commentary, and translations by Alfred T. Hennelly, S.J. (Maryknoll, NY: Orbis Books, 1990), p. xv.

31. "The Ecumenical Calling of the Christian Church Today: Ecumenism and Paradigm-Shifts," ER 2/1989, p. 255.

32. Quoted in H. Rosin, "Reactions to Melbourne and Pattaya," EXCHANGE 10, no. 28, Sept. 1981, p. 2.

33. Leonardo Boff, ECCLESIOGENESIS: The Base Communities Re-invent the Church (London: Collins, 1985); CHALLENGE OF THE BASE CHRISTIAN COMMUNITIES, edited by Sergio Torres and John Eagleson (Maryknoll, NY: Orbis Books, 1981); Bibliography on Basic Christian Communities in Africa: Theology in Context Supplements (Aachen: Missio A.V., 1993).

34. TENSIONS BETWEEN THE CHURCHES OF THE FIRST WORLD AND THE THIRD WORLD, edited by Virgil Elizondo & Norbert Greinacher (Edinburgh: T. & T. Clark, 1981), p. vii.

35. Tissa Balasuriya, "The Need for Another Ecumenical Council," in

CATALYSING HOPE FOR JUSTICE, pp. 3-7.

36. Barry Till, THE CHURCHES SEARCH FOR UNITY (London: Penguin Books, 1972), pp. 272, 273; Mercy Amba Oduyoye, "The Development of the Ecumenical Movement in Africa with Special Reference to the AACC 1958-1974," ATJ, 3/1980, pp. 30-40.

37. Efiong S. Utuk, "A Reassessment of the African Contribution to the Development of the Ecumenical Movement: Edinburgh, 1910," ATJ 2/1989, pp. 89-104; T. V. Philip, "Church History in Ecumenical Perspective," ER 4/1987, p. 419.

38. WORLD CONFERENCE ON CHURCH AND SOCIETY, Geneva July 18-26, 1966. The Official Report with a description of the Conference by M. M. Thomas and Paul Albrecht (Geneva: WCC, 1967).

39. THE UPPSALA REPORT 1968, edited by Norman Goodall (Geneva: WCC, 1968), para. 59, p. 376.

40. Richard D. N. Dickinson, TO SET AT LIBERTY THE OPPRESSED: Towards an Understanding of Christian Responsibilities of Development/Liberation (Geneva: WCC, 1975), p. 43.

41. Philip Potter, "Doing Theology in a Divided World," ATJ 1/1984, p. 12.

42. Reinhard Frieling, BEFREIUNGSTHEOLOGIEN: Studien zur Theologie in Lateinamerika, Bensheimer Hefte 63 (Goettingen: Vandenhoeck und Ruprecht, 1986), p. 6.

43. Constitution of the Commission of Faith and Order, in David P. Gaines, THE WORLD COUNCIL OF CHURCHES: A Study of Its Background and History (Peterborough, New Hampshire: Richard R. Smith, Noon House, 1966), pp. 1116, 1117.

44. Cf. the special issue of ER 1/1993.

45. Harvey L. Perkins, "Towards an Ecumenical Movement for Justice," in CATALYSING HOPE FOR JUSTICE, pp. 49, 37.

46. Grigorios Larentzakis, "Die Konvergenz Erklaerungen ueber Taufe, Eucharistie, und Amt der Kommission fuer Glauben und Kirchenverfassung als Ansporn zur intensiveren oekumenischen Arbeit der Kirchen," OR 4/1985, p. 434.

47. Guenther Gassmann, "Lima—Vancouver—und danach: Zur Rolle von Glauben und Kirchenverfassung," OR 3/83, p. 260.

48. Wolfhart Pannenberg, "Die Arbeit von Faith and Order im Kontext der oekumenischen Bewegung," OR 1/1982, pp. 52ff.

49. Charles Angell, "The Catholic Church in Dialogue Today: Introduction," OIC 1982-3, p. 193.

50. J. D. G. Dunn, UNITY AND DIVERSITY IN THE NEW TESTAMENT: An Inquiry into the Character of Early Christianity (London: SCM Press, 1986), p. 1.

51. Alister McGrath, THE GENESIS OF DOCTRINE (Oxford: Basil Blackwell, 1990), p. 38.

52. Anastasios Kallis, "Papsttum und Orthodoxie," OR 1/1981, pp. 34, 35.

53. George A. Lindbeck, THE NATURE OF DOCTRINE: Religion and Doctrine in a Post-liberal Age (London: SPCK, 1984), p. 107.

54. S. Mark Heim, "The WCC Faith and Order Plenary Session in Budapest," ET 1/1990, pp. 10-12.

55. Harvey Cox, RELIGION IN THE SECULAR CITY: Towards a Post-modern Theology (New York: Simon and Schuster, 1984), p. 220.

56. Nils Ehrenstroem and Guenther Gassmann, CONFESSIONS IN DIA-

LOGUE: A Survey of Bilateral Conversations among World Confessional Families 1959-1974 (Geneva: WCC, 1975), p. 9.

57. George H. Tavard, "The Bi-lateral Dialogues: Speaking Together," OIC 1980/ 1-2, p. 30.

58. Harding Meyer, "Basic Theological Concerns of World Confessional Families," in THE HISTORY AND THEOLOGICAL CONCERNS OF WORLD CONFESSIONAL FAMILIES, edited by Yoshiro Ishida, Harding Meyer, Edmond Perret (Geneva: LWF Report 5, August 1979), pp. 25f.; "The investment of people and money in these dialogues is evidence of the commitment to the cause of Christian unity the Christian World Communions share" (Kevin McDonald, "Fifth Forum on Bilateral Conversations, Budapest," MSt 4/1991, p. 356).

59. J. M. R. Tillard, "The Ecclesiological Implications of Bilateral Dialogues," JES 3/1986, p. 415.

60. Ibid.

61. Ibid., p. 416.

62. W. Pannenberg, "Die Antwort der Kirchen auf die Herausforderung der Zeit: Ueberwindung der Spaltung," in Heinrich Fries (ed.), DAS RINGEN UM DIE EINHEIT DER KIRCHEN (Duesseldorf: Patmos Verlag, 1983), p. 162.

63. Ibid., p. 161.

64. W. Pannenberg, "Unity of the Church—Unity of Humankind: A Critical Appraisal of a Shift in Ecumenical Direction," MSt 4/1982, pp. 485-490.

65. Erich Geldbach, OEKUMENE IN GEGENSAETZEN, Bensheimer Hefte 66 (Goettingen: Vandenhoeck & Ruprecht, 1987), p. 15.

66. Harding Meyer, "Weltweite christliche Gemeinschaften (WCG)," in OEKUMENE LEXICON: Kirchen—Religionen—Bewegungen (Frankfurt: Verlag Otto Lembeck, 1983), pp. 1260-1266.

67. Lukas Vischer, "The Ecumenical Movement and the Roman Catholic Church," in A HISTORY OF THE ECUMENICAL MOVEMENT: 1948-1968: The Ecumenical Advance, p. 348.

68. Edmond Perret, "The Conference of Secretaries of World Confessional Families 1957-1977," in HISTORY AND THEOLOGICAL CONCERNS, pp. 65-68.

69. Gassmann, "Lima-Vancouver-und danach," p. 267.

70. Ibid., p. 268. Alan D. Falconer, "En Route to Santiago," ER 1/1993, p. 45.

71. J. M. R. Tillard, "The Contribution of the Disciples of Christ/Roman Catholic Dialogue for the Ecclesiology of the Ecumenical Movement," MSt 1/1992, p. 25 (emphasis in the original); Geoffrey Wainwright, "Faith and Order within or without the WCC," ER 1/1993, pp. 118-121.

72. Lukas Vischer, "A Privileged Instrument of the Ecumenical Movement?" ER 1/1991, p. 96.

73. Michael Kinnamon, TRUTH AND COMMUNITY: Diversity and Its Limits in the Ecumenical Movement (Geneva: WCC, 1988), p. 82.

74. Perret, "Conference of Secretaries," p. 68.

75. Quoted in Harold E. Fey, "Confessional Families and the Ecumenical Movement," in A HISTORY OF THE ECUMENICAL MOVEMENT, vol. 2, p. 120.

76. BREAKING BARRIERS: NAIROBI 1975, pp. 196, 197.

77. "It would seem that God has chosen to come among us in the poor, and even to die 'outside the camp' (Heb. 13:13). From a feminist/liberation perspective this is an issue that calls for much consideration. Yet those who write about this in Black Theology, Minjung Theology, Latin American Theology, and Feminist Theology

seem to find very few dialogue partners among the white, western, male theological establishment" (Letty M. Russell, "Unity and Renewal in Feminist Perspective," MSt 1/1989, p. 65).
   78. Cf. Erhard Camphausen, "Eigenstaendigkeit und Dialog," OR 2/1982, pp. 205-223; "Theologie und Praxis in einer geteilten Welt," OR 2/1983, pp. 208-224.
   79. Raiser, "Einheit der Kirche und Einheit der Menschheit: Ueberlegungen zum Thema oekumenischer Theologie," OR 1/1986, p. 37.
   80. Anton Houtepen, "Oekumenische Hermeneutik: Auf der Suche nach Kriterien der Kohaerenz im Christentum," OR 3/1990, pp. 294f.

1. The Interconfessional Dialogues

   1. See the Festschrift on his sixtieth birthday, EINHEIT DER KIRCHE: Neue Entwicklungen und Perspektiven, edited by G. Gassmann and Peder Norgaard-Hojen (Frankfurt am Main: Verlag Otto Lembeck, 1988).
   2. Harding Meyer, "Lutheranism in the Ecumenical Movement," in THE LUTHERAN CHURCH: PAST AND PRESENT, edited by Vilmos Vajta (Minneapolis: Augsburg Publishing House, 1977), p. 247.
   3. David Willis, "BEM, Reception, and the Bilaterals," JES 1/1984, pp. 104-105.
   4. "Another problem is whether bilateral conversations and agreements between the various CWCs are as conclusive as the multilateral efforts of the Faith and Order movement" (Ans van der Bent, "Christian World Communions," in THE DICTIONARY OF THE ECUMENICAL MOVEMENT, edited by Nicholas Lossky et al. [Geneva: WCC, 1991], p. 157).
   5. Guenther Gassmann, "The Nature and Function of Bilateral and Multilateral Dialogues and Their Interrelation," MSt 3/1986, p. 300.
   6. THE THREE REPORTS of the Forum on Bilateral Conversations, F&O Paper no. 107 (Geneva: WCC, 1981), p. 2.
   7. FOURTH FORUM ON BILATERAL CONVERSATIONS REPORT, F&O Paper no. 125 (Geneva: WCC, 1985); FIFTH FORUM ON BILATERAL CONVERSATIONS—REPORT—International Bilateral Dialogues 1965-1991; List of Commissions, Meetings, Themes and Reports, compiled by Guenther Gassmann. F&O Paper no. 156 (Geneva: WCC Publications, 1991).
   8. The only other "unique ecumenical action" was the one organized in 1984 on the level of department heads to organize a common response to the drought in Africa. (Cf. Carl H. Mau, "Report of the General Secretary," in BUDAPEST 1984 LWF Report 19/20 (Geneva: The Lutheran World Federation, 1985), p. 170.
   9. Harding Meyer, "Dialog II. Bilaterale Dialoge," in OEKUMENE LEXICON, p. 225.
   10. Quoted in Barry Till, THE CHURCHES SEARCH FOR UNITY (Penguin Books, 1972), p. 207.
   11. Harding Meyer, "The Future of the Bilaterals and the Bilaterals of the Future," LUTHERAN WORLD, 3/1975, p. 233.
   12. Nils Ehrenstroem and Guenther Gassmann, CONFESSIONS IN DIALOGUE: A Survey of Bilateral Conversations among World Confessional Families 1959-1974, 3d ed. (Geneva: WCC, 1975), p. 15.
   13. ECUMENICAL RELATIONS OF THE LUTHERAN WORLD FED-

ERATION: Report of the Working Group on the Interrelations between the Various Bilateral Dialogues (Geneva: LWF, 1977), p. 11 (emphasis in the original).

14. Ecumenical Documents II GROWTH IN AGREEMENT: Reports and Agreed Statements of Ecumenical Conversations on a World Level, edited by Harding Meyer and Lukas Vischer, F&O Paper no. 108 (Geneva: WCC, 1984), p. 14.

15. Ibid., p. 132.

16. For a Catholic evaluation see Johannes Kardinal Willebrands, "Der oekumenische Dialog zwanzig Jahre nach dem zweiten vatikanischen Konzil," CATHOLICA, 4/1985, pp. 336ff; Karl Lehmann, "Evangelium und Dialog," HK 2/1991, p. 87; Dale M. Schlitt, "Ecumenism from a Renewed Catholic Perspective," OIC 1/1984, pp. 48-61.

17. Cf. DOCUMENTS OF VATICAN II, edited by Walter M. Abbott, S.J. (London: Geoffrey Chapman, 1967), p. 336.

18. Aloys Klein, "Dialogue between the Roman Catholic Church and the Lutheran World Federation," OIC 3/1982, p. 204.

19. Eleuterio F. Fortino, "The Catholic-Orthodox Dialogue," OIC 3/1982, p. 195.

20. Decree on Ecumenism, nos. 21, 24, in Abbott, DOCUMENTS OF VATICAN II, p. 365; Robert McAfee Brown, THE ECUMENICAL REVOLUTION: an Interpretation of the Catholic-Protestant Dialogue (New York: Doubleday, 1967).

21. Harding Meyer, "The Decree on Ecumenism: A Protestant View," ER 1985, p. 320.

22. G. Gassmann, "The Decree on Ecumenism: The Churches of the Reformation," OIC 1,2/1990, pp. 32-39.

23. ECUMENICAL RELATIONS LWF, p. 3.

24. Paul Ladriere, "Le decret du concile Vatican II sur l'oecumenisme: Ouverture et blocage," in VERS DE NOUVEAUX OECUMENISMES, edited by Jean-Paul Willaime (Paris: Cerf, 1989), p. 94.

25. Karl Lehmann, "How Can the Unity of the Church Be Achieved? The Next Step on the Road to Unity: An Attempt at a Roman Catholic Answer," in UNITING IN HOPE, Commission on Faith and Order, Accra 1974. F&O Paper no. 72 (Geneva: WCC, 1975), p. 96.

26. Nils Ehrenstroem, "Churches and Confessional Families in Bilateral Dialogues," MSt 4/1976, p. 346.

27. Meyer/Vischer, GROWTH IN AGREEMENT, p. 232.

28. INFORMATION SERVICE, Vatican Secretariat for Christian Unity, no. 64, 11/1987, p. 68; "Summons to Witness to Christ in Today's World: A Report on the Baptist-RC International Conversations, 1984-88," OIC 3/1990, p. 238.

29. Meyer/Vischer, GROWTH IN AGREEMENT, p. 422.

30. Ibid., p. 24.

31. "Ways to Community," in Meyer/Vischer, GROWTH IN AGREEMENT, p. 225.

32. FACING UNITY: Models, Forms, and Phases of Catholic-Lutheran Church Fellowship (Geneva: WCC, 1985), p. 6.

33. Ibid., p. 13.

34. Fortino, "The Catholic-Orthodox Dialogue," p. 194.

35. Colin Davey, "Orthodox-Roman Catholic Dialogue," OIC 4/1984, p. 351.

36. Dom Emmanuel Lanne, "Catholic-Orthodox Dialogue: In Search of a New Direction," OIC 1/1985, p. 19.

37. "Inwieweit sind die Dialoge und ihre Ergebnisse verbindlich fur die Kirchen?" in LES DIALOGUES OECUMENIQUES HIER ET AUJOURD'HUI (Chambesy-Geneva: Centre Orthodoxe du Patriarcat Oecumenique, 1985), p. 263.

38. For a presentation of some of the related issues involved in the Reformation era, see G. R. Evans, PROBLEMS OF AUTHORITY IN THE REFORMATION DEBATES (Cambridge: Cambridge University Press, 1992).

39. Meyer/Vischer, GROWTH IN AGREEMENT, p. 173.

40. THE THREE REPORTS, p. 22.

41. Meyer/Vischer, GROWTH IN AGREEMENT, p. 248.

42. Andre Birmele, Thomas Ruster, VEREINT IM GLAUBEN -GETTRENT AM TISCH DES HERRN (Goettingen: Vandenhoeck und Ruprecht, 1987), pp. 40-79.

43. Christopher J. Schreck, "The Eucharist in International Bilateral Dialogues," JES 3/1986, p. 464.

44. THE THREE REPORTS, pp. 26f.

45. Commission on Faith and Order: Baptism, Eucharist, Ministry. Report of the Faith and Order Commission, World Council of Churches, Lima, Peru, 1982, in Meyer/Vischer, GROWTH IN AGREEMENT, p. 482.

46. J. Robert Nelson, "The Holy Eucharist in Bilateral Conversations," JES 3/1986, pp. 449-461.

47. George H. Tavard, "The Recognition of Ministry: What Is the Priority?," OIC 1,2/1987, p. 26.

48. Meyer/Vischer, GROWTH IN AGREEMENT, p. 266; THE NIAGARA REPORT: Report of the Anglican-Lutheran Consultation on Episcope 1987 (Geneva: LWF, 1988), pp. 30, 31.

49. THE THREE REPORTS, p. 33.

50. Cf. also BEM, in Meyer/Vischer, GROWTH IN AGREEMENT, pp. 487f.

51. "Towards a Statement on the Church: Report on the Joint Commission between the Roman Catholic Church and the World Methodist Council, 1982-1986 (Fourth Series)," OIC 3/1986, p. 258.

52. "The Ministry in the Church," in Meyer/Vischer, GROWTH IN AGREEMENT, pp. 271, 184.

53. Peder Norgaard-Hojen, "Das Papstamt bleibt bestimmend. Zur Revision des katholischen Kirchenrechts," LM 24 (1985) 5, pp. 129ff; and "Wege und Irrwege des katholisch-lutherischen Dialogs," OR 4/85, p. 419: "Even in view of the latest reservation, this is for Lutheran ears an astounding and striking statement indeed."

54. "Authority in the Church (Windsor Statement) 1981," in Meyer/Vischer, GROWTH IN AGREEMENT, p. 110.

55. Anastasios Kallis, "Papstum und Orthodoxie: Das Papst und die Kircheneinheit aus orthodoxer Sicht," OR 1/1981, p. 37.

56. Colin Davey, "Orthodox-Roman Catholic Dialog," OIC 4/1984, p. 362.

57. THE NIAGARA REPORT, p. 43.

58. Thomas Rausch, "Episcopacy in Ecumenical Dialogue," ET 7/1991, p. 105.

59. Werner Voelker, "Mariendogma und Marienverehrung im Dialog der Kirchen seit 1950," OR 1/1981, pp. 16-17. For a further discussion, cf. THE ONE MEDIATOR, THE SAINTS AND MARY: Lutherans and Catholics in Dialogue VIII, edited by George F. Anderson, J. Francis Stafford, and Joseph A. Burgess (Minneapolis: Augsburg Publishing House, 1992).

60. Harding Meyer, "The Ecumenical Unburdening of the Mariological Prob-

lem," JES 4/1989, pp. 681-696; Andre Birmele, "La mere du Seigneur dans la theologie protestante," L&V 189, pp. 33-48.

61. Margaret O'Gara, "Infallibility in the Ecumenical Crucible," OIC 4/1984, pp. 325-345.

62. Norgaard-Hojen, "Wege und Irrwege," p. 403.

63. Heinrich Doering, "Nahziel: 'Schwesterkirchen,' zum Stand des offiziellen katholisch-lutherischen Dialogs," OR 3/1985, p. 283.

64. BANGALORE 1978 SHARING IN ONE HOPE: Reports and Documents from the Meeting of the F&O Commission. F&O Paper no. 92 (Geneva: WCC, 1978), p. 236.

65. THE THREE REPORTS, p. 8; see also the comments of Gassmann and Ehrenstroem: "At their meeting in 1971, the secretaries of the World Confessional Families (also called Christian World Communions) resolved among others that the principal topic for all bilateral dialogues will evermore be clearly seen to be a common vision of the unity of the church at every level in obedience to the Faith" (CONFESSIONS IN DIALOGUE, p. 262).

66. Minutes of the Standing Committee on F&O—1981. F&O Paper no. 106 (Geneva: WCC, 1981), p. 22.

67. FACING UNITY, p. 11.

68. See Harding Meyer, "Einheit in versoehnter Verschiedenheit—konziliare Gemeinschaft—organische Union," OR 3/1978, pp. 377ff.; and "Einheit der Kirch I, Einigungsbestrebungen," OEKUMENE LEXICON, pp. 295ff.

69. Konrad Raiser, "Modeller kirchlicher Einheit," OR 2/1987, pp. 195ff.

70. Norman Goodall, ECUMENICAL PROGRESS: A Decade of Challenge in the Ecumenical Movement, 1961-1971 (London: Oxford University Press, 1972), p. 62.

71. For an extensive presentation, see J. Robert Nelson, "Konziliaritaet—Konziliare Gemeinschaft," OR 3/1978, pp. 358-377.

72. BREAKING BARRIERS: NAIROBI 1975, p. 60.

73. Minutes and Reports of the 13th Meeting of the Central Committee of the WCC (Geneva: WCC, 1980), p. 183.

74. FAITH AND ORDER: LOUVAIN 1971. F&O Paper no. 79 (Geneva: WCC, 1971), pp. 138-158.

75. Ibid., p. 226.

76. Quoted in BANGALORE 1978 SHARING IN ONE HOPE, p. 237.

77. UPPSALA TO NAIROBI: 1968-1975: Report of the Central Committee to the Fifth Assembly of the WCC, edited by D. E. Johnson (NY Friendship Press, 1975), p. 79. See also Lesslie Newbigin, "What Is a 'Local Church Truly United'?" ER 1977, p. 117.

78. Harding Meyer, "Das Konzept der versoehnten Verschiedenheit als oekumenische Strategie," in EINHEIT DER KIRCHE, (edited by) Friedrich-Otto Scharbau (Hannover: Lutherisches Verlagshaus, 1985), pp. 35ff.

79. Guenther Gassmann, "Die Bedeutung der bilateralen Konfessionsgespraeche und ihr Einfluss auf die Rolle der konfessionelle Weltbunde innerhalb der oekumenische Bewegung," in DARSTELLUNG UND GRENZEN DER SICHTBAREN EINHEIT (Erlangen: Martin Luther Verlag, 1982), pp. 88-89.

80. Guenther Gassmann/Harding Meyer, THE UNITY OF THE CHURCH: Requirements and Structure, LWF Report 15, June 1983 (Stuttgart: Kreuz Verlag, 1983), p. 9.

81. Meyer/Vischer, GROWTH IN AGREEMENT, p. 236.

82. Gassmann/Meyer, UNITY OF THE CHURCH, p. 31.

83. See the whole discussion in Ulrich Duchrow, CONFLICT OVER THE ECUMENICAL MOVEMENT: Confessing Christ Today in a Universal Church (Geneva: WCC, 1981), pp. 182-204. For the story of the discussion, see also Meyer's article, "Das Konzept der versoehnten Verschiedenheit," pp. 35-68; and Gassmann/ Meyer, UNITY OF THE CHURCH, pp. 8ff.

84. THE THREE REPORTS, p. 10.

85. Harding Meyer, "Unity in Diversity: A Concept in Crisis," OIC 2/1988, p. 132.

86. Ibid., p. 133.

87. Gassmann/Meyer, UNITY OF THE CHURCH, pp. 15ff.; Bangalore 1978: SHARING IN ONE HOPE, pp. 235ff.

88. Harding Meyer, "Unite dans la diversite reconciliee," IRENIKON, 1/1984, pp. 45f.; Mark E. Chapman, "The Unity of the Church and the Truth of the Gospel," OIC 1,2/1990, pp. 68-79.

89. See "The Leuenberg Concord," in AN INVITATION TO ACTION: The Lutheran/Reformed Dialogue, series 3, 1981-1983, edited by James E. Andrews and Joseph A. Burgess (Philadelphia: Fortress Press, 1984), pp. 61ff.

90. Ibid. p. 60.

91. "The Leuenberg Agreement from 1973-1988," in THE LEUENBERG AGREEMENT AND LUTHERAN-REFORMED RELATIONSHIPS: Evaluations by North American and European Theologians, edited by William G. Rusch and Daniel F. Martensen (Minneapolis: Augsburg Publishing House, 1989), p. 39.

92. Ibid., p. 48.

93. "Unity and Renewal: The Ecclesiological Significance of the Churches' Involvement in Issues of Justice," MSt 1/1988, p. 81.

94. Thomas F. Best, "Doing Theology . . . and Justice," MSt 3/1988, p. 320.

95. "Living Today towards Visible Unity," MSt 3/1988, p. 302.

96. Ferdinand Hahn, "Das apostolische und das nachapostolische Zeitalter als oekumenisches Problem," OR 2/1981, p. 154.

97. DAS NEUE TESTAMENT ALS KANON: Documentation und kritische Analyse zur gegenwaertigen Diskussion, edited by Ernst Kaesemann (Goettingen: Vandenhoeck & Ruprecht, 1970), p. 131. Translation taken from Leonhard Goppelt, "The Plurality of New Testament Theologies and the Unity of the Gospels as an Ecumenical Problem," in THE GOSPEL AND UNITY, edited by Vilmos Vajta (Minneapolis: Augsburg Publishing House, 1971), p. 106.

98. Edition of the Interuniversitair Instituut Utrecht, 21, 22, quoted in J. A. Hebly, "Die oekumenische Bewegung in Wandel ihrer historischen Perspektiven," OR 4/1979, p. 433.

99. Oscar Cullmann, UNITY THROUGH DIVERSITY (Philadelphia: Fortress Press, 1988), p. 8.

100. James D. G. Dunn, UNITY AND DIVERSITY IN THE NEW TESTAMENT: An Inquiry into the Character of Early Christianity (London: SCM Press, 1977), p. 379.

101. James Dunn, "Unity and Diversity in the Church: A New Testament Perspective," GREGORIANUM 71/4 (1990), p. 647.

102. Ibid., p. 648. See further, James Dunn, "Instruments of Koinonia in the Early Church," OIC, 3/1989, pp. 204-216.

103. Guenther Gassmann, "Einheit der Kirche—die Notwendigkeit einer neuen Klaerung," in Gassman/Norgaard-Hojen, EINHEIT DER KIRCHE, p. 20.

2. Problems and Promises of the Dialogues

1. Harding Meyer, "Die Dynamik des Dialogs," US 1985, pp. 286ff.

2. For arguments for and against, see the articles of Peter Hocken, "Bilateral or Multilateral?" OIC 4/1970, pp. 496-524; and Rupert E. Davies, "Multilateral and Bilateral Conversations," OIC 4/1979, pp. 334-335.

3. BREAKING BARRIERS: NAIROBI 1975, p. 198.

4. Guenther Gassmann, "The Relation between Bilateral and Multilateral Dialogues," and J. M. R. Tillard, "The Ecclesiological Implications of Bilateral Dialogues," JES 3/1986, pp. 365-373, 412-423.

5. FOURTH FORUM ON BILATERAL CONVERSATIONS REPORT, p. 5.

6. NAIROBI TO VANCOUVER—1975-1983 (Geneva: WCC, 1983), p. 10.

7. GATHERED FOR LIFE: Official Report, VI Assembly World Council of Churches, edited by David Gill (Geneva: WCC, 1983), p. 122.

8. Ibid., p. 123.

9. VANCOUVER TO CANBERRA 1983-1990: Report of the Central Committee of the World Council of Churches to the Seventh Assembly, edited by Thomas F. Best (Geneva: WCC, 1990), p. 11.

10. SIGNS OF THE SPIRIT, p. 176.

11. UNITY IN EACH PLACE. . . IN ALL PLACES. . .: United Churches and Christian World Communions. F&O Paper no. 118, edited by Michael Kinnamon (Geneva: WCC, 1983), p. 1.

12. Ibid., p. 2.

13. THE NEW DELHI REPORT: The Third Assembly of the World Council of Churches 1961 (London: SCM Press, 1962), p. 132.

14. BREAKING BARRIERS: NAIROBI 1975, p. 197.

15. Kinnamon, UNITY IN EACH PLACE, p. 2.

16. "WHAT UNITY REQUIRES: Papers and Reports on the Unity of the Church. F&O Paper no. 77 (Geneva: WCC, 1975), p. 21.

17. Duchrow, CONFLICT OVER THE ECUMENICAL MOVEMENT, p. 143; John S. Mbiti, BIBLE AND THEOLOGY IN AFRICAN CHRISTIANITY (Nairobi: Oxford University Press, 1986), pp. 214f.

18. Cf. also BREAKING BARRIERS: NAIROBI 1975, p. 197.

19. "Growing towards Consensus and Commitment: Report of the Fourth Consultation of United and Uniting Churches," in UNITY IN EACH PLACE. . . IN ALL PLACES. . ., pp. 123-124.

20. Cf. SENT INTO THE WORLD: The Proceedings of the Fifth Assembly of the Lutheran World Federation, Evian, France, July 14-24, 1970, edited by La Vern K. Groc (Minneapolis: Augsburg Publishing House, 1971), pp. 139ff. For an opposite view, cf. Duchrow, CONFLICT OVER THE ECUMENICAL MOVEMENT, pp. 139ff.

21. Mary Tanner, "Steps Towards Unity," OIC 3/1987, p. 194.

22. LIVING TODAY TOWARDS VISIBLE UNITY: Fifth International Con-

sultation of United and Uniting Churches. F&O Paper no. 142, edited by Thomas Best (Geneva: WCC, 1988), p. 15.

23. Mary Tanner, "Anglicans and the Ecumenical Future after Lambeth 1988," OIC 2/1989, p. 133.

24. Cf. the discussion in Harding Meyer, "Die weltweiten christlichen Gemeinshaften: Oekumenischer Auftrag und Identitaet," OR 4/1992, pp. 419-434.

25. WHAT UNITY REQUIRES, p. 26.

26. Meyer, FUTURE OF THE BILATERALS, pp. 234ff.

27. Willem Visser't Hooft, "The Place of Bilateral Conversations in the Ecumenical Movement," in LES DIALOGUES OECUMENIQUES HIER ET AUJOURD'HUI, p. 140.

28. Roger Mehl, "Oecumenisme et strategies confessionnelles," in VERS DE NOUVEAUX OECUMENISMES, p. 190.

29. Duchrow, CONFLICT OVER THE ECUMENICAL MOVEMENT, p. 134.

30. NEW DELHI REPORT, p. 23.

31. THE THREE REPORTS, p. 49.

32. Aloys Klein, "The Dialogue between Roman Catholics and Reformed," OIC 3/1982, p. 243.

33. Yacob Tesfai, "The Church in Focus: The Importance of Ecclesiology in Contemporary-Ecumenical Discussions," OIC 2/1991, p. 139.

34. John R. Arnold, "Eine Konsultation in Basel—Erwiderung auf zwei Vortraege," OR 1/1992, p. 76.

35. Ruediger Schutz, "Glaube in der Kultur: Die Funktion der Religionen fuer die Zukunft Europas," EvKomm 4/1991, pp. 219f. Cf. also Jean Fisher, "Address Given in Rome on 2 December 1991 to the Special Assembly for Europe of the Synod of Bishops," CEC DOCUMENTATION SERVICE 17, nos. 3, 32, June/December 1991, p. 60.

36. Aloys Klein, "Oekumene—Quo Vadis? Identitaetsprobleme in der Kirchen: Zur Lage der Oekumene heute," MATERIALDIENST der oekumenischen Centrale, 2/1990, no. 8, p. 31.

37. Walter J. Hollenweger, "The Ecumenical Significance of Oral Christianity," ER 1989, p. 263.

38. Paul F. Knitter, NO OTHER NAME? A Critical Survey of Christian Attitudes towards World Religions (Maryknoll, NY: Orbis Books; London: SCM Press, 1985), p. 222.

39. "The Future Role of Faith and Order," in FAITH AND ORDER 1985-1989: The Commission Meeting at Budapest 1989, edited by Thomas F. Best. F&O Paper no. 148 (Geneva: WCC Publications, 1990), p. 229.

40. W. Pannenberg, CHRISTENTUM IN EINEN SAEKULARISIERTEN WELT (Freiburg: Herder, 1988).

41. Cf. the discussion in Walter Sundberg, "Ecumenism and the Conflict over Modernity," LQ 4/1990, pp. 398ff.

42. Douglas John Hall, HAS THE CHURCH A FUTURE? (Philadelphia: Westminster Press, 1980), p. 28; THE FUTURE OF THE CHURCH: Where Are We Headed? (United Church Publishing House, 1989).

43. Jean Delumeau, LE CHRISTIANISME VA-T-IL MOURIR? (Paris: Librairie Hachette, 1977), p. 18.

44. Lange, AND YET IT MOVES: Dream and Reality of the Ecumenical Movement, translated by Edwin Robertson (Geneva: WCC, 1978), p. 73.

45. A DOCUMENTARY HISTORY OF THE FAITH AND ORDER MOVEMENT 1927-1963, edited by Lukas Vischer (St. Louis, Missouri: Bethany Press, 1963), pp. 104, 111ff.

46. INSTITUTIONALISM AND CHURCH UNITY, edited by Nils Ehrenstroem and Walter G. Muelder (London: 1963).

47. THE FOURTH WORLD CONFERENCE ON FAITH AND ORDER: The Report from Montreal 1963. F&O Paper no. 42, edited by P. C. Roger and L. Vischer (London: SCM Press, 1964), p. 57.

48. Kondothera M. George, "Looking beyond Doctrinal Agreements," ER 1/1992, p. 4.

49. Andre Birmele, "De l'heresie doctrinale a l'heresie ethique?" in VERS DE NOUVEAUX OECUMENISMES, pp. 242, 243.

50. Cyrille Argent, "Why We Are Divided," in WHAT UNITY REQUIRES, p. 50.

51. Metropolitan Emilianos Timiadis, "Seeking Unity in Each Place: Issues Emerging from Dialogues Involving Orthodox," in UNITY IN EACH PLACE. . . IN ALL PLACES . . ., p. 80.

52. Ibid., p. 79.

53. Ernst Lange, AND YET IT MOVES, p. 37. Cf. also Marc Lienhard, "Clivages doctrinaux et conflits de pouvoir: La rupture du XVIeme siecle," in VERS DE NOUVEAUX OECUMENISMES, pp. 53-77; Mark V. Edwards, Jr., LUTHER'S LAST BATTLES: Politics and Polemics (Leiden: E. J. Brill, 1983).

54. THE CHURCH, F&O Paper no. 7 (Rochester, Kent: Staples Printers, 1952), p. 26.

55. Richard Schluetter, "Die 'Grunddifferenz' zwischen den Konfessionen: Zur bisherigen roemisch-katholischen Diskussion als Frage nach moeglichen Motiven und Zielen," OR 3/1987, p. 304.

56. Ibid., p. 307. Cf. Edward Schillebeeckx, JESUS: Die Geschichte von einem Lebenden (Freiburg: Verlag Herder, 1975), p. 597.

57. Ibid., p. 318.

58. Ibid.

59. Letty M. Russell, "Women and Unity: Problem and Possibility," in MSt 3/1982, p. 298.

60. Lange, AND YET IT MOVES, p. 96.

61. Melanie May, "Response to Gunther Gassmann," JES 3/1986, p. 373.

62. Schuelte F. Berge, "Nichttheologische Konflikfelder der Oekumene," US 1/1980, p. 25.

63. Johannes Kardinal Willebrands, "Der Paepstliche Rat fuer die Foerderung der Einheit der Christen im Jahre 1990" CATHOLICA vol. 45, 1991, p. 173.

64. Letty M. Russell, "Unity and Renewal in Feminist Perspective," MSt 1/1988, p. 64.

65. John Baycroft, "Inclusive Episcopacy and Koinonia," OIC 1/1988, p. 10.

66. Johannes Cardinal Willebrands, "Der Paepstliche Rat fuer die Foerderung der Einheit der Christen im Jahre 1990," CATHOLICA vol. 45/1991, p. 173.

67. George H. Tavard, "The Ordination of Women," OIC 3/1987, p. 200.

68. "The Church of England Is to Ordain Women as Priests," CHURCH

TIMES, no. 6770, 13 November 1992, p. 1.

69. Monique Hebard, "Les femmes dans l'Eglise," ETUDES, Janvier 1993 (3781), pp. 97-105.

70. Dom Emmanuel Lanne, "Catholic-Orthodox Dialogue," OIC 1/1985, pp. 28, 29.

71. Dom Emmanuel Lanne, "Eastern Catholics: Religious Freedom and Ecumenism," OIC 4/1990, pp. 308-327.

72. Mircea Basarab, "Uniatismus und Proselytismus auf der Tagesordnung des internationalen katholisch/orthodoxen Dialogs," US, 4/1990, p. 321-329, p. 323.

73. Colin Davey, "Orthodox-Roman Catholic Dialogue, 1983-1990," OIC 4/1990, p. 289.

74. Paul A. Crow, "After All These Years . . . Why Isn't Church Unity More Visible?"; Harding Meyer, "Fundamental Difference—Fundamental Consensus"; and J.M.R. Tillard, "We Are Different," MSt 3/1986, pp. 247-259.

75. IN SEARCH OF CHRISTIAN UNITY: Basic Consensus/Basic Differences, Joseph A. Burgess (ed.) (Minneapolis: Fortress Press, 1991).

76. BEM, in Meyer/Vischer, GROWTH IN AGREEMENT, pp. 466-503.

77. CHURCHES RESPOND TO BEM, edited by Max Thurian. F&O Papers nos. 129, 132, 135, 137, 143, 144 (Geneva: WCC, 1986-1988).

78. FAITH AND ORDER 1985-1989; The Commission Meeting at Budapest 1989, edited by Thomas F. Best. F&O paper no. 148 (Geneva: WCC, 1990), p. 25.

79. Guenther Gassmann, "Report of the Secretariat," in FAITH AND RENEWAL: Reports and Documents of the Commission on Faith and Order, Stavanger 1985, Norway 13-25 August 1985, edited by Thomas F. Best. F&O Paper no. 131 (Geneva: WCC, 1986), p. 33.

80. Andre Birmele, LE SALUT EN JESUS CHRIST DANS LES DIALOGUES OECUMENIQUES (Paris: Editions du Cerf, 1986), pp. 47ff. Also Harding Meyer, "Rechtfertigung," in OEKUMENE LEXICON, p. 1003. JUSTIFICATION BY FAITH: Lutherans and Catholics in Dialogue, edited by George Anderson, T. Austin Murphy, and Joseph A. Burgess (Minneapolis: Augsburg Publishing House, 1985), pp. 17ff.

81. "The Malta Report," in Meyer/Vischer, GROWTH IN AGREEMENT, p. 174.

82. Harding Meyer, "The Doctrine of Justification in the Lutheran Dialogue with Other Churches," OIC 2/1981, pp. 86ff.

83. "Dialogue between the RCC and LWF," OIC 3/1982, p. 209.

84. Lutheran/Catholic Discussion on the Augsburg Confession: Documents 1977-1981, edited by Harding Meyer (Stuttgart: Kreuz Verlag, 1982), p. 6.

85. "All under One Christ," in Meyer/Vischer, GROWTH IN AGREEMENT, pp. 5, 24ff.

86. Cf. Gassmann/Meyer, RECHTFERTIGUNG IM OEKUMENISCHEN DIALOG: Dokumente und Einfuehrung. Oekumenische Perspektiven 12, edited by Harding Meyer and Guenther Gassmann (Frankfurt am Main: Verlag Otto Lembeck, 1987); and George Tavard, "Justification in Dialogue," OIC 4/1989, pp. 299-310.

87. "Salvation and the Church: An Agreed Statement by ARCIC II," OIC 1,2/1987, p. 158.

88. Ibid., p. 171.

89. FACING UNITY, p. 34.

90. Quoted in D. Hermann Dietzfelbinger, "Das katholisch-lutherisch Gespraech," in DARSTELLUNG UND GRENZEN DER SICHTBAREN EINHEIT DER KIRCHE, p. 93.

91. RECHTFERTIGUNG IM OEKUMENISCHEN DIALOG, p. 54.

92. THE CONDEMNATIONS OF THE REFORMATION ERA: Do They Still Divide? edited by Karl Lehmann and Wolfhart Pannenberg, translated by Margaret Kohl (Minneapolis: Fortress Press, 1989), pp. 29-69. For a convenient summary, see Yacob Tesfai, "Justification and Justice: An Ecumenical Focus," ET 10/1991, pp. 154-158.

93. "Observations of the Congregation for the Doctrine of the Faith on the Report of ARCIC-II: 'Salvation and the Church,' " OIC 4/1988, p. 379.

94. J. M. R. Tillard, "The Problem of Justification: A New Context of Study," OIC 4/1990, pp. 328-338.

95. SIND WIR UNSERES HEILES SCHMIED? (Gottingen: Vandenhoeck & Ruprecht, 1987), p. 53.

96. "Luther et l'unite des chretiens," DC 1866/1984, pp. 121-128. Gerharde Forde, "A Movement without a Move," DIALOG 30, no. 2, Spring 1991, pp. 84f.

97. Johannes Cardinal Willebrands, "The Catholic Church and the Ecumenical Movement," MSt 1/1988, pp. 24ff.

98. Cf. the discussion in Tavard, "Justification in Dialogue," pp. 299f.

99. Malta Report, in Myer/Vischer, GROWTH IN AGREEMENT, p. 175.

100. See the extensive discussion of the pros and cons in Andre Birmele, LE SALUT EN JESUS CHRIST DANS LES DIALOGUES OECUMENIQUES, pp. 45-125.

101. "An Opinion on *The Condemnations of the Reformation Era* Part One: Justification. The Theological Faculty, Georgia Augusta University, Goettingen," LQ 1/1991, pp. 1-62.

102. Meyer, THE FUTURE OF THE BILATERALS, p. 228. Andre Birmele and Thomas Ruster, BRAUCHEN WIR DIE EINHEIT DER KIRCHE? (Gottingen: Echter, Vandenhoeck und Ruprecht, 1986), p. 24; Andre Birmele, CONSENSUS OECUMENIQUE ET DIFFERENCE FONDAMENTALE (Paris: Editions du Centurion, 1987), p. 36.

103. THE THREE REPORTS, p. 27.

104. "All under One Christ," p. 242.

105. Fortino, "The Catholic-Orthodox Dialogue," pp. 194, 198.

106. BAPTISM, EUCHARIST, AND MINISTRY 1982-1990, p. 13.

3. Reception and the Dialogues

1. Doesta, "Theologie der oekumene—Oekumenische Theoriebildung," OR 2/1988, p. 218, quoted in Raiser, ECUMENISM IN TRANSITION, p. 16 (emphasis in the original).

2. G. Gassmann,"Die Rezeption der Dialoge—eine lutherische Perspektive," in LES DIALOGUES OECUMENIQUES HIER ET AUJOURD'HUI, pp. 306, 308.

3. Meyer/Vischer, GROWTH IN AGREEMENT, p. 8.

4. J. M. R. Tillard, "Reception—Communion," OIC 4/1992, p. 307.

5. Harding Meyer, "Rezeption von Konsens zur Gemeinschaft," DAS RINGEN

UM DIE EINHEIT DER CHRISTEN, p. 171.

6. "Inaugural Peter Ainslie Lecture: Called to Unity and Wholeness," MSt 1/ 1983, p. 1.

7. Meyer/Vischer, GROWTH IN AGREEMENT, p. 469.

8. FAITH AND ORDER 1985, pp. 33, 34.

9. Gassmann, "Die Rezeption der Dialoge," p. 311.

10. BAPTISM, EUCHARIST, AND MINISTRY 1982-1990: Report on the Process and Responses. F&O Paper no. 149 (Geneva: WCC, 1990), p. 13.

11. Emmanuel Sullivan, "Reception: Factor and Moment in Ecumenism," ET 7/ 1986, p. 105; W.-A. Purdy, "The Reception of the Dialogues—A Roman Catholic Account," in LES DIALOGUES OECUMENIQUES HIER ET AUJOURD'HUI, p. 294.

12. COUNCILS AND THE ECUMENICAL MOVEMENT, F&O Paper no. 5 (Geneva: WCC, 1968), p. 15.

13. Ion Bria, "La 'Reception' des resultats des dialogues," in LES DIALOGUES OECUMENIQUES HIER ET AUJOURD'HUI, pp. 288f.

14. Harding Meyer, "Wenn Verluste drohen: Oekumene in Uebergang," LM 5/ 90, p. 206.

15. William G. Rusch, RECEPTION: An Ecumenical Opportunity (Geneva: Lutheran World Federation, 1988), pp. 22ff.

16. Peter Neuner, "Konvergenzen im Verstaendnis des geistlichen Amtes— Moeglichkeiten zur Rezeption . . .," US 38 (1983), p. 198.

17. Walter Lindemann, "Notwendige Stufen eines oekumenischen Dialogs," LM 5/90, p. 209.

18. THE THREE REPORTS, p. 38.

19. Johannes Cardinal Willebrands, "The Ecumenical Dialogue and its Reception," BULLETIN/CENTRO PRO UNIONE 27/1985, p. 5.

20. Lukas Vischer, "Consensus in the Ecumenical Movement," OIC 4/1981, pp. 302-304.

21. John Zizioulas, "The Theological Problem of 'Reception,' " BULLETIN/ CENTRO PRO UNIONE 26/1984, pp. 3-6.

22. Mgr. Richard Stewart, "Reception: What Do the Churches Do with Ecumenical Agreements?," BULLETIN/CENTRO PRO UNIONE 25/1984, pp. 2-7.

23. COMMISSION ON FAITH AND ORDER: Minutes of the Standing Committee on F & O—1981, Annecy (Geneva: WCC, 1981), p. 25.

24. Harding Meyer and Aloys Klein, LUTHERAN/ROMAN CATHOLIC DISCUSSIONS ON THE AUGSBURG CONFESSION, p. 10.

25. Gassmann/Ehrenstrom, CONFESSIONS IN DIALOGUE, pp. 139, 141.

26. Raiser, ECUMENISM IN TRANSITION, p. 16. Cf. also Kinnamon: "These conversations [bilaterals], far from undermining confessional identity have strengthened it in recent years" (TRUTH AND COMMUNITY, p. 80).

27. Raiser, ECUMENISM IN TRANSITION, p. 16. In this connection, cf. the discussion of James Dunn, "Unity and Diversity in the Church: A New Testament Perspective," GREGORIANUM 71/4 (1990), pp. 629-656.

28. Gerhard Voss, "Canberra '91: Oekumenische Rechenschaft und Neuorientierung," KNA 5, 23 January 1991, pp. 14, 15.

29. "Reform and Recognition of Church Offices," JES 2/1973, pp. 390-401.

30. Ibid., pp. 400, 401.

31. Heinrich Fries, "Die dogmatische Relevanz der Ergebnisse theologischer Gespraeche zwischen roemisch-katholischen und evangelischen Theologen," OR 3/1980, pp. 267-269.

32. "What Kind of Unity: The Dialogue between the Traditions of East and West," in LAUSANNE 77: Fifty Years of Faith and Order. F&O Paper no. 82 (Geneva: WCC, 1977), p. 39.

33. Rusch, RECEPTION: An Ecumenical Opportunity, p. 71.

34. Heinrich Fries and Karl Rahner, UNITY OF THE CHURCHES—AN AC-TUAL POSSIBILITY (Philadelphia: Fortress Press, 1985), pp. 7-10; Heinrich Fries, "Einigung der Kirchen—reale Moeglichkeit," in Scharbau, EINHEIT DER KIRCHE, pp. 69-105.

35. Aidan Nichols, "Einigung der Kirchen—An Ecumenical Controversy," OIC 2/1985, pp. 139-166.

36. "Luther und die Einheit der Kirchen," IKZ 12/1983, pp. 568-582.

37. Heinrich Fries and Otto Hermann Pesch, STREITEN FUER DIE EINE KIRCHE (Muenchen: Koesel, 1987), pp. 13-84.

38. Harold Ditmanson, "Response to the Fries-Rahner Proposal for Church Unity," LQ 3/1987, pp. 375ff.

39. Reinhard Slenczka, "Die dogmatische Relevanz der Ergebnisse theologische Gespraeche zwischen roemisch-katholischen und evangelischen Theologen," OR 4/1980, p. 454.

40. Ibid., p. 455.

41. Ibid., p. 456.

42. Wolfgang Seibel, "Einheit der Kirchen," SdZ 2/1993, p. 74.

43. Robert W. Jenson, "The Elusive Bottom Lines," DIALOG 29, Spring 1990, p. 112; THE UNBAPTIZED GOD: The Basic Flaw in Ecumenical Theology (Minneapolis: Fortress Press, 1992), pp. 3f.

44. Mary Tanner, "Eighth Peter Ainslie Lecture on Christian Unity: Ecumenical Attitudes at the End of the Ecumenical Century," MSt 2/1990, p. 111.

45. Karl Lehmann, "How Can the Unity of the Church Be Achieved? The Next Steps on the Road to Unity: An Attempt at a Roman Catholic Answer," in Accra 1974 UNITING IN HOPE: Reports and Documents from the Meeting of the F&O Commission. F&O Paper no. 72 (Geneva: WCC, 1975), p. 96.

46. Aloys Klein, "Dialogue between the Roman Catholic Church and the Lutheran World Federation," OIC 3/1982, p. 209.

47. Patrick G. Henry, "From Breakthrough to Breakthrough," ER 43, pp. 29, 30.

48. Raiser, ECUMENISM IN TRANSITION, p. 25.

49. "Church as Communion: An Agreed Statement by ARCIC II," OIC 1/1991, p. 78.

50. For a critical assessment from an Anglican perspective, cf. Paul Avis, ECU-MENICAL THEOLOGY AND THE ELUSIVENESS OF DOCTRINE (London: SPCK, 1986).

51. Johannes Cardinal Willebrands, "Called to Unity and Wholeness," MSt 1/1983, p. 1.

52. Edward I. Cassidy, "The Catholic Church and Ecumenism as We Approach the Third Christian Millennium," BULLETIN/CENTRO PRO UNIONE 39/1991, p. 16.

53. For background information, cf. Kevin McDonald, "Development of Response to ARCIC-I: Background Information on Holy See's Reply," L'OSSERVATORE

ROMANO, weekly edition, no. 4, 29 February 1992, pp. 5-6.

54. "The Official Response of the Catholic Church to ARCIC I," OIC 1/1992, p. 38; also "Vatican Responds to ARCIC I Final Report," ORIGINS 21, no. 28, 19 December 1991, pp. 441ff.

55. "Anglican Theologian Comments on Vatican Response to ARCIC Agreements," ET 1/1992, p. 14.

56. Hugh Montefiore, "A Douche of Cold Water," CHURCH TIMES, no. 6722, 13 December 1991, p. 10.

57. Canon Michael Richards, "Twenty-five Years of Anglican-Roman Catholic Dialogue—Where Do We Go from Here?" OIC 2/1992, p. 126.

58. Canon Christopher Hill, "The Fundamental Question of Ecumenical Method," OIC 2/1992, p. 138.

59. R. T. Greenacre, "Diversity in Unity: A Problem for Anglicans," BULLETIN/CENTRO PRO UNIONE 39/1991, p. 5.

60. W.-A. Purdy, "Dialogue with the Anglican Communion," OIC 3/1982, p. 219.

61. Ibid.

62. Greenacre, "Diversity in Unity," p. 8.

63. Ibid.

64. Ibid.; cf. also Martin Dudley, "Waiting on the Common Mind: Authority in Anglicanism," OIC 1/1984, pp. 62-77.

65. Henry Chadwick, "A Retrospect on the Consequences of the 1988 Lambeth Conference for Anglican Ecumenism," MSt 2/1989, p. 211.

66. Garreth Bennett, "The Church of England and the Royal Supremacy," OIC 4/1986, pp. 304-313.

67. Cardinal Joseph Ratzinger, "Le dialogue Anglican-Catholique: Problemes et espoirs," DC, no. 1880, 2 September 1984, pp. 854-862.

68. J. M. R. Tillard, "La lecon oecumenique de Lambeth 88," IRENIKON 4/1988, p. 534.

69. Cassidy, "The Catholic Church and Ecumenism," p. 18.

70. Guenther Gassmann, "Rezeption im oekumenischen Kontext," OR 3/1977, p. 315.

71. Cf. "I Have Heard the Cry of My People," LWF REPORT, no. 28/29, December 1990, p. 127.

72. "*Facing Unity*—for What?," ET 11/1986, p. 177; also Hojen, "Wege und Irrwege," p. 406.

73. Eugene L. Brand, "The Lutheran World Federation: Communion and Structure," in GEMEINSAMER GLAUBE UND STRUKTUREN DER GEMEINSCHAFT, edited by Harding Meyer (Frankfurt am Main: Verlag Otto Lembeck, 1991), pp. 157-167.

74. Ibid., p. 166.

75. Lukas Vischer, "The Ecumenical Commitment of the World Alliance of Reformed Churches," in REFORMED WORLD 38, no. 5, p. 263, quoted in Alan D. Falconer, "How Do the Reformed Churches Now See the Roman Catholic Church?" OIC 1,2/1990, p. 60.

76. "The Leuenberg Concord," in INVITATION TO ACTION, 71. Dietrich Gang, "Strassburg 1987—Vollversammlung der Leuenberger Unterzeichnerkirchen," OR 3/1987, pp. 361-364.

77. Cf. pp. 36ff. above.

78. Cf. LEUENBERG—KONKORDIE ODER DISKORDIE? Oekumenische Kritik zur Konkordie reformatorischen Kirchen in Europa, edited by Ulrich Asendorf & F. W. Kuenneth (Berlin: Verlag die Spur, 1974).

79. Wenzel Lohff, "Ekklesiologische Konsequenzen der Leuenberger Konkordie," OR 2/1983, p. 207.

80. Hojen, "Wege und Irwege," OR 4/1985, p. 417.

81. Lukas Vischer, "Visible Unity—Realistic Goal or Mirage?" OIC 1/1982, p. 25.

82. Archm. Placide Deseille, "Point de vue orthodoxe sur l'unite de chretiens," LE MESSAGERE ORTHODOXE, no. 105, II-1987, p. 6.

83. "The Struggle for Justice and the Unity of the Church," in WHAT UNITY REQUIRES, p. 41.

84. Cf. SOEPI, no. 15, 2 May 1986, quoted in Roger Mehl, "Oecumenisme et strategies confessionnelles," in VERS DE NOUVEAUX OECUMENISMES, p. 189.

85. Robert Hotz, "Der Standpunkt der Orthodoxie (Statement)," in NEUE OEKUMENISCHE EISZEIT? edited by Hans Halter Benziger (Zuerich: Benziger Verlag, 1989), pp. 147-152.

86. Johannes Cardinal Willebrands, "Vatican II's Ecclesiology of Communion," OIC 3/1987, pp. 179-191. Cf. also Council for Promoting Christian Unity, "Directory for the Application of the Principles and Norms of Ecumenism," L'OSSERVATORE ROMANO, English edition, no. 24 (1295, 16 June 1993.

87. Francis A. Sullivan, S.J, "Subsistit in: The Significance of Vatican II's Decision to Say of the Church of Christ Not That It 'Is' but That It 'Subsists in' the Roman Catholic Church," OIC 2/1986, p. 119.

88. Ibid., p. 190.

89. Bent Dalsgaard Larsen, "Le ministere dans l'Eglise: A propos d'un document oecumenique," StT 1/1987, pp. 59-64.

90. J. M. R. Tillard, "The Eucharist in Apostolic Community," OIC 1/1988, p. 23 (emphasis in the original). Concerning other structural problems, cf. Lukas Vischer, "The Holy See, the Vatican State, and the Churches' Common Witness: A Neglected Ecumenical Problem," JES 11/1974, pp. 617-636; Donald P. Warwick, "Organizational Politics and Ecumenism," JES 11/1974, pp. 293-308.

91. "Letter to the Bishops of the Catholic Church on Some Aspects of the Church Understood as Communion," ET 9/1992, pp. 145/13.

92. See the reaction of some Protestants to this letter: K. Ruediger Durth, "Enttaeuschte Protestanten. Das Communio-Schreiben und die evangelische Kirche in Rheinland," KNA, no. 5, 27 January 1993, pp. 17-19.

93. Eilert Herms, EINHEIT DER CHRISTEN IN DER GEMEINSCHAFT DER KIRCHEN (Goettingen: Vandenhoeck & Ruprecht, 1984); VON DER GLAUBENSEINHEIT ZUR KIRCHENGEMEINSCHAFT: Plaedoyer fuer eine realistische Oekumene (Marburg: N. G. Elwert Verlag, 1989); Guenther Gassmann, Ein alter oekumenischer Hut. Anmerkungen zu Eilert Herms' 'Einigkeit im Fundamentalen,' " OR 3/88, pp. 340-342.

94. Ulrich Kuehn, "Das reformatorisches Proprium und die Oekumene." K&D, 32 (1986), pp. 171f.

95. Quoted in Heinrich Doering, "Einheit durch Vielfalt? Ueberlegungen zum gegenwaertigen Stand der Oekumene," US 2/89, p. 102.

96. "Bilaterals and the Uniting and United Churches," JES 3/1985, p. 385.

97. Andre Birmele and Thomas Ruster, BRAUCHEN WIR DIE EINHEIT DER KIRCHE? (Goettingen: Vandenhoeck & Ruprecht, 1986), p. 49.

4. Third World Reactions to the Dialogues

1. Cf. Yacob Tesfai, "Interconfessional Doctrinal Dialogue and Concerns of the Third World," ET 9/1991, pp. 135-138.
2. The Three Reports of the FORUM ON BILATERAL CONVERSATIONS. F&O Paper no. 107 (Geneva: WCC, 1981), p. 47 (emphasis added).
3. Ibid., p. 49.
4. FOURTH FORUM ON BILATERAL CONVERSATIONS REPORT. F&O Paper no. 125 (Geneva: WCC, 1985), p. 6.
5. LUTHERAN CONVERGENCE? An Analysis of the Lutheran Responses to the Convergence Document "Baptism, Eucharist, and Ministry" of the WCC Faith and Order Commission, LWF Report 25 (Geneva: LWF, 1988), p. 16.
6. John Deschner, "More than Inclusiveness: The New Christian Majority and the Shift in the Ecumenical Conversation on Church Unity," ER 1/1991, p. 58.
7. G. Gassmann, "Introduction: The Lima Process Continues," in CHURCHES RESPOND TO BEM, vol. 4, edited by Max Thurian (Geneva: WCC, 1987), p. x.
8. BAPTISM, EUCHARIST, AND MINISTRY 1982-1990: Report on the Process and Responses. F&O Paper no. 149 (Geneva: WCC, 1990), p. 11.
9. Irmgard Kind-Siegwalt, "Responses to Baptism, Eucharist, and Ministry," MSt 3/1989, p. 240.
10. "A 'Third World' Perspective on the Ecumenical Movement," in TOWARDS VISIBLE UNITY: Commission on F&O Lima 1982, Vol. 1: Minutes and Addresses, edited by Michael Kinnamon. F&O Paper no. 112 (Geneva: WCC, 1982), p. 61.
11. Ans van der Bent, VITAL ECUMENICAL CONCERNS: Sixteen Documentary Surveys (Geneva: WCC, 1986), p. 92.
12. Kind-Siegwalt, "Responses to Baptism, Eucharist, and Ministry," p. 243.
13. UNITING IN HOPE, Commission on F&O Accra 1974, pp. 33f.
14. FAITH AND RENEWAL, p. 233.
15. Mark S. Heim, "The WCC Faith and Order Plenary Session in Budapest," ET 19/1990, pp. 11-12.
16. Lukas Vischer, "Europaeische Theologie—weltweit gefordert?" OR 3/1979, pp. 233-247; THEOLOGIEN DER DRITTEN WELT: EATWOT als Herausforderung westlicher Theologie und Kirche, edited by Giancarlo Collet (Freiburg, 1990).
17. Bruno Chenu, THEOLOGIES CHRETIENNES DES TIERS MONDES (Paris: Le Centurion, 1987), pp. 11-16; Rosino Gibellini, THE LIBERATION THEOLOGY DEBATE (London: SCM Press, 1986), p. vii.
18. Erhard Kampenhausen, "Theologische Praxis in einer geteilten Welt," OR 2/1983, pp. 208-224.
19. IRRUPTION OF THE THIRD WORLD: Challenge to Theology, edited by Virginia Fabella and Sergio Torres (Maryknoll, NY: Orbis Books, 1983), p. xvi.
20. Cardinal Joseph Ratzinger, "Liberation Theology (March 1984)," in Hennelly, LIBERATION THEOLOGY: A DOCUMENTARY HISTORY, p. 368.
21. Norbert Greinacher, DIE KIRCHE DER ARMEN: Zur Theologie der Befreiung (Muenchen: R. Piper Verlag, 1980), p. 63.

22. Tissa Balasuriya, "Das akute Evangelium," in HERAUSGEFORDERT DURCH DIE ARMEN: Dokumente der oekumenischen Vereinigung von Dritte-Welt-Theologen 1976-1983, Theologie der Dritten Welt 4 (Freiburg: Herder Verlag, 1983), p. 28.

23. Per Frostin, LIBERATION THEOLOGY IN TANZANIA AND SOUTH AFRICA: A First World Interpretation, Studia Theologica Lundensia 42 (Lund: Lund University Press, 1988), pp. 1-13.

24. Sebastian Kappen, "Orientations for an Asian Theology," in ASIA'S STRUGGLE FOR FULL HUMANITY, edited by Virginia Fabella (Maryknoll, NY: Orbis Books, 1980), p. 117.

25. Ibid., p. 22. What Greinacher says about German theology is typical of "Western theology." He writes: "German theology lives to a certain degree in an academic ghetto. It often finds itself in the danger of withdrawing in an ivory tower and doing theology for the sake of theology. Its communication with the praxis of the church's rank and file and with the problems of the society is often very small. It is often the case that answers are given to questions which no one other than the researcher himself is interested in. It is also the case that these have very rarely to do with a critical reflection on the situation of the church and its place in society" (DIE KIRCHE DER ARMEN, p. 124). And also Walter Hollenweger: "Whatever one may say against it [i.e, Western theology], one thing is sure: it has become a highly specialized academic discipline which no longer serves the community for which it was once intended" ("The Ecumenical Significance of Oral Christianity," ER 1989, p. 263).

26. "Final Statement," Ecumenical Dialogue of Third World Theologians, Dar es Salaam, Tanzania, August 5-12, 1976, in THE EMERGENT GOSPEL: Theology from the Underside of History, edited by Sergio Torres and Virginia Fabella (Maryknoll, NY: Orbis Books, 1978), p. 269.

27. Sergio Torres, "Einfuehrung: Die oekumenische Vereinigung von Dritte-Welt-Theologen," in HERAUSGEFORDERT DURCH DIE ARMEN, p. 15.

28. Kappen, "Orientations for an Asian Theology," in ASIA'S STRUGGLE FOR FULL HUMANITY, edited by Fabella, p. 122.

29. Balasuriya, "Towards the Liberation of Theology in Asia," in ASIA'S STRUGGLE FOR FULL HUMANITY, edited by Fabella, p. 25.

30. "The Confessing Church in Asia and Its Theological Task," A C.C.A. Statement, in WHAT ASIAN CHRISTIANS ARE THINKING: Readings from Asian Theologians, edited by Douglas J. Elwood (Manilla: New Day Publishers, 1976), p. 44.

31. Jean-Marc Ela, MY FAITH AS AN AFRICAN (Maryknoll, NY: Orbis Books, 1988), p. 99.

32. Ibid., p. 153.

33. Balasuriya, "Towards the Liberation of Theology in Asia," p. 19.

34. WHAT ASIAN CHRISTIANS ARE THINKING, p. 42.

35. Ibid., p. 44.

36. ASIAN VOICES IN CHRISTIAN THEOLOGY, edited with an introduction by Gerald H. Anderson (Maryknoll, NY: Orbis Books, 1976), p. 105.

37. WHAT ASIAN CHRISTIANS ARE THINKING, p. 45.

38. UNITING IN HOPE, Accra 1974, p. 126.

39. Saphy F. Athyl, "Toward an Asian Christian Theology," in WHAT ASIAN CHRISTIANS ARE THINKING, p. 82.

40. Manas Buthelezi "Towards Indigenous Theology in South Africa," in THE

EMERGENT GOSPEL, edited by Torres and Fabella, p. 72.

41. Manas Buthelezi, "In Christ—One Community in the Spirit," in CHRIST A NEW COMMUNITY: The Proceedings of the Sixth Assembly of the Lutheran World Federation, Dar-es-Salaam, Tanzania, June 13-25, 1977, edited by Arne Sovik (Geneva: LWF, 1977), p. 94.

42. Ibid., p. 90.

43. John Gatu, "Response," ibid., p. 53.

44. Note the tragicomic story related by the late president of the LWF, Bishop Josiah Kibira from Tanzania: "Has Luther Reached Africa?: The Testimony of a Confused Lutheran," ATJ 1/1983, pp. 6-15.

45. Kevin Ward, "Catholic-Protestant Relations in Uganda: An Historical Perspective," ATJ 3/1984, p. 180.

46. Ibid., p. 183.

47. Manas Buthelezi, "A Voice from South Africa," in WHAT UNITY REQUIRES, p. 48.

48. Mercy Amba Oduyoye, HEARING AND KNOWING: Theological Reflections on Christianity in Africa (Maryknoll, NY: Orbis Books, 1986), p. 68.

49. Samuel Rayan, "Theological Priorities in India Today," in IRRUPTION OF THE THIRD WORLD, edited by Fabella and Torres, p. 40.

50. "Why Planetary Theology?" in THIRD WORLD LIBERATION THEOLOGIES, A Reader, edited by Deane William Ferm (Maryknoll, NY: Orbis Books, 1986), p. 326.

51. Rayan, "Theological Priorities in India Today," p. 40.

52. Manas Buthelezi, "Commentary on an African-American Perspective on the Text 'The Church as Mystery and Prophetic Sign,' " MSt 4/1989, p. 353.

53. L. Vischer, "Europaeische Theologie," p. 243.

54. Geoffrey Wainright, "Rain Stopped Play? The Anglican Communion at Lambeth 1988," MSt 2/1989, p. 211.

55. C. S. Song, THIRD-EYE THEOLOGY: Theology in Formation in Asian Settings, rev. ed. (Maryknoll, NY: Orbis Books, 1990), p. 27.

56. James Cone, "Reflections from the Perspective of U.S. Blacks: Black Theology and Third World Theology," in IRRUPTION OF THE THIRD WORLD, edited by Fabella and Torres, p. 240.

57. Gustavo Gutierrez, "Two Theological Perspectives: Liberation Theology and Progressivist Theology," in THE EMERGENT GOSPEL, edited by Torres and Fabella, p. 249; for another perspective, cf. Walter Altmann, LUTHER AND LIBERATION: A Latin American Perspective, translated by Mary M. Solberg (Minneapolis: Augsburg Fortress, 1992).

58. Virgil Elizondo, "Towards an American-Hispanic Theology of Liberation in the U.S.A.," in Ferm, THIRD WORLD LIBERATION THEOLOGIES, p. 54.

59. J. Russel Chandran, "A Methodological Approach to Third World Theology," in IRRUPTION OF THE THIRD WORLD, edited by Fabella and Torres, p. 82.

60. "Final Statement," ibid., p. 204.

61. Gustavo Gutierrez, A THEOLOGY OF LIBERATION: History, Politics and Salvation (London: SCM Press, rev. ed. Maryknoll, NY: Orbis Books, 1988), p. 104.

62. For what follows, cf. Yacob Tesfai, "Concepts of Division and Unity in the Ecumenical Movement," ET 3/1993, pp. 9/41-15/47.

63. Edmund Schlink, THE THEOLOGY OF THE LUTHERAN CONFES-SIONS (Philadelphia: Muhlenberg Press, 1961), pp. 207f. Richard John Neuhaus, THE CATHOLIC MOMENT: The Paradox of the Church in the Postmodern World (San Francisco: Harper & Row, 1987), p. 93.

64. "The Road to Damascus: Kairos and Conversion," in KAIROS: Three Prophetic Challenges to the Church, edited by Robert McAfee Brown (Grand Rapids, Michigan: William B. Eerdmans, 1990), pp. 113, 137.

65. Jon Sobrino and Juan Hernandez Pico, THEOLOGY OF CHRISTIAN SOLIDARITY, translated from the Spanish by Phillip Berryman (Maryknoll, NY: Orbis Books, 1985), p. 30.

66. "The Kairos Document," in Brown, KAIROS, p. 27.

67. Robin Peterson, "Unity in Struggle: The Church and Ecumenism in South Africa," ET 11/1990, p. 161.

68. Gutierrez, THEOLOGY OF LIBERATION, p. 75.

69. Paul A. Crow, "Ecumenics as Reflection on Models of Christian Unity," ER 1987, pp. 401-402.

70. "The Kairos Document," p. 26.

71. Sobrino and Pico, THEOLOGY OF CHRISTIAN SOLIDARITY, p. 27.

72. "The Kairos Document," p. 62.

73. Jose Miguez Bonino, DOING THEOLOGY IN A REVOLUTIONARY SITUATION (Philadelphia: Fortress Press, 1975), p. 170.

74. Sobrino and Pico, THEOLOGY OF CHRISTIAN SOLIDARITY, p. 31.

75. Peterson, "Unity in Struggle," p. 164.

76. J. N. J. Kritzinger, "The Kairos Document—a Call to Conversion," MISSIONALIA 16:3 (November 1988), pp. 126-145.

77. Jose Miguez Bonino, "A Latin American Attempt to Locate the Question of Unity," ER 1974, pp. 210-221.

78. Lysaneas Maciel, "The Struggle for Human Rights: An Ecumenical Event," in FAITH BORN IN THE STRUGGLE FOR LIFE: A Re-reading of Protestant Faith in Latin America, edited by Dow Kirkpatrick (Grand Rapids, Michigan: William B. Eerdmans, 1988), p. 292.

79. Jean-Pierre Sebastian, "Welche Oekumene fuer Lateinamerika?" OR 3/1983, p. 316.

80. Juan Luis Segundo, THE LIBERATION OF THEOLOGY (Maryknoll, NY: Orbis Books, 1988), p. 149.

81. Sebastian, "Welche Oekumene?" p. 316.

82. COMMISSION ON FAITH AND ORDER 1981, Annecy, pp. 29f.

83. Cf. Aloysius Pieris, THEOLOGIE DER BEFREIUNG IN ASIEN: Christentum im Kontext der Armut und der Religionen (Freiburg: Herder, 1986), pp. 239ff.; "Oekumenismus angesichts der Suche Asiens nach Christus," US 1979, pp. 319-332.

84. Pieris, THEOLOGIE DER BEFREIUNG IN ASIEN, p. 247 (emphasis in the original).

85. Cf. J. Paul Rajashekar, "Dialogue with People of Other Faiths and Ecumenical Theology," ER 1987, p. 457.

86. M. M. Thomas, "Christlicher Oekumenismus und Saekularoekumenismus," OR 2/1979, p. 174. Cf. the reaction of Wolfhart Pannenberg: "Die 'westliche,' Christenheit in der Oekumene: Eine Antwort an M. M. Thomas," OR 3/1979, pp. 306-316.

5. Common Emerging Themes

1. Cf. Francois Biot, "The Idea of Orthodoxy in Cardinal Ratzinger's Book: Conversation on the Faith," in ORTHODOXY AND HETERODOXY: Concilium, edited by Johann-Baptist Metz and Edward Schillebeeckx (Edinburgh: T. & T. Clark, 1987), p. 126.

2. All in LIBERATION THEOLOGY: A Documentary History, edited with Introductions, Commentary and Translations by Alfred T. Hennelly, S.J. (Maryknoll, NY: Orbis Books, 1990), pp. 393-414, 461-497, and 367-374 respectively.

3. Cardinal Joseph Ratzinger, "Liberation Theology," in ibid., pp. 373, 374.

4. Carl E. Braaten, "Liberation Theology Coming of Age," DIALOG 4/1989, p. 242.

5. Cf. the discussion in Craig L. Nessan, ORTHOPRAXIS OR HERESY: The North American Theological Response to Latin American Liberation Theology (Atlanta, Georgia: Scholars Press, 1989).

6. Richard John Neuhaus, THE CATHOLIC MOMENT: The Paradox of the Church in the Post-Modern World (San Francisco: Harper and Row Publishers, 1987), p. 187.

7. Jeffrey Gros, "Discovering the Gospel: Dialogue in the Catholic Church," THE CHRISTIAN CENTURY, 2 May 1990, p. 460.

8. Leonardo Boff, "Vatican Instruction Reflects European Mind-Set," in Hennelly, LIBERATION THEOLOGY, pp. 415-418.

9. Tissa Balasuriya, "Liberation Theology on Trial," LOGOS 23, no. 4 (December 1984), pp. 67ff.

10. Gustavo Gutierrez, "Criticism Will Deepen, Clarify Liberation Theology," in Hennelly, LIBERATION THEOLOGY, p. 423.

11. "The Poor Judge: The Magisterium and Liberation Theologians," in Metz/Schillebeeckx, ORTHODOXY AND HETERODOXY, p. xii.

12. "The Red-Hot Issue: Liberation Theology," ibid., p. 508.

13. Ibid., p. 508.

14. Theo Witvliet, A PLACE IN THE SUN: Liberation Theology in the Third World (London: SCM Press, 1985), p. 167.

15. Maria Clara Lucchetti Bingemer, "Preface: Third World Theologies: Conversion to Others," in THIRD WORLD THEOLOGIES: Commonalities and Divergences, edited by K. C. Abraham (Maryknoll, NY: Orbis Books, 1986), p. xii.

16. Cf. Cone, "Reflections from Perspectives of U.S. Blacks," pp. 235-245; "From Geneva to Sao Paulo: A Dialogue between Black Theology and Latin American Liberation Theology," in THE CHALLENGE OF BASIC CHRISTIAN COMMUNITIES, edited by Sergio Torres and John Eagleson (Maryknoll, NY: Orbis Books, 1988), pp. 265-281.

17. Mercy Amba Oduyoye, "Reflections from a Third World Woman's Perspective: Women's Experience and Liberation Theologies," in IRRUPTION OF THE THIRD WORLD, edited by Fabella and Torres, pp. 246-255.

18. DOING THEOLOGY IN A DIVIDED WORLD, edited by Virginia Fabella and Sergio Torres (Maryknoll, NY: Orbis Books, 1985), p. ix.

19. Dirk Doering and Erhard Kamphausen, "EATWOT and Its Significance: A European Perspective," in IRRUPTION OF THE THIRD WORLD, edited by Fabella and Torres, p. 270.

20. Erhard Kamphausen, "Eigenstaendigkeit und Dialog: Zum Weg kontextueller Befreiungstheologien in Sued und Nord," OR 31/2 (April 1982), pp. 205-222; Per Frostin, "The Hermeneutics of the Poor—The Epistemological 'Break' in Third World Theologies," ST 2/1985, pp. 127-150; Lars Thunberg, "Third World Theologies and the Appeal to History," ST 1986, pp. 95-113.

21. Heinrich Doering, "Die Communio—Ekklesiologie als Grundmodell und Chance der oekumenische Theologie," in COMMUNIO SANCTORUM: Einheit der Christen—Einheit der Kirche. Festschrift fuer Bischof Paul-Werner Scheele, edited by Joseph Schreiner and Klaus Wittstadt (Wuerzburg: Echter Verlag, 1988), pp. 439-468.

22. Cullmann, UNITY THROUGH DIVERSITY, p. 35.

23. Adelbert Denaux, "L'Eglise comme Communion," NRT 110, 1988, pp. 16-37 and 161-180.

24. J. M. R. Tillard, "L'Eglise de Dieu est une Communion," IRENIKON 4/1980, pp. 451ff.

25. VINGT ANS APRES VATICAN II: Synod extraordinaire Rome 1985, edited by Jaques Potin and Documentation Catholique (Paris: Le Centurion, 1986), especially p. 231.

26. International Bilateral Dialogues 1965-1991—Commissions, Meetings, Themes and Reports: Fifth Forum on Bilateral Conversations Report, compiled by Guenther Gassmann. F&O Paper no. 156 (Geneva: WCC, 1991), pp. 45f. Cf. GROWTH IN AGREEMENT, and DOKUMENTE WACHSENDER UEBEREINSTIMMUNG, vol. 2, 1982-1990, edited by Harding Meyer et al. (Paderborn: Bonifatius Verlag, 1992).

27. George H. Tavard, "Tradition as Koinonia in Historical Perspective," OIC 2/1988, p. 97.

28. "The Unity of the Church as Koinonia: Gift and Calling," in SIGNS OF THE SPIRIT, pp. 172-174.

29. TOWARDS KOINONIA IN FAITH, LIFE, AND WITNESS, draft of a working document, Dublin, Ireland, April 1992, WCC, Commission on F&O.

30. Martin H. Cressey, "A Vital Role in the Whole Ecumenical Movement: The Faith and Order Commission Takes up Its Tasks after Canberra," MSt 1/1992, p. 40.

31. SIGNS OF THE SPIRIT, 139.

32. Mary Tanner, "The Time Has Come: A Vision of the Fifth World Conference on Faith and Order," ER 1/1993, p. 6. Cf. Aram Keshishian, "Growing Together towards a Full Koinonia," MSt 1/1993, pp. 31-49.

33. COMMUNIO—KOINONIA: A Study by the Institute for Ecumenical Research in Strasbourg (Strasbourg, 1990), pp. 9, 10.

34. L'OSSERVATORE ROMANO, no. 24, 17 June 1992, pp. 8-10.

35. Basel Final Document, no. 22; cf. Anna Marie Aagaard, "The Common Good, Structures of Resistance, and the Politics of Greed: On Church and Economy," ST 45 (1991), pp. 3-17.

36. Gutierrez, A THEOLOGY OF LIBERATION, p. 150.

37. Oduyoye, HEARING AND KNOWING, pp. 109ff.; John S. Mbiti, "Eucharistie, Koinonia, und Gemeinschaft in der afrikanischen Christenheit," ZfM 3/1990, pp. 149-154.

38. M. M. Thomas, ER 1989, pp. 177-183.

39. BEM, in GROWTH IN AGREEMENT, p. 479.

40. GROWTH IN AGREEMENT, p. 65.

41. Ibid., p. 69.

42. Konrad Raiser, "Towards a Sharing Community," in SHARING LIFE: Official Report of the WCC Consultation on Koinonia: Sharing Life in a World Community, El Ascorial, Spain, October 1987, edited by Huibert van Beck (Geneva: WCC, 1989), p. 17.

43. Mercy Amba Oduyoye, "The African Family as a Symbol of Ecumenism," OIC 3/1989, p. 250.

44. Oduyoye, HEARING AND KNOWING, p. 111.

45. Gutierrez, A THEOLOGY OF LIBERATION, p. 149.

46. Ibid., p. 150.

47. Enrique Dussel, "Das Brot der Feier: Gemeinschaftszeichen der Gerechtigkeit," CONCILIUM 2/1982, pp. 120-129.

48. WHAT UNITY REQUIRES, p. 48.

49. Ulrich Duchrow, GLOBAL ECONOMY: A Confessional Issue for the Churches? (Geneva: WCC, 1987), p. 111.

50. Ela, MY FAITH AS AN AFRICAN, p. 98; cf. also Ela, AFRICAN CRY (Maryknoll, NY: Orbis Books, 1986), pp. 1-8.

51. BEM, in GROWTH IN AGREEMENT, p. 479. Cf. also Juergen Moltmann, NEUER LEBENSSTIL: Schritte zur Gemeinde (Muenchen: Chr. Kaiser Verlag, 1977), pp. 96-113.

52. F&O Porto Alegre (1987) Consultation, MSt 1/1989, p. 112.

53. For a succinct history of the first phase of the studies of this issue, see Gieko Mueller-Fahrenholz, UNITY IN TODAY'S WORLD: The Faith and Order Studies on Unity of the Church—Unity of Humankind. F&O Paper no. 88 (Geneva: WCC, 1978).

54. Meredith B. Handspicker, "Faith and Order, 1948-1968," in A HISTORY OF THE ECUMENICAL MOVEMENT: The Ecumenical Advance 1948-1968, vol. 2, edited by Harold E. Fey, p. 170.

55. John Deschner, "The Unity of the Church and the Unity of Mankind: An Appraisal of the Study," in UNITING IN HOPE, Commission on Faith and Order, Accra 1974, F&O Paper no. 72 (Geneva: WCC, 1975), p. 81.

56. Ibid., p. 83.

57. "Towards Unity in Tension: Statement of the Conference," in UNITING IN HOPE, ACCRA 1974, p. 93.

58. COMMISSION ON F&O 1981, Annecy, p. 31.

59. Duchrow, CONFLICT OVER THE ECUMENICAL MOVEMENT, pp. 333, 335.

60. COMMISSION ON F&O 1981, Annecy, pp. 31, 36.

61. John Deschner, in TOWARDS VISIBLE UNITY, Commission on F&O Lima 1982, vol. 2: Study Papers and Reports (Geneva: WCC, 1982), p. 187.

62. Ibid., pp. 184, 185.

63. Thomas F. Best, "Listening and Learning in Harlem: The WCC Faith and Order/Black Churches in the U.S. Consultation," MSt 4/1989, p. 333.

64. Wolfhart Pannenberg, "Unity of the Church—Unity of Mankind," MSt 4/1982, p. 185.

65. Paul A. Crow, "Unity and Renewal: Introductory Reflections," in FAITH AND ORDER Commission on F&O, Stavanger 1985, p. 166.

66. COMMISSION ON FAITH AND ORDER: Minutes of the Meeting of

the Standing Commission 1984, Crete. F&O paper no. 21 (Geneva: WCC, 1984), p. 34.

67. SEPARATION WITHOUT HOPE? Julio de Santa Ana (ed.) (Geneva: WCC, 1978), p. 185.

68. CHURCH AND WORLD: The Unity of the Church and the Renewal of Human Community. A Faith and Order Study Document. F&O Paper no. 151 (Geneva: WCC, 1990).

69. Konrad Raiser, "Einheit der Kirche—Einheit der Menschheit: Ueberlegungen zum Thema oekumenischer Theologie," OR 1/1986, p. 19.

70. Manas Buthelezi, "Commentary on an African-American Perspective on the Text 'The Church as Mystery and Prophetic Sign,' " MSt 4/1989, p. 353.

71. "An African-American Perspective on the Unity of the Church and the Renewal of Human Community," MSt 4/1988, p. 339.

72. "Unity and Renewal: The Ecclesiological Significance of the Churches' Involvement in Issues of Justice, the Singapore Consultation, Nov. 1986," MSt 1/1988, p. 79.

73. "Report of the Porto Alegre, Brazil (1987) Unity and Renewal Consultation," MSt 1/1989, p. 104.

74. UNITY IN TODAY'S WORLD: The F&O Studies on "Unity of the Church—Unity of Mankind," edited by Geiko Mueller-Fahrenholz. F&O Paper no. 88 (Geneva: WCC, 1978), p. 210.

75. Deschner, TOWARDS VISIBLE UNITY, vol. 2, p. 193.

76. Paul A. Crow, Jr., "The Unity of the Church and the Renewal of Human Community: A Perspective from Budapest," MSt 2/1991, p. 138.

77. Hennelly, LIBERATION THEOLOGY, p. xii.

78. D. Preman Niles, RESISTING THE THREATS OF LIFE: Covenanting for Justice, Peace, and the Integrity of Creation (Geneva: WCC, 1991), p. 11.

79. Duchrow, GLOBAL ECONOMY, p. 72.

80. GOOD NEWS TO THE POOR, edited by Julio de Santa Ana (Geneva: WCC, 1978).

81. SEPARATION WITHOUT HOPE? edited by Julio de Santa Ana (Geneva: WCC, 1978).

82. Martin E. Marty, THE MODERN SCHISM: Three Paths to the Secular (London: SCM Press, 1969), pp. 61ff.

83. Wolfgang Schweitzer, "Sind wir eine mit der Armen solidarische Kirche? Anmerkungen zu dem Beitrag von Hebly und Houtepen," OR 2/1981, p. 183.

84. J. A. Hebly and Anton W. J. Houtepen, "Eine mit der Armen solidarische Kirche?" OR 1/1981, p. 87.

85. Paul A. Crow, "Editorial: The Church and the Poor," MSt 4/1981, p. 365.

86. A. Bellagamba, "Preferential Option for the Poor: African Perspective," AFRICAN CHRISTIAN STUDIES 3/1987, pp. 19-47.

87. Julio de Santa Ana, "An Open Letter to the Churches in the USA," MSt 4/1981, p. 367.

88. Letty Russell, "Unity and Renewal," p. 65.

89. NAIROBI TO VANCOUVER: 1975-1983 Report of the Central Committee to the Sixth Assembly of the WCC (Geneva: WCC, 1983), p. 160.

90. THE PREFERENTIAL OPTION FOR THE POOR, edited by Richard John Neuhaus (Grand Rapids, Michigan: William B. Eerdmans, 1988).

91. Wolfgang Schweitzer, "Was hoffen wir wirklich?" OR 3/1979, p. 255.

92. Mueller-Fahrenholz, UNITY IN TODAY'S WORLD, p. 43.

93. Peter Sandner, "Melbourne—Mission und Eucharistie," OR 4/1980, p. 483; cf. further, THY KINGDOM COME: Mission Perspectives, Report on the World Conference on Mission and Evangelism, Melbourne, Australia, 12-25 May 1980 (Geneva: WCC, 1980).

94. Deschner, "The Unity of the Church and the Renewal of Human Community," in TOWARDS VISIBLE UNITY, vol. 2, p. 195.

95. FAITH AND ORDER LOUVAIN 1971. F&O Paper no. 60 (Geneva: WCC, 1971), p. 191.

96. Deschner, "The Unity of the Church," p. 86.

97. COMMISSION ON 1981, Annecy, pp. 36f.

98. F&O Porto Alegre Consultation (1987). MSt 1/1988, p. 112.

99. Raiser, "Einheit der Kirche," p. 27.

100. GLOBAL ECONOMY, pp. 191f. (emphasis in the original).

101. Quoted in Nolan, GOD IN SOUTH AFRICA, p. 192.

102. Thomas Rayan, "La 7e Assemblee generale du Conseil oecumenique des Eglises," OECUMENISME, no. 101, March 1991, pp. 31-37.

103. GATHERED FOR LIFE, p. 255.

104. Konrad Raiser, "Growing into Ecumenical Covenant," in CATALYSING HOPE FOR JUSTICE, p. 57.

105. Wolfgang Huber, "Mangel an Klarheit," EvKomm 23/1990, p. 289.

106. Georg Hintzen, "Die ekklesiologische Bedeutung des konziliaren Prozesses fuer Gerechtigkeit, Frieden, und Bewahrung der Schoepfung," OR 3/1989, p. 289.

107. Lukas Vischer, "Is This Really the Unity We Seek?" ER 4/1992, pp. 467ff.

108. Guenther Gassmann, "Canberra Erklaerung sur Einheit der Kirche," OR 2/1991, p. 179.

109. Janice Love, "JPIC, the WCC, and the Future of the Ecumenical Movement," OR 4/1990, pp. 396-414.

110. FINAL DOCUMENT of the European Ecumenical Assembly PEACE WITH JUSTICE, 15-21 May 1989, Basel, Switzerland.

111. Walter Klaiber, "Die Zukunft der oekumenischen Bewegung," US 4/1991, p. 276.

112. Aloys Klein, "Oekumene—Quo Vadis?," MATERIALDIENST der oekumenischen Centrale 2/1990, no. 8, p. 30.

113. Michael Strauss, OEKUMENE AUF DER WEG: Der konziliarer Prozess zwischen Vancouver und Canberra (Bielefeld: Luther-Verlag, 1991); BETWEEN THE FLOOD AND THE RAINBOW: Interpreting the Conciliar Process of Mutual Commitment (Covenant) to Justice, Peace, and the Integrity of Creation, compiled by D. Preman Niles (Geneva: WCC, 1992).

114. Cf. Yacob Tesfai, "JPIC—the Seoul Convocation of the WCC," ATJ 1/1991, pp. 17-27.

115. SIGNS OF THE SPIRIT, p. 187.

116. SIGNS OF THE SPIRIT, p. 174.

117. Raiser, ECUMENISM IN TRANSITION, p. 17.

118. Heinz Joachim Held, "Forderungen des Evangeliums: Neutestamentliche Gedanken zum Thema der Gerechtigkeit in der oekumenische Debatte," OR 2/1988, p. 164.

119. Cf. the special issue "Justice, Peace, and the Integrity of Creation: Looking to the Future," ER 3/1992.

120. Quoted in Anton Houtepen, "Key Issues in Some JPIC Texts—a Theological Evaluation," EXCHANGE 19, no. 3 (December 1990), p. 244.

121. Raiser, ECUMENISM IN TRANSITION, p. 18.

122. Konrad Raiser, "Buerge der Kirche—im Licht ihrer oekumenischen Moeglichkeit: Zum Gedanken an Ernst Lange," OR 3/1987, p. 287.

123. COSTLY UNITY: A WCC Consultation on Koinonia and JPIC, Ronde Folk High School, Ronde, Denmark, February 24-28, 1993 (Geneva: WCC, 1993), p. 5.

124. THE COMMUNITY OF WOMEN AND MEN IN THE CHURCH, edited by Constance F. Parvey (Geneva: WCC, 1981), pp. 9-13.

125. COMMISSION ON F&O 1981, Annecy, pp. 53-57.

126. Bangalore 1978 SHARING IN ONE HOPE, p. 163.

127. Constance E. Parvey, "The Community Study: Its Mixed Meanings for the Churches," in BEYOND UNITY-IN-TENSION: Unity, Renewal, and the Community of Women and Men, edited by Thomas F. Best. F&O Paper no. 138 (Geneva: WCC, 1988), p. 40.

6. Concluding Remarks

1. THE CHURCHES SEARCH FOR UNITY, p. 290.

2. "Die eine Welt als Herausforderung an das westliche Christentum," US 2/1989, pp. 314-322.

3. Walbert Buehlmann, "Komm, heiliger Geist! Visionen einer Weltkirche," in GOTT KOMMT AUS DER DRITTEN WELT: Erfahrungen und Zeugnisse, edited by Johannes Roeser (Freiburg: Herder, 1988), p. 213.

4. Ernest W. Lefever, AMSTERDAM TO NAIROBI: The World Council of Churches and the Third World (Washington: Ethics and Public Policy Center of Georgetown University, 1979); NAIROBI TO VANCOUVER: The World Council of Churches and the World, 1975-87 (Washington: Ethics and Public Policy Center, 1987), pp. 81f.

5. Wolfhart Pannenberg, "Unity of the Church—Unity of Humankind: A Critical Appraisal of a Shift in Ecumenical Direction," MSt 4/1982, pp. 485-490.

6. Enrique Dussel, "The Ebb and Flow of the Gospel," VOICES FROM THE THIRD WORLD 10, no. 4, pp. 31-40.

7. Norman Goodall, ECUMENICAL PROGRESS: A Decade of Change in the Ecumenical Movement 1961-1971 (London: Oxford University Press, 1972), p. 6 (emphasis added).

8. David J. Bosch, TRANSFORMING MISSION: Paradigm Shifts in Theology and Mission, American Society of Missiology Series, no. 16 (Maryknoll, NY: Orbis Books, 1992), pp. 7, 363ff.

9. Constance Colonna-Cesari, URBI ET ORBI: Enquete sur la Geopolitique Vaticane (Paris: Editions La Decouverte, 1992), pp. 171-221.

10. Jan Heijke, "African Synod—Colonization of Africa?" EXCHANGE 21, no. 3, December 1992, pp. 177-230.

11. Dean Peerman, "CELAM IV: Maneuvering and Marking Time in Santo Dominigo," CHRISTIAN CENTURY 110, no. 5, 17 February 1993, pp. 180-185.

12. Douglas J. Elwood, "Riding the Third Wave," INTERNATIONAL BUL-

LETIN OF MISSIONARY RESEARCH, January 1992, p. 24.

13. Ludwig Ruetti, "Westliche Identitaet und weltweite Oekumene," in OEKUMENISCHE THEOLOGIE: Ein Arbeitsbuch, edited by Peter Lengsfeld (Stuttgart: Verlag W. Kohlhammer, 1980), p. 286 (italics in the original).

14. Ulrich Duchrow, EUROPE IN THE WORLD SYSTEM 1492-1992: Is Justice Possible? (Geneva: WCC, 1992).

15. Yacob Tesfai, "Invasion and Evangelization: Reflections on a Quincentenary," IRM 81, no. 324 (1992), pp. 525-541; "African and Asian Spirituality: New Awareness and Orientation," VOTW 2/1992, pp. 189-221.

16. Heinrich Balz, "Mission und Kolonialismus," ZfM 3/1991, pp. 175-181; also Ruetti, "Westliche Identitaet," pp. 288ff.

17. Ludwig Ruetti, "Westliche Identitaet als theologisches Problem," ZfM 2/1978, pp. 97-107.

18. CHINA AND CHRISTIANITY: Historical and Future Encounters, James D. Whitehead, Yu-Ming Shaw, and N. J. Girardot, editors (Notre Dame, Indiana: Notre Dame University Press, 1979).

19. David M. Paton, CHRISTIAN MISSION AND THE JUDGMENT OF GOD (London: SCM Press, 1953), p. 53.

20. Lawrence J. Burkholder, "Rethinking Christian Life and Mission in the Light of the Chinese Experience," in CHINA AND CHRISTIANITY, p. 208.

21. Konrad Raiser, ECUMENISM IN TRANSITION (Geneva, WCC, 1991), p. 35.

22. Philip Potter, "Preface," in Elizabeth Adler, A SMALL BEGINNING: An Assessment of the First Five Years of the PCR (Geneva: WCC, 1974), p. v.

23. Adler, A SMALL BEGINNING, p. 7; and "Evaluation of Combatting Racism in Europe: PCR and the Churches in Europe," in RACISM IN EUROPE: Final Report, European Church Consultation on Combatting Racism, Stockholm, March 2-9, 1980 (Sigtuna: Nordic Ecumenical Institute, 1980), pp. 30-34.

24. Roger Williamson, "Die EKD in Deutschland, die Oekumene, und das institutionelle Dilemma: Das Programme zur Bekaempfung des Rassismus als Fallstudie," OR 3/1988, p. 298.

25. Mercy Amba Oduyoye, "A Decade and a Half of Ecumenism in Africa," in VOICES OF UNITY, p. 77.

26. Bosch, TRANSFORMING MISSION: Paradigm Shifts in Theology of Mission, American Society of Missiology Series, no. 16 (Maryknoll, New York: Orbis Books, 1991), pp. 363ff.

27. Richard D. N. Dickinson, TO SET AT LIBERTY THE OPPRESSED: Towards an Understanding of Christian Responsibilities of Development/Liberation (Geneva: WCC, 1975), p. 44 (emphasis added).

28. THE SILENCING OF LEONARDO BOFF: The Vatican and the Future of World Christianity (London: Collins, 1989), pp. 12, 13.

29. Dorothee Soelle, "Dialectics of Enlightenment," in DOING THEOLOGY IN A DIVIDED WORLD, p. 84.

30. Philip Potter, "The Third World in the Ecumenical Movement," ER 1/1972, pp. 70f.

31. James Cone, "Black Ecumenism and the Liberation Struggle," in SPEAKING THE TRUTH: Ecumenism, Liberation, and Black Theology (Grand Rapids, Michigan: William B. Eerdmans, 1986), p. 142.

32. Nils Ehrenstroem, "Movements for International Friendship and Life and Work 1925-1948," in A HISTORY OF THE ECUMENICAL MOVEMENT, vol. 1, p. 569.

33. Ruetti, "Westliche Identitaet," p. 284.

34. J. A. Hebly, "Die oekumenische Bewegung in Wendel ihrer historischen Perspektiven," OR 4/1979, pp. 421-439.

35. Melanie May, "Fire or Ice? Or, How Will We Stay Together?" ER 1/1993, p. 115.

36. Barry Till, THE CHURCHES SEARCH FOR UNITY, p. 289.

37. Barbara Rogers, RACE: No Peace without Justice—Churches Confront the Mounting Racism of the 1980s (Geneva: WCC, 1980), p. 3.

38. Jose Miguez Bonino, "A Latin American Attempt to Locate the Question of Unity," ER 26/1974, p. 219.

39. "Is Fellowship Possible: Extracts from a Discussion in the Central Committee," ER 24, 4/1972, pp. 459ff.

40. John Deschner, "More than Inclusiveness: The New Christian Minority and the Shift in the Ecumenical Conversation about Church Unity," ER 43, no. 1, January 1991, p. 59.

41. Ibid., p. 67 (emphasis added).

42. Ibid., pp. 60, 61, 63.

43. John Deschner, "The Changing Shape of the Church Unity Question," MSt 1/1990, p. 23.

44. ER 43, no. 1, January 1991, p. 63.

45. Walter J. Hollenweger, "The Ecumenical Significance of Oral Christianity," ER 1989, p. 261.

46. John May, "Sprache der Einheit—Sprache der Zwietracht. Der Rassismus als Testfall oekumenischer Kommunikation," in OEKUMENISCHE THEOLOGIE, p. 251.

47. WORLD CHRISTIAN ENCYCLOPAEDIA, edited by David B. Barrett (Oxford: Oxford University Press, 1982), p. 5.

48. John Kenneth Galbraith, THE CULTURE OF CONTENTMENT.

49. Cox, THE SILENCING OF LEONARDO BOFF, p. 117.

50. Cf. Jon Sobrino, THE TRUE CHURCH AND THE POOR (London: SCM Press, 1985).

51. Gutierrez, A THEOLOGY OF LIBERATION, pp. 162ff.

52. Thomas D. Hanks, GOD SO LOVED THE THIRD WORLD: The Bible, the Reformation, and Liberation Theology (Maryknoll, NY: Orbis Books, 1983), pp. 61-69, 109-119.

53. Ronald J. Sider, RICH CHRISTIANS IN AN AGE OF HUNGER (London: Hodder and Stoughton, 1990).

54. M. Darroll Bryant, A WORLD BROKEN BY UNSHARED BREAD (Geneva: WCC, 1970).

55. "It must become clear that church members who deny in fact their responsibility for the needy in any part of the world are just as much guilty of heresy as those who deny this or that article of the faith" (Norman Goodall, ed., THE UPPSALA REPORT 1968 [Geneva: WCC, 1968], p. 320).

56. THE POLITICS OF CHURCH AID (Geneva: LWF, 1977), p. 21.

57. Pablo Richard, DEATH OF CHRISTENDOMS, BIRTH OF THE CHURCH: Historical Analysis and Theological Interpretation of the Church in Latin

America, translated by Phillip Berryman (Maryknoll, NY: Orbis Books, 1987), p. 158.

58. Thomas F. Best, "The Community Study: Where Do We Go from Here?" ER 1/1988, p. 56.

59. Constance F. Purvey, "The Continuing Significance of the Community of Women and Men in the Church Study: Its Mixed Meaning for the Churches," pp. 35ff; and Janet Crawford, "The Continuing Significance of the Community Study: Sheffield and Beyond." Both in BEYOND UNITY-IN-TENSION, pp. 45ff.

60. Rosemary Radford Ruether, TO CHANGE THE WORLD: Christology and Cultural Criticism (London: SCM Press, 1981); Elizabeth Schussler Fiorenza, "Biblical Interpretation and Critical Commitment," StT 1/1989, p. 6.

61. Letty M. Russell, "Introduction: Liberating the Word," in FEMINIST INTERPRETATION OF THE BIBLE (London: Basil Blackwell, 1985), p. 12.

62. Elizabeth Schussler Fiorenza, "Text and Reality—Reality as Text," StT 1/1989, p. 20.

63. Thomas F. Best, "The Prague Consultation in Ecumenical Perspective," in BEYOND UNITY-IN-TENSION, p. 13.

64. "Baptism, Eucharist, and Ministry and the Community of Women and Men Study," MSt 3/1984, p. 245.

65. Paul A. Crow, "The Unity of the Church and the Renewal of Human Community: A Perspective from Budapest," in FAITH AND ORDER 1985-1989: The Commission Meeting at Budapest 1989, edited by Thomas F. Best. F&O Paper no. 148 (Geneva: WCC, 1990), p. 142.

66. "A Missionary's Dream," ER 43, no. 1, p. 4.

67. Norman Goodall, THE ECUMENICAL MOVEMENT: What It Is and What It Does (London: Oxford University Press, 1964), p. 64.

68. "Fire or Ice?" ER 1/1993, p. 115.

69. W. A. Visser't Hooft, THE GENESIS AND FORMATION OF THE WCC (Geneva: WCC, 1982), pp. 58-60.

70. W. A. Visser't Hooft, "The Genesis of the World Council of Churches," in A HISTORY OF THE ECUMENICAL MOVEMENT, 1517-1948, vol. 1, p. 709.

71. Oliver Stratford Tomkins, "The Roman Catholic Church and the Ecumenical Movement 1910-1948," in A HISTORY OF THE ECUMENICAL MOVEMENT, vol. 1, p. 688.

72. Visser't Hooft, "The Genesis of the World Council of Churches," pp. 711, 712.

73. THE CHURCH: A Report of the Theological Commission of the F&O Commission of the WCC in Preparation for the Third World Conference on F&O to Be Held at Lund, Sweden in 1952. F&O Paper no. 7 (Rochester, Kent: Staples Printers, 1952), p. 35.

74. THE CHRISTIAN HOPE AND THE TASK OF THE CHURCH (New York: Harper and Bros., 1954), p. 42f, quoted in Mueller-Fahrenholz, UNITY IN TODAY'S WORLD, p. 19.

75. COMMISSION ON FAITH AND ORDER, 1984, Crete, p. 35.

76. LUND, Third World Conference on Faith and Order, August 15-28, 1952, quoted in A DOCUMENTARY HISTORY OF THE FAITH AND ORDER MOVEMENT 1927-1963, edited by Lukas Vischer (St. Louis, Missouri: Bethany Press, 1963), p. 105.

77. Raiser, ECUMENISM IN TRANSITION, p. 24.

78. THE FOURTH WORLD CONFERENCE ON FAITH AND ORDER: The Report from Montreal 1963, edited by P. C. Roger and L. Vischer. F&O Paper no. 42 (London: SCM Press, 1964), p. 44.

79. Paul A. Crow, "The Unity of the Church and the Renewal of Human Community: A Perspective from Budapest," MSt 2/1991, p. 138.

80. Efiong Utuk, FROM NEW YORK TO IBADAN: The Impact of African Questions on the Making of Ecumenical Mission Mandates, 1900-1958, American University Studies (New York: Peter Lang, 1991), p. 38.

81. Jean-Paul Willaime, LA PRECARITE PROTESTANTE: Sociologie du Protestantisme contemporain (Geneva: Labor et Fides, 1992), pp. 161ff.

82. Quoted in Heinz-Guenther Stobbe, "3 Konflikte um Identitaet. Eine Studie zur Bedeutung von Macht in interkonfessionellen Beziehungen und in oekumenischen Prozess," in OEKUMNISCHE THEOLOGIE, p. 197.

83. Hebly, "Die oekumenische Bewegung," pp. 434f.

84. Jose Miguez Bonino, "A Mirror of the Ecumenical Movement?," VOICES OF UNITY, p. 52.

85. Anton Houtepen, "Europe beyond 1992: The Redefining of the Ecumenical Quest," EXCHANGE 2/1992, pp. 100ff.

86. Eberhard Juengel, "The Christian Understanding of Suffering," JOURNAL OF THEOLOGY FOR SOUTHERN AFRICA, no. 65, December 1988, p. 13 (emphasis in the original).

87. Konrad Raiser, "Einheit der Kirche—Einheit der Menschheit: Ueberlegungen zum Thema oekumenischer Theologie," OR 1/86, p. 27.

88. COMMISSION ON F&O 1981, Annecy, p. 37.

89. NAIROBI TO VANCOUVER, p. 83.

90. Ibid., p. 84.

91. COMMISSION ON F&O 1981, Annecy, p. 37. Taking note of the fact that the Reformed Christians are among the richest in the world (whether it be in South Africa or elsewhere) and relating this to the issue of the unity of the church, Lukas Vischer writes: "The fact has directly to do with the unity of the church. For the unity of the churches can grow and become a sign of reconciliation in the present world only when one works on the removal of the inequalities among classes" ("Der Auftrag der reformierten Kirche in der oekumenischen Bewegung," OR 4/1979, p. 419).

92. Letty M. Russell, "Unity and Renewal," p. 63. Paul Tillich noted:"But let us consider ourselves, and what we feel, when we read, this morning and tonight, that in some sections of Europe all the children under the age of three are sick or dying, or that in some sections of Asia millions without homes are freezing and starving to death. The strangeness of life to life is evident in the strange fact that we can know all this, and yet can live today, this morning, tonight, as though we were completely ignorant. And I refer to the most sensitive people amongst us. In both humankind and nature, Life is separated from life" (quoted in Bill Lesher, "Reflections on the aftermath of Global Conflict," CURRENTS in Theology and Mission 18, no. 4, August 1991, p. 320).

Index

Aagaard, Anna Marie: on the Lutheran World Federation, 81-82
Africa: Christianity in, 102-103; churches in, 95-96; and liberation theology, 5-7
Africa, East: and dialogues, 23
African-American Christians, 125, 141
Anglican Church: autonomy in, 79-80; and the British Parliament, 80; crisis in, 79; dialogue with the Lutheran World Federation, 23; dialogue with the Roman Catholic Church, 27, 63, 117-118; and the ministry, 30; and the ordination of women, 58-59; on the papacy, 31; relations with the Roman Catholic Church, 58-59
Apartheid, 106, 107
ARCIC I, 78-82, 100, 120
Asia: and Christian World Communions, 17-18; churches in, 104-105, 124; dialogues in, 111; and liberation theology, 5-7
Augsberg Confession (Lutheranism), 63, 97
Authority (bilateral dialogues), 28-30

Balasuriya, Tissa: on liberation theology, 114; on Third World churches, 101-102
Bangladesh: Anglican communities in, 48-49
Baptism, 147
Baptism, Eucharist, and Ministry (BEM) document (Lima, Peru, 1982), 9, 61-62, 67, 69, 71, 77, 90: and the Eucharist, 120, 122; and Third World churches, 89-92
Baptist Church: dialogue with the Reformed Church, 24, 26; dialogue with

the Roman Catholic Church, 26
Barrett, David: on the poor, 146
Basel document, 119
Batak Church (Indonesia), 97
Baum, Gregory: on liberation theology, 113
BEM. *See* Baptism, Eucharist, and Ministry (BEM) document (Lima, Peru, 1982)
Bent, Ans van der: on Baptism, Eucharist, and the Ministry (BEM), 90-91
Bible, 28: and the poor, 126; and women, 134, 148. *See also* New Testament
Bilateral dialogues: on authority, 28-30; and Christian World Communions, 12-13, 21-22; on communion, 117; definition of, 12; on the Eucharist, 29-30; and the Faith and Order Commission, 12, 15-16; goals of, 25-27; on the ministry, 30-33; effect on multilateral dialogues, 23, 45-46; and organic union, 33-34; purpose of, 22, 44-47; rise of, 22-25; and the Third World, 87-88; topics of, 27-33; on unity, 33-36; and the World Council of Churches, 21-22. *See also* Dialogues; Multilateral dialogues
Birmele, Andre: on justice, peace and the integrity of creation (JPIC), 54; on the Leuenberg Agreement, 37; on the Malta Report, 64
Black churches in the United States, 141. *See also* African-American Christians
Blasphemy, 108
Boff, Leonardo: on Catholic Church, 5; on liberation theology, 114, 115
Bonhoeffer, Dietrich: on Jesus Christ, 130
Book of Common Prayer, 80